SOUNDWRITING

SOUNDWRITING

A GUIDE TO MAKING
AUDIO PROJECTS

TANYA K. RODRIGUE AND KYLE D. STEDMAN

broadview press

BROADVIEW PRESS – www.broadviewpress.com
Peterborough, Ontario, Canada

Founded in 1985, Broadview Press remains a wholly independent publishing house. Broadview's focus is on academic publishing; our titles are accessible to university and college students as well as scholars and general readers. With over 800 titles in print, Broadview has become a leading international publisher in the humanities, with world-wide distribution. Broadview is committed to environmentally responsible publishing and fair business practices.

Library and Archives Canada Cataloguing in Publication

Title: Soundwriting : a guide to making audio projects / Tanya K. Rodrigue and Kyle D. Stedman.
Names: Rodrigue, Tanya K., author. | Stedman, Kyle D., author.
Description: Includes bibliographical references and index.
Identifiers: Canadiana (print) 20220420947 | Canadiana (ebook) 20220421072 | ISBN 9781554815111 (softcover) | ISBN 9781770488724 (PDF) | ISBN 9781460408087 (EPUB)
Subjects: LCSH: Podcasting. | LCSH: Podcasting—Sound effects. | LCSH: Podcasts. | LCSH: Rhetoric. | LCSH: Authorship.
Classification: LCC PN4567.7 .R63 2022 | DDC 791.46—dc23

Broadview Press handles its own distribution in North America:
PO Box 1243, Peterborough, Ontario K9J 7H5, Canada
555 Riverwalk Parkway, Tonawanda, NY 14150, USA
Tel: (705) 743-8990; Fax: (705) 743-8353
email: customerservice@broadviewpress.com

For all territories outside of North America, distribution is handled by Eurospan Group.

Broadview Press acknowledges the financial support of the Government of Canada for our publishing activities.

Canada

Edited by Tania Therien

Book design by Chris Rowat Design

PRINTED IN CANADA

CONTENTS

A companion website offers template documents for brainstorming,
pitching, and peer reviewing your work; links to websites that host
downloadable sounds; and audio-editing tutorial GIFs and videos.

https://sites.broadviewpress.com/soundwriting/
Access code: m592ft

ACKNOWLEDGMENTS

Thanks first to our students at Salem State University and Rockford University. They've dreamed and brainstormed and recorded and edited and published sound-writing that surprised and enthralled us. Thanks for testing out our ideas, giving us feedback on our teaching and textbook-writing, and motivating us to keep going through a pandemic and beyond.

Thanks to all the staff and board at Broadview for believing in this unusual, exciting book, especially Brett McLenithan and Marjorie Mather. And thank you to Robin Meyer for designing the artwork for the companion website.

Thanks to Amy Cicchino for her kind permission to let us share her sound-mapping exercise in chapter two, and to Janine Butler for helping us clarify some of our language.

Tanya: I want to give a special thanks to the cowriters of "Navigating the Sound-scape, Composing with Audio" in *Kairos*: Kate Artz, Danah Hashem, Anne Mooney, Julia Bennet, M.P. Carver, Megan Grandmont, Mike Rand, Dan Harris, and Amy Zimmerman. Our many hours of work (and fun!) together in and out of class forever changed the way I think about soundwriting and the teaching of it. I also want to thank Rob Rosenthal and the whole crew at the 2019 Transom Traveling Workshop (Radio!) as well as all the sonic rhetoric scholars and their smart work; I am indebted to you for all you've taught me about soundwriting and pedagogy. A huge thanks to my friends and colleagues at Salem State University, especially Jan Lindholm and Amy Minett. I am so grateful for your continuous support, for your brilliance, and for all you've done to help me be a better writer, a better teacher, and a better human. And the most special thanks goes to my family, the ones who make me smile, hold my hand, and smother me with love. Mom, Pete, Aedan, and Rowan: you're the best!

Kyle: I especially want to thank the crew of sonic rhetoric scholars who have encouraged my weirdest ideas at so many conferences over the last decade. There are too many to name, but a few have been there for me since the beginning, especially Kati Fargo Ahern, Steph Ceraso, Harley Ferris, Steven Hammer, Jon Stone, and Crystal

VanKooten—and always with the support and encouragement of Dan Anderson over our shoulders. Special thanks to Courtney Danforth and Michael Faris, who have worked with me on the longest and most rewarding publishing journeys of my life; you've both been important to me as a scholar, soundwriter, collaborator, and person. Thanks too to the most supportive conference karaoke singers (I'm looking at you, Matt Gomes and Kate Pantelides), the most inspiring and innovative podcasts, and all the film and videogame soundtracks that played as these chapters were drafted and revised. And of course, Margo, who taught me to invest in people who are smart, witty, and thoughtful—like you, and like everyone in this list.

PREFACE

This is an exciting moment for sound.

People are increasingly listening to podcasts in the car, on walks, and lying in bed, and many want to create their own—or have already begun. Creators are playing with sound on social media, layering it over video, and sharing audio snippets from their life adventures. Scholars are studying and writing about sound in different disciplines and at interdisciplinary intersections. Teachers are assigning what the field of writing studies has started to call soundwriting: audio projects made by "manipulating recorded sound and making something new from it" (Danforth and Stedman). Students from every major are making powerful audio projects like podcast episodes, audio essays, personal narratives, and documentaries that they're proud of and want to share with the world.

This textbook is about how to compose with sound—how to make the kind of podcasts you listen to late at night in your bed and the powerful audio projects (like sonic remixes and audio stories) that so many of our own college students have created in our classes. It's about how to approach the world with a listening ear and body, target the perfect audience, and play around in audio editing software.

We're excited to make some noise with you.

A Note for Composers

This book focuses on a primary audience: undergraduate college students enrolled in writing and rhetoric courses like the ones we teach. However, we also can see it being useful to students in classes—across the disciplines and at any level—that focus on sound or incorporate soundwriting assignments.

This book is also for people beyond the classroom who are or want to be composers of sound: podcasters, artists, storytellers, performing arts professionals, radio journalists, and sound-focused individuals across disciplines and industries. Sure, there are other books and websites out there to support you in those specific contexts, resources that we could never replace (and indeed, we cite many of them in this book's pages), but we think our book's rhetorical framework offers something unique. Our flexible approach can be applied to any context and audience, exciting your listeners and keeping them wanting more.

No matter who you are, we write to you throughout with a playful, engaging, and accessible voice. While this book is research-based, it's not heady: it's straight-forward, clear, and practical. To make it even more practical, we've supplemented the textbook with a companion website that gives you all the things that wouldn't fit as well in these pages, such as documents to support your soundwriting process, links to websites that host sounds you can download, and audio-editing tutorial videos. You'll see quickly that the site focuses largely on an audio editor called Audacity, a free cross-platform open-source program commonly used in classrooms across the country, but the approaches we offer can be adapted to other audio-editing programs.

What will you actually find in this book? The focus is always on helping you compose audio that helps you achieve *your* goals for *your* audience. Here's how we'll get there:

- Chapter one introduces what we mean by soundwriting, as well as a term we'll use throughout, "the rhetorical situation." It's a phrase that encompasses the purpose, audience, context, and genre of any piece of communication, which we think should guide the choices you make to achieve your goals.
- Chapter two invites you to become a better listener in general, but especially a better listener to the strategies others have used in their own audio produc-tions, so you can follow their lead in your own soundwriting.
- Chapter three offers specific strategies for using the sonic rhetorical tools of voice, music, sound effects, and silence—again, giving you advice about how to best impact your audience.
- Chapter four suggests brainstorming techniques that can help you discover and sharpen your ideas, and then it offers advice for gathering and recording all the sounds you might want to use in an audio project.
- Chapter five guides you to put all those sounds together, editing them into a masterpiece, getting feedback, and sharing your soundwriting with the world.
- Interludes between each chapter give you a chance to read extended personal narratives from each of us about some of our own soundwriting experiences. We hope they'll give you a glimpse into the different ways people approach audio production in different genres, provide models for possible composing processes, and spark ideas that will inspire your own work.

How you navigate this textbook depends on why you're reading it. If you're read-ing it for a class, your instructor will likely direct you toward what to read, when to read it, and why—maybe in order, maybe jumping around, maybe completing the suggested exercises we call "try-its," maybe offering their own. If you're not reading this for a class, you have the same option: read it in order or by focusing only on the sections you think would be most helpful for you. We've added notes throughout to direct you to complementary material in other chapters to encourage that kind of jumping around.

With that said, this textbook isn't designed to be a one-and-done reading experience; it will serve you best as a reference book that you continuously draw on when questions emerge during your soundwriting composing process. Say you're composing an introduction for a podcast and you want to know more about how to create an engaging, playful vibe. Head to chapter three and check out what sonic strategies you could use for your desired effect, chapter four for advice on reading narration well, and chapter five for suggestions on layering your voice and music. Or say you're in the editing phase of your project and can't remember how to cut up and arrange tracks in the audio editor. Flip to chapter five for guidance—but maybe pop back to chapter one for reminders about making editing decisions that match your rhetorical situation. Don't put this book on the shelf to gather dust; keep it next to you while you compose.

0.1 Suggested Reading for New Podcasters

We write a lot about podcasts in this book, since we know that for many of you, podcasts are likely to be the model of soundwriting you're most familiar with—and also the model you'd most like to create for yourself.

What chapters and sections give you the most direct path toward better understanding and making podcasts? Here are some suggestions:

- **Listen**: Tip 1.3 introduces you to some of the many genres of podcasts, some of which might surprise you if you're used to listening to a particular type of show. Then, Tip 2.4 introduces a list of shows and episodes that reward careful listening. And Tip 4.1 suggests ways to find the best podcasts for you.
- **Analyze**: Try-Its 1.3 and 2.1 ask you to listen to podcasts to analyze them in particular ways, which might help you better understand how podcasters affect their audiences.
- **Read a case study**: Interlude C tells Kyle's story of producing a collaborative podcast episode, including his real experience gathering audio assets, editing it all together, and sharing it on a podcast platform. Don't miss the section at the end of that interlude with details about the genre features of a podcast.
- **Plan**: Skim the four main sections of chapter three (on using voice, music, sound effects, and silence) for tips that will help you make the kind of podcast you want. For instance, if you're planning on a podcast that features mostly

speaking, focus on the Voice section. Chapter four also has a lot to offer you as you're dreaming and planning, especially in the sections on Generating Ideas, Planning and Pitching Your Ideas, and Scripting.

- **Interviewing**: If your show will include interviews, be sure to read chapter four's section on Interviewing.
- **Editing**: Browse the sections in chapter five for focused advice on editing your digital audio, including sections on Editing Basics, Editing Voice, Layering Together Multiple Tracks, and more.
- **Sharing**: Chapter five introduces the basics of how to start a new podcast in the Podcasting section toward the end of the chapter. (In fact, you might want to start here if you're not familiar with the basic way podcasts are distributed to listeners!)

A Note for Instructors

We've heard the same story over and over: writing and rhetoric instructors have started asking their students to compose with digital audio but are unsure what the best practices are, if they're doing it right, or if audio editing is even allowed in a writing class. Maybe you love podcasts and want your students to learn how to make them, or maybe you've seen the growing focus on sound in scholarly conversations about multimodal composition, or even the growing interdisciplinary field of sound studies writ large. We've gotten to know many of you instructors (and count ourselves among you!), and we know you need support.

We wrote this textbook to offer that support. And while other textbooks exist that support multimodal composing practices in general, we think it's time for a textbook that draws on the insights of scholars in writing and rhetoric to inform soundwriting instruction and support rhetoric-centered pedagogies. We think it's time for a textbook that uses the unifying power of rhetoric and rhetorical vocabulary to speak to students and non-students who are studying and composing with sound, but with a special focus on the composition classroom. We also believe it's time for a textbook that is influenced by our field's call for sonic literacy (Comstock and Hocks), by renewed attention to sound in our scholarship and teaching (Selfe), and by theoretical investigations of both linguistic and non-linguistic uses of sound (Katz).

We think we're the right people to offer this textbook. While teaching soundwriting in digital writing courses for years, Tanya's strong interest in sonic rhetoric began to develop while cowriting and later publishing "Navigating the Soundscape, Composing with Audio" in *Kairos* with eight of her graduate students in a Digital Writing class (Rodrigue et al.). That led her to more sound: facilitating faculty workshops on soundwriting, teaching sound-specific classes, producing more scholarship related to sonic rhetoric, and crafting multiple audio documentaries that have been aired on the radio and played on podcasts. Kyle's creative-critical podcasts and publications helped inspire his teaching and his work on the three collections he coedited with Courtney S. Danforth and Michael J. Faris (*Soundwriting Pedagogies, Tuning in to Soundwriting,* and *Amplifying Soundwriting Pedagogies: Integrating Sound into Rhetoric and Writing*), all of which share theories and pedagogies of soundwriting for a teacher/scholar audience (unlike the student/practitioner audience of this book). We've studied and taught at small, medium, and large universities, where we've worn a number of administrative hats that we believe broaden our understanding of the various needs of rhetoric and writing instructors today as well as instructors across the disciplines, especially those who want to bring the study of sound and soundwriting into their classes.

Our background in rhetoric and writing is infused throughout the book. Indeed, while this book is designed to teach students about soundwriting specifically, it also teaches them more broadly about writing and communication because of its rhetorical lens. It helps students understand that writers make rhetorical choices to impact their audience and achieve their purpose while engaging in a multistep composing process. With that said, this textbook can prepare students for other kinds of writing; we hope you'll reference it throughout the semester in conversations about rhetoric, rhetorical strategies, genre, purpose, audience, context, composing processes, reading strategies, and the transformation of what it means to write in the digital age—including changes to what writing looks like, how it functions and is created, and where it is produced, read, shared, distributed, and circulated. As much as possible, we've written the book for all students, including those who are d/Deaf and hard of hearing; we regularly suggest assignments that work when attending to audible sound, reading transcripts of sound, or watching visualizations of sound.

This textbook, we imagine, is best used as a supplemental text for a unit in a writing class or as the primary text in a class that specifically focuses on sound, perhaps in courses called Audio Storytelling, Sonic Rhetoric, Writing with Sound, or even Radio Journalism. The way you use the textbook will depend on your pedagogical goals and rhetorical context; see our summary of the contents above for an overview of where to look as you plan whether to assign it in order.

Here's one more note about the "interludes," the personal narratives of our own soundwriting experiences that are found between each chapter. These narratives take a different style from the rest of the book: detailed accounts of the various struggles and choices we made in some of our early soundwriting experiences. Rather than including direct, "do this" language, these narratives are meant to be teaching tools in their own right, using the power of story. They concretize some of the concepts and ideas we discuss throughout the book, like how to use genre and rhetorical analysis to guide one's composing process or how to work collaboratively on a soundwriting project. They also bring attention to the different kinds of composing processes of soundwriting and how different genres and people can approach a task, especially when audio production isn't their day job. We see these interludes as humanizing the experience of soundwriting, which can often be challenging and frustrating, especially for beginners.

You'll also find "try-its" scattered throughout the chapters—exercises that can accommodate all learners and be used as in-class activities, homework assignments, or can be adapted to high-stakes assignments. We've included variations for most activities so you can accommodate all learners in your class. They represent a blend of activities we've used in our own classes and new ideas we developed just for this book.

And don't forget the companion website we described above. We hope that whenever the content in the book feels too limiting—too print-centric, too general—you'll turn there with your students to watch our videos, listen to sonically rich soundwriting, and click our links.

The Term Soundwriting

We want to acknowledge that we're not the first people to use the word *soundwriting* in the field of writing studies or the world in general. In fact, people have blended versions of the word *sound* and the word *writing* to describe overlapping projects for years—just think of the word *phonograph*, which blends the Greek words for sound and writing.

For a deep dive into the global history of the term, we recommend the introduction that Kyle cowrote with Courtney S. Danforth for the digital book *Soundwriting Pedagogies* (Danforth and Stedman). But in writing studies, it's easier to trace the word: in 2008, both Danforth and writing scholar Will Burdette started using the word independently and in about the same way: to describe the audio production projects they were asking students to do in the context of college courses in writing and rhetoric. As far as we can tell, that's when students first came to a writing class and heard a professor say, "Let's work on your soundwriting project!" Since then, soundwriting has increasingly been the word used by teachers of writing and rhetoric to refer to audio projects. (Chapter one of this book explains more about why we like the term in this context.)

We're especially grateful to Courtney and Will for bringing the term into use in our field. It's hard to imagine calling this work anything else.

Works Cited

Comstock, Michelle, and Mary E. Hocks. "Voice in the Cultural Soundscape: Sonic Literacy in Composition Studies." *Computers and Composition Online*, Fall 2006, cconlinejournal.org/comstock_hocks/index.htm.

Danforth, Courtney S., and Kyle D. Stedman. "Introduction." *Soundwriting Pedagogies*, edited by Courtney S. Danforth et al., Computers and Composition Digital Press/Utah State UP, 2018, ccdigitalpress.org/book/soundwriting/introduction/index.html.

Danforth, Courtney S., et al., editors. *Soundwriting Pedagogies*. Computers and Composition Digital Press/Utah State UP, 2018, ccdigitalpress.org/book/soundwriting/.

Faris, Michael J., et al., editors. *Amplifying Soundwriting: Integrating Sound into Rhetoric and Writing*. WAC Clearinghouse, forthcoming.

Katz, Steven B. "Sonic Rhetorics as Ethics in Action: Hidden Temporalities of Sound in Language(s)." *Humanities*, vol. 9, no. 1, 2020, https://doi.org/10.3390/h9010013.

Rodrigue, Tanya K., et al. "Navigating the Soundscape, Composing with Audio." *Kairos: A Journal of Rhetoric, Technology, and Pedagogy*, vol. 21, no. 1, 2016, kairos.technorhetoric.net/21.1/praxis/rodrigue/index.html.

Selfe, Cynthia L. "The Movement of Air, the Breath of Meaning: Aurality and Multimodal Composing." *College Composition and Communication*, vol. 60, no. 4, 2009, pp. 616–63.

Stedman, Kyle D., et al., editors. *Tuning in to Soundwriting*. enculturation/Intermezzo, 2021, intermezzo.enculturation.net/14-stedman-et-al.htm.

Chapter One

SOUND, SOUNDWRITING, AND RHETORIC

INTRODUCTION: SOUND SURROUNDS US

Have you ever thought about all the sounds around you? Take a moment and listen—with your ears if you're able, and with your whole body attuned to the vibrations of the air and the resonances surrounding you.

Figure 1.1
We choose the sounds we hear in our headphones, and our bodies feel the vibrations of the other sounds around us.

What do you hear? Near you, do you sense the creak of a chair, the click of a computer mouse, the footsteps of a person or animal walking by, the notifications on your phone, the beats and melodies of a song, or perhaps other furnace-whooshes, house-creaks, and tree-rustles nearby? What about when you direct your attention further away: are there cars, planes, distant rumbles of thunder, unidentifiable groans of the earth? Or try directing your attention inward to the sounds of your body: your breath, the creaks of your back, the shifts in your belly, and the moisture in your mouth.

Figure 1.2
There's more
to hear than
we sometimes
realize.

These sounds are natural and human-made, ongoing and fitful, rhythmic and random, expected and surprising. Sounds warn of danger, announce upcoming pleasures, invite us to feel emotions, and hint at things our other senses don't notice. Sounds construct our experience of reality, guiding us to think and feel and understand things in the world that we otherwise might miss. They resonate through our entire bodies, not just our ears, telling us just how loudly that door was slammed, just what kind of music is in the room, and how and when we ought to move.

For ages, people have been fascinated by sound and have theorized and explored what sound is and how it plays a role in our lives. For instance, from a scientific perspective sound can be described by focusing on its transmission as waves. Or, as NASA describes it, "Sound waves are longitudinal waves that travel through a medium like air or water. When we think about sound, we often think about how loud it is (amplitude or intensity) and its pitch (frequency)" ("What's the Science of Sound?"). Sound is also intimately connected to humanness, to our existence, identities, and life experiences. Professor and author Deborah Kapchan claims "the body begins with sound, in sound" (33) in utero, while musician Saul Williams claims every person is a "being of sound" (21). Music philosopher David Burrows describes sound as "invasive," since it's "experienced as going on inside the listener as well as outside" (70). Sonic vibrations are simply a part of who we are as humans.

Whether we focus on the subjective experiences of sound or the objective physics of sound, it's important to all of our lives. But instead of focusing on all the ways sound impacts us, this book tunes into a particular aspect of sound: the way composers use sound to have an impact on their audience. That is, we're interested in sound *as communication*.

Figure 1.3
A 1921 book (Bragg) illustrates the effect of rubbing a violin bow across the edge of a glass filled with water.

FIG. 47.—The vibration is here so violent that the surface of the water breaks into spray.

THE AFFORDANCES OF SONIC COMMUNICATION

Yes, sound envelops us and shapes our experience of the world—but sound also gives us a chance to communicate in unique ways. The messages we send and receive through the vibrations of sound waves—whether heard through the ears or felt in the body—are filled with meanings that tell us what to do, how to feel, and how to understand something. Some of those messages come from the natural world, like when the sound of wind signals a storm is coming or when birds call each other to alert. And of course humans also communicate with sound, intentionally using the sounds of their voices and bodies (like clapping, snapping, or clicking tongues) with purpose, adding new layers to what can be conveyed through other means of communication like movement or writing.

We don't want to suggest that communicating in sound is *better* than other kinds of communication, though. There's a reason that humans surround themselves with messages of all kinds, encoded into sounds, words, images, and gestures: those different vehicles of communication all carry inherent features that enable composers to make and not make certain communicative moves. Depending on your purpose and audience, you might find yourself choosing to write an email or text, make a phone or video call, or visit your audience in person to share the full experience of your body language. And it's not just individuals: organizations decide what vehicle of communication works best for their purposes too, like when advertisers try to reach different audiences in different ways on social media, radio, podcasts, television, and print newspapers and magazines.

Figure 1.4
Speaking is only one
of many ways we
communicate.

Scholars of communication and rhetoric (a word we'll define below) call these different vehicles of communication **modes**, a word that can be tricky to define. Linguist Gunther Kress defines modes as "resources of meaning making" that enable people to communicate and express themselves in various ways (54). Or sometimes we describe modes to our students as "particular ways of encoding messages for audiences"—as in, *I have these things I want you to know or experience, and I have to decide how to help you know or experience those things, so I encode my ideas into words, sounds, images, and movements in ways that I hope you'll decode and make sense of.* The authors of the popular rhetoric textbook *Writer/Designer* describe five modes, following the work of a group of scholars called The New London Group: the linguistic mode (spoken and written alphabetic words), aural mode (voiced and unvoiced sounds), visual mode (images and other design elements), spatial mode (the physical arrangement of objects in space), and gestural mode (movement and interactivity) (Ball et al.). Those modes are all tools that help us communicate with others and shape how others experience our communication.

1.1 Further Reading on Modes and Multimodality

For further reading on modes and multimodality, check out:
- Ball, Cheryl E., et al. *Writer/Designer*. 3rd ed., Bedford/St. Martin's, 2021.
- *Glossary of Multimodal Terms*. National Centre for Research Methods, 2012, multimodalityglossary.wordpress.com.

- Kress, Gunther, and Theo van Leeuwen. *Multimodal Discourse: The Modes and Media of Contemporary Communication.* Bloomsbury, 2001.

You may have already anticipated one interesting thing about modes: they're rarely used in isolation. Communicators almost always use a combination of modes to make their points and affect their audiences. That's where the word **multimodal** comes from: the blending and interplay of modes for communicative purposes. Consider the multimodal nature of the examples we mentioned above: an email blends the linguistic mode with the visual mode, because those words are laid out on a screen in fonts and colors, while a phone call blends the linguistic mode with the aural mode, since the words spoken are blended with the sound of the speaker's voice. They're all multimodal; most communication is.

Modes and combinations of modes have a set of **affordances**, or in other words, unique and inherent capabilities that they can *offer* or *do* to help someone communicate and express themselves. A mode "affords"—*allows, invites,* or *encourages*—particular types of communication. Think of a lengthy novel that takes many hours to read in its print form. We'd call this a multimodal blend of the linguistic mode (words) and the visual mode (the layout of the words on the page or screen, using fonts, colors, and columns). The linguistic mode affords the composer the opportunity to present ideas in alphabetic language in a linear way in structures like paragraphs and sentences; these words and the familiar way they are chunked together can be engaged with again and again. In turn, a reader has the option to read and reread at their own pace. They can skip passages or move throughout the text in any way they wish. The linguistic mode also invites readers to activate their imagination and prior knowledge, as they are implicitly encouraged to infuse characters with voices or fill in gaps not explicitly stated in the text. Plus, if the book is printed on paper, the reader can easily underline passages or flip back and forth quickly to find a particular spot. A novel, in other words, affords the communicator the opportunity to craft a particular experience for the reader and invites the reader to engage with the text in different ways.

Yet a novel might also take the form of an audiobook, with its linguistic content encoded into the aural mode instead of the visual mode on the page. That audiobook also has certain affordances—certain strengths in its communicative capabilities—that aren't the same as a print book. For example, the aural mode invites voices to be utilized in different ways, such as when a voice is infused with emotion or fluctuates in tone. The aural mode also invites listening in contexts where print books don't fit: in earbuds, while walking across campus, or in the car during a commute. Yet an audiobook is harder to experience nonlinearly; you can't flip back and forth as easily as with a print book, and it's harder to imagine highlighting an audio passage or writing something in the margins. Let's call the things the audiobook can't or won't do constraints of the aural mode. Think of **constraints** as limitations that prevent the mode from working to communicate in some way. For example, a recording of spoken audio without a transcript would deny people who are d/Deaf or hard-of-hearing the experience of engaging with it. Knowing the affordances and constraints of a mode helps writers determine how to best convey their message to achieve their goals.

Figure 1.5
Books use the linguistic mode whether they're on the page (with the visual mode) or read aloud (with the aural mode).

Even this textbook was designed with affordances and constraints in mind. After all, we get the irony: we're writing linguistic words on a visual page in a book about aural sounds. Yet we made the choice to write a textbook for similar reasons to a novelist's: we want you to have the experience of reading slowly and interactively, with the easy ability to move back and forth quickly between sections and mark important moments with notes in the margins and dog-eared pages. We want you to have the chance to return to different parts of this textbook when composing your own audio projects, perhaps to find answers to questions or review something you learned about soundwriting. Sure, we recognize that those affordances aren't perfect for every situation or every learner's style and body, so we're supplementing this written text with an online companion website with its own affordances. There, audio and video files use combinations of sound and movement to offer the kinds of teaching that words *can't* do very well. Knowing the affordances and constraints of different modes helped us make strategic decisions about which mode to use when and for what purpose. Neither is better all on its own; "better" is always contextual when it comes to communication.

We encourage you to imagine the affordances of various combinations of multi-modal communication, especially when you add or remove certain modes from the mix. Whether a novel is in print or audio form, the **linguistic mode** is always present, since words are part of the communication whether they're on the page or read aloud. But don't forget all the affordances of the other **nonlinguistic modes** too, like the ways the visual, aural, and gestural modes can communicate *without* words. We're thinking of the paint color of a room, the subtle eyebrow scrunch of our friend, the ominous bass notes in a movie soundtrack, the arrangement of desks in a classroom, the overly cheerful music of your phone's alarm sound, the sleek look of the car you're going to buy one day, the arrangement of streets in a suburban neighborhood, the cry of a baby, the "don't cross this line" message when your grandmother holds up her finger and gives you *the look*. These messages, whether with or without words, all have affordances and can affect audiences in their own particular ways. As scholars and composers of sound, we're captivated by the rich results when we use the aural mode to communicate both linguistically and nonlinguistically. That is, we love the experience of hearing spoken, sung, and shouted words, but we also love the experience of instrumental music, layered sound effects, and sudden silences. This book will guide you toward using both kinds of sound in your soundwriting projects to help you achieve your communication goals.

Wait, did we just say "soundwriting"? Let's take a minute to explain that word and why we're using it to describe the audio projects this book will help you create.

Try-It 1.1 Modes and Affordances with Texts and Selfie Videos

The following activity will help you better understand how the aural mode can be blended with other modes as well as the various affordances and constraints of different mode combinations. For this activity, you will need a word processor or messaging app, a voice recording device, and a video recording device.

1. Type a text message (either in a word processor or actual messaging app) that you could send to someone you know well, telling them about something unusual you did or saw today. Just use words.
2. Now write a text on the same topic, but add a bunch of emojis. You can imagine this text is being sent to the same person or a different person.
3. Next, use your voice or someone else's voice to convey the same content in a recording. Think of it as a brief voice message that they would listen to instead of read on the screen.
4. Now, do the same thing (yes, we know it's getting old) in a selfie video: video yourself telling the same story with words or sign language. Be sure your face is visible. Add filters and effects and text to your selfie video, if you'd like.

After you've composed these messages, respond to the following questions:

1. Would some of these messages feel more appropriate for certain people you know (certain audiences)? Why?

2. As you used different blends of modes in each message, did any feel odd or unusual to you? Which felt most natural and comfortable? Does that answer change depending on your audience?

3. For each of the four messages, list the affordances and constraints of communicating in that way in general. That is, what are the capabilities and limitations of texting with words alone? What is added or lost when you add emojis? And so on. Push yourself to go beyond the obvious answers.

4. You used the aural mode in messages three and four, but both times blended with the linguistic mode (words). What might the effect of those messages be if you tried to use the aural and visual modes without relying on the linguistic mode—that is, without using any spoken, written, or signed words?

Try-It   1.2 Modes and Affordances in the Audio Editor

The following activity asks you to hone in on the aural mode, thinking carefully about its affordances and constraints in relation to the linguistic mode. For this activity, you will need a computer with access to the internet as well as an audio editing program. Follow the steps below:

1. Go to a website that hosts sound effects, such as freesound. org or sounddogs.com.

2. Search for and download the following sound effects: a barking dog, a meowing cat, footsteps, wind, a scream, and a knock on a door.

3. Import the sound effects into the audio editing program and, if necessary, trim each clip to 3–5 seconds.

4. Now, create a "sound effect story" by rearranging the clips in whatever way you want—back to back, layered, repeated.

5. After you create your story using only sound effects, write a linguistic version of the same story with words on the page or screen.

6. Consider the linguistic version of your sound effect story in relation to your soundwriting. What are some of the unique affordances and constraints of telling stories with the aural mode alone, as compared to telling them with the linguistic mode? Be sure to consider your audience; from a listener's perspective, what is gained and lost when engaging with each type of story?

> **Learn More**
> See chapter four for guidance on how to download sound from the internet and chapter five for learning how to trim, split, and layer clips.

> **Learn More**
> See the "Sound Effects" section in chapter three for more about the rhetorical functions of sound effects.

Figure 1.6
Writing and
sound have more
in common than
you might think.

WHY "SOUNDWRITING"?

What do we mean by **soundwriting**? It's a complicated word that can refer to both the *product* and *process* of composing with sound.

When we focus on soundwriting *products*, we emphasize audio projects that exist in the world and invite engagement. In that sense, soundwriting describes compositions that employ sonic strategies such as voice, sound effects, music, and silence, and which are often crafted using audio editing software and meant to be engaged with on a sound-playing device like a radio, smart phone, or computer (or even a stereo that plays records and cassettes). But soundwriting can also refer to a *process*, emphasizing the actions taken to create the soundwriting, as in this shorter definition: "manipulating recorded sound and making something new from it" (Danforth and Stedman). Thus, *soundwriting* has the grammatical flexibility of the word *writing*, describing both the product and the process; we can say both "check out my soundwriting" and "my soundwriting process is wild." We soundwrite as a verb to produce soundwriting, the noun.

Though some might disagree, we distinguish soundwriting from activities like giving live speeches (since the sound itself isn't revised before sharing with an audience, even if the *script* is) or playing someone else's recording (since you're not the one who soundwrote it). Instead, soundwriting describes all the things you could create in a digital audio editing program, whether you're using linguistic or nonlinguistic modes: a podcast episode, an audio essay, a radio drama, or a soundscape that combines multiple kinds of effects, for example.

But why call it *soundwriting* instead of something like "making, editing, or producing audio projects"? We like the deliberate parallel with the word *writing*. Think of the process that many of us take when writing an essay:

- We brainstorm ideas that will best help us achieve our purpose for our reader.
- We research to find conversations we can participate in and quote from.
- We organize those ideas in outlines and messy first drafts.
- We read and reread our drafts, clarifying our ideas and organization while editing our expression of those ideas.
- We share our writing with others to see if it's achieving the goals we intended.
- We revise again, formatting our pages for the expectations of our audience.
- We share our best work by sending it to a professor, friend, or publication.

Think of how many of those tasks are analogous to the process of crafting soundwriting: we still brainstorm, gather the sounds of those who went before us, plan our project, draft by combining and layering various audio clips, get revision ideas from others, edit the whole into a perfect final draft, and send it out for others to hear. So much of what we know and love about the writing process can also apply to what we know and love about working in sound.

The word *soundwriting* also emphasizes where we're coming from as authors. We're scholars and teachers in writing studies; our degrees are in English and in rhetoric and composition, not sound engineering or sound studies. We teach writing classes, direct writing centers, and train college professors to teach writing in their own courses. We're part of a growing community of writing scholars who are studying and practicing digital audio and entering the interdisciplinary conversations of sound studies. We're coming to sound with many of the assumptions and knowledge that comes from our professional lives studying the practice, impact, and teaching of writing in the world. So by using the word *soundwriting* throughout the book, we're also staking a claim to the particular areas of the sonic world we're interested in: those areas that have parallels to the teaching and practice of writing.

SOUNDWRITING AND RHETORIC

Our understanding of writing and soundwriting is largely informed by one of the oldest academic disciplines in history: rhetoric. The discipline of rhetoric is ancient and global, going back to "Mesopotamia, Egypt, China, and ancient Israel" (Lipson and Binkley 3), though we got the word *rhetoric* from ancient Greece about 2,500 years ago, when teachers began systematizing ways to effectively communicate in the burgeoning democracy of Athens. Of course, definitions of rhetoric have evolved since then, but we can still say that **rhetoric**, in the most general sense, is the art and practice of effective communication. People who create rhetorical communication (called "rhetors") do so by making choices that impact or affect an audience to achieve a purpose.

Ancient Greek rhetors improved their speeches in their democratic assembly by studying proven strategies for finding the best ideas, organization, words, and delivery for their specific purposes and audiences—and it's the same for today's soundwriters. That is, this book uses the language of rhetoric to help you use proven strategies that you can flexibly apply to your own contexts for your own communication goals.

You'll notice that when we talk about rhetoric, we often use words like *flexible* and *contextual*. That's a core assumption of the study of rhetoric: that there's never a single best rhetorical choice that will apply to every situation. That's why we want to introduce **the rhetorical situation**, a term often used to describe the full, rich context of our ever-changing communication settings. The four factors of the rhetorical situation include the rhetor's purpose, audience, context, and genre of communication. Fluency with these factors is useful both for analyzing the communication of others and as a checklist when trying to create your own soundwriting. For example, I can listen to a favorite episode of a podcast and ask myself, "Why do I love this episode so much? Why did it make such an impact on me?" I can understand it better by thinking about what purpose it's trying to achieve, what audience it's designed for, what larger context it fits into, and how the soundwriters used this genre of podcast so effectively—all of which are part of the rhetorical situation. I can also explore these same factors when composing my own podcast, thinking carefully about how to make my audience feel the way I did when listening to that podcast episode.

> **Learn More**
>
> We use the term "podcast" to describe an entire show, a serialized (multipart) collection of episodes that can be subscribed to through a podcast app or accessed on a website. When we're just talking about a single part of that podcast, we call it an "episode," just as we use the word "episode" to talk about a single part of a larger TV show.

Let's go through the factors of the rhetorical situation one at a time, but with this warning in mind: while each factor is discussed separately below, they are intimately connected. They often work together and can be explained and explored in relation to each other, making these individual sections handy as a checklist but somewhat artificial in practice.

Purpose

Let's start with purpose, and for a good reason: you could say that composing with a purpose is what makes soundwriting rhetorical. That is, *what you're trying to achieve* shapes every choice you make; it's a key part of any rhetorical situation.

A focus on purpose reminds us that writing (and soundwriting) often *does something*. It helps us accomplish goals and impact audiences (even when we write to ourselves). We write grocery lists to identify what we need to buy, to remember what to buy when we get to the store, and ultimately, to purchase groceries. You record an audio message to send to your friend on their birthday with the purpose of making that friend feel loved and celebrated on their special day. The purpose of the writing acts as a guiding light, directing the rhetor in every aspect of the composing process, from brainstorming to creating to assessing its effectiveness.

As a soundwriter, you might know your purpose right away, but you also might discover your purpose in the process of composing. Your purpose might be given to you, like when your teacher asks you to create a public service announcement (PSA) for a local radio station to draw attention to a problem in the community. Or maybe you're driven by a personal purpose, like a desire to create a personal audio essay that conveys a belief or value in the same genre as *This I Believe*, a popular public radio show that ended in 2009. In that case, you could adopt the purpose of that show: to contribute to ongoing discussions about people's different beliefs and present different perspectives on how people exist in the world. In some cases, your purpose will feel less clear, at least at the beginning of a project. For example, let's say you attend a pride festival in your town and you decide to record the festival on your phone in hopes of getting some interesting material to work with for an audio project. You might only discover your purpose after listening to the tape and brainstorming ways to manipulate that tape to produce a piece of soundwriting.

> **Learn More**
> See the Scripting section in chapter four for an explanation of how to write a script that "lets the tape lead."

As elusive as purpose sometimes feels, it's still useful to try to nail it down. Knowing your purpose has the potential to help you:

- Select a topic or subject area
- Determine the genre and modes for your project
- Consider listeners' needs and interests
- Choose sonic tools that work best to accomplish your purpose
- Make other writerly decisions such as organization and structure

Audience

Purpose is inextricably tied to audience—or in the case of soundwriting, to *listeners* (or readers of a transcript). After all, we can determine whether soundwriting is effective by judging the extent to which it impacts or influences an audience in the way it was intended to.

The identification and exploration of an audience can be tricky, though, since a soundwriter often can't predict exactly who will hear a finished product. It can help to think of these overlapping categories of audiences:

Figure 1.7
Rhetoric is all about impacting an audience—whoever they might be.

- Intended audience: the listeners you expect or know will engage with your soundwriting; you make decisions hoping to achieve your purpose with them.
- Actual audience: the listeners who *actually hear* your soundwriting, like it or not; they're not always the people you primarily have in mind, but if they accidentally encounter your work, you still want to engage them.

For instance, let's say your professor asks you to plan and record a brief audio response to a reading. Your audio recording critiques the limitations of the reading, and as you do so you find yourself relying on terminology and assumptions that the class has shared over the past few weeks. And in the context of your class, your piece achieves its purpose for this intended audience: a lot of your classmates agree with your critiques. It goes over so well that you post it to your personal SoundCloud account and link to it on social media, only to find that a few people on Twitter critique your understanding of the text. This feels annoying, since this actual audience has lost the nuance that comes from weeks of being in the class together. You resolve to keep those kinds of people in mind the next time you record an audio response; you plan to compose primarily for the intended audience of your classmates as always, but while remembering to predict the responses of the actual audience as well.

That example emphasizes how your mind *predicts* your audience's responses as you plan and compose your soundwriting. Those predictions don't have to be random; you can mentally "assign" listeners to certain roles as you compose, making choices that will help them trust your authority on the subject, imagine themselves in the middle of the story you're telling, or predict solutions to a problem you're posing. Your plans can assume that those kinds of listeners might be out there.

And like it or not, listeners will assign themselves their own roles, consciously or not, making decisions about what kinds of connections they want to have with your soundwriting. Those roles may be influenced by where or how they are listening, their mood, their likes or dislikes, or even their personality. They might become "outsiders" if they feel like they have no point of reference to the content in the audio project, or they may become "skeptics" if they think the composer isn't credible. Maybe they are "detached listeners" as they engage with soundwriting while multitasking with long bouts of distraction, or maybe they are "intent listeners" as they listen to a newscast on the radio driving down a road they've driven down a thousand times. There are endless possibilities to how your intended and actual audiences might encounter your work.

It might sound like we're describing an impossibly messy situation: soundwriters create something and can't predict who will hear it and how they'll interpret it? Is communication really that unpredictable? Well, yes and no. To some extent you just can't know who your actual audience is; you can't control everything once you start sharing your work with audiences. But you could also choose to see that uncertainty as an opportunity or a challenge. You could creatively try to anticipate all the various kinds of actual audiences who might encounter your work, always making sure that your purposes will be achieved for as many of them as possible.

But start by focusing on your intended audience, either as identified in an assignment or chosen yourself. Then you can gather information about your intended audience and reflect on how that information may guide your decisions while composing your audio project.

> **Learn More**
>
> See the Rhetorical Analysis section in chapter four for an exercise that will help you better understand your intended audience.

Context

A soundwriter's purpose for an audience is never achieved in isolation; people experience audio in time and space, affecting how it impacts them—and ideally, affecting the choices the soundwriter makes. Like all the parts of the rhetorical situation, context is a slippery term, referring to several different kinds of contexts: social and cultural context, timing, location, and means of engagement. As with audience, the more the soundwriter can plan for these contexts, the greater likelihood of rhetorical success.

Context can refer to the social and cultural happenings in a person's community (like the city or town in which they live) or in the larger community (like a country or even the world). The systems, structures, events, attitudes, and behaviors related to people within the immediate and larger contexts all influence the creation and reception of soundwriting. So does the moment in time in which something is created or engaged, fitting the soundwriting into a broader cultural conversation or concern.

Consider how important context was in the effectiveness of an episode of the popular radio show and podcast *Radiolab*. In the summer of 2020, the show released an episode called "Nina," described like this on *Radiolab*'s website (where you can hear the entire story):

> Producer Tracie Hunte stumbled into a duet between Nina Simone and the sounds of protest outside her apartment. Then she discovered a performance by Nina on April 7, 1968—three days after the assassination of Dr. Martin Luther King Jr. Tracie talks about what Nina's music, born during another

time when our country was facing questions that seemed to have no answer, meant then and why it still resonates today. (Hunte)

The "sounds of protest" in the description references a string of protests that occurred for several months across the country following the death of George Floyd, a Black man killed by a white police officer in Minnesota. The protests, fueled by the social and political movement Black Lives Matter, sought to bring awareness and attention to systemic racism and police brutality. The situation prompted the focus of this podcast episode as well as the sonic rhetorical strategies included in the episode, such as the use of silence and sound effects of the protest. The episode was released on June 6th, 2020, the day half a million protesters gathered in 550 places across the country to fight for equality (Buchanan et al.). The timing of the episode's release couldn't be more perfect, as many Americans were aware of and even participating in the protests when it was released; the episode was extremely relevant to the time by adding to the cultural conversation producer Tracie Hunte's unique experience and understanding of the situation as a Black woman. Her personal context and the national context added power to the episode's purpose.

Figure 1.8
Nina Simone's music brings awareness to past and present struggles for justice.

While soundwriters should consider how their work will be heard in their particular cultural time and place, they should also think smaller, predicting the literal types of spaces where their work will be heard and through what speakers it will be played. Do you think your audience will hear your soundwriting through computer speakers, a car radio, headphones, or a cell phone propped up in a cup? On the street, in an office, blasted through huge speakers in a massive space? While reading along with your transcript and taking notes, or while doing dishes or feeding children? Sure, you can't pinpoint every location or medium where your work will be heard, but you can make educated guesses, based on where you'll publish your work and who your intended and actual audiences are likely to be.

Tanya recently experienced the power of context when listening to a student's soundwriting project. She first listened to it through earbuds while hiking in the woods, taking advantage of one of the affordances of the aural mode: its portability and amenability to multitasking. But when she listened to the same project at a listening party in class, giving it a different kind of attention and surrounded by others also focusing on the project, her body physically reacted to several parts of the soundwriting in a way that it hadn't when she was multitasking earlier, giving her the feeling of chills during some of the most powerful moments of the story.

How and where and when do you want your soundwriting to be heard? What choices can you make to help it work most powerfully wherever and whenever it's encountered?

Genre

Genre, the fourth factor of the rhetorical situation, flows naturally with the previous three: soundwriters achieve a *purpose* for an *audience* in a *context*—but how can they strategically make something that fits that audience's expectations? Shouldn't their soundwriting match certain categories and do certain things that an audience expects it to do? That's where genre comes in: it's the category that the soundwriting fits into. Soundwriters can use genre knowledge to think about how to recognize and determine what kind of writing most appropriately fits in their rhetorical situation; this helps their work be all the more successful.

This probably isn't a surprise, since you've seen genres used to categorize books, movies, music, podcasts, and more. Those genres tend to gather entire collections of traits that often match up. Romantic Christmas movies usually feature a straight, white couple who fall in love by the end of the movie, kissing in the snow, advertised with an image of a man wearing green and a woman wearing red. Horror movies of course rely on characters making bad decisions, tense music, supernatural mysteries, and bloody endings, advertised with images that use a lot of black. Sure, any individual item could be changed and it could still fit in the genre; genres can't describe every possible divergence, instead acting as a sort of summary of commonalities that make it easier for people to decide how to spend their time. That is, if you're looking for a romantic Christmas movie or horror movie, it's not hard to find them, since the genre is marked in so many obvious ways.

The reasons for these similarities aren't arbitrary: they exist because they have come to be known over time to be effective in accomplishing common goals in social situations that happen again and again. People test what works and what doesn't, learn to do what works, and others follow suit. Using a haiku to land a job? Not effective. Using a resume that details education and work experience to land a job? Effective. Using oral history to tell a story about current events? Not effective.

Using an audio documentary to tell a story about current events? Effective. When writers know why a genre is used and how people generally react to that genre, they can draw on this knowledge to determine the most appropriate and fitting response to their situation.

Don't miss that: people designing movie posters, writing resumes, and making oral documentaries are *intentionally* and *rhetorically* using genres because they know how powerful they can be. Here's an example of how a soundwriter's knowledge of genre leans effectively on an audience's expectations for a category of listening. Say you're browsing the "true crime" podcast genre in your podcast app; don't you have a certain set of expectations of what you'll hear in the podcast? Most would agree that listeners expect to hear about a real-life crime, perhaps a murder or assault, along with the details of what happened before and after the crime happened. They not only expect a certain kind of content, they expect to feel a certain way: shocked, surprised, appalled, curious, upset, or even angry. Soundwriters can cater to their audience by knowing what they expect. They can give listeners what they want, anticipate, or need, which ultimately helps in accomplishing their goals.

1.2 Soundwriting Genres

This list of genres is necessarily incomplete. You could imagine a wealth of subgenres under each of these categories; for example, "audio short stories and novels" could include historical fiction, science fiction, romance, and so on, while "soundscapes" might include sounds recorded and edited in the field, sounds designed to be played in a particular space, or sounds meant to evoke a specific, real location.

Our point: don't let this list hold you back. See it as a playful beginning, as a list of forms that are meant to be used rhetorically, yes, but also combined and broken.

- Archival audio remix
- Audio postcards
- Audio short stories and novels
- Audio tours
- Documentaries
- Dramas
- Feature stories
- Histories
- Interviews
- Literary/rhetorical/genre analyses
- Mashups/collages
- Memoirs
- Mixtapes

- Music
- Narrative journalism
- Newscasts
- Oral histories
- Personal essays
- Podcasts (with all of their sub-genres)
- Public service announcements
- Radio commercials
- Remediations of written works
- Remixes
- Researched scholarly audio essays
- Sound art
- Sound portraits
- Soundscapes
- Soundtrack replacements

For more on the conventions used in many different soundwriting genres, see the interludes between each of the chapters in this book. There, you'll find advice on using the soundwriting genres of audio memoirs, narrative journalism, academic podcasts, and radio feature stories, as well as ways to blend and disrupt genres.

Yet all of this is not to say that soundwriting in all genres is exactly the same. Knowing a genre and its conventions only gives soundwriters a loose guide for approaching a project, as compositional decisions are largely based on *all* the unique factors of a rhetorical situation. Writing studies scholar Amy Devitt explains:

> Different grocery stores make for different grocery lists. Different law courts make for different legal briefs. And different college classes make for different research papers. Location may not be the first, second, and third most important qualities of writing, as it is for real estate, but location is surely among the situational elements that lead to expected genres and to adaptations of those genres in particular situations. (218)

Devitt uses "location" broadly here, referring to both "its literal sense of physical environment" and "its more metaphorical sense of cultural and institutional setting, a component of each rhetorical situation" (218). In other words, she's talking about what we called *context* above; she's saying that how we use genre is like how we use context: flexibly, situationally.

You've likely heard a saying that goes something like this: learn the rules so you can break them. This saying sums up the last thing soundwriters can take away from the study of genre. Once a soundwriter is able to recognize genre conventions, they can make strategic decisions about how they might disrupt those conventions, push the boundaries of that genre, or even create new genres for creative expression. Although genres may seem rigid, they are really dynamic, fluid entities that beg to be played and experimented with; play leads to creativity, which leads to strong listener engagement.

> **Learn More**
>
> For advice on analyzing genre conventions, see the section on Rhetorical Analysis in chapter four.

1.3 Podcast Genres

Podcasts are one of the most common ways that many of us compose and consume soundwriting—and there are a lot of ways to categorize all of them! As rhetors, this means that there are many different lists of genre conventions to follow when composing in any of these podcast genres.

At the time of writing, Apple Podcasts (one of the largest podcast distributors) categorizes podcasts into 19 main categories (Arts, Business, Comedy, Education, Fiction, Government, Health & Fitness, History, Kids & Family, Leisure, Music, News, Religion & Spirituality, Science, Society & Culture, Sports, TV & Film, Technology, True Crime) and 91 sub-categories (Arts: Books, Design, Fashion & Beauty, etc.) ("Podcasts Downloads").

Or, to look at podcast genres another way, here's what Radiotopia Executive Producer Julie Shapiro called "A New Taxonomy of Podcast Genres for the 20-Teens":

- CRIMEcast
- DAILYcast
- CELEBcast
- BACKcast
- CULTcast
- DATAcast
- CHUMcast
- KIDcast
- POLITIcast
- HOWTOcast
- FEMcast
- FICTIONcast

If that feels overwhelming, rhetoric scholar Eric Detweiler, in "The Bandwidth of Podcasting," categorizes podcasts into just four main categories: educational, interview, discussion, and narrative. See his article for a list of podcasts that fit into each of those genre categories, allowing you to study them and find the genre conventions you might want to follow when composing in those genres.

Try-It 1.3 **Analyzing the Rhetorical Situation of a Podcast Episode**

As we wrote above, the rhetorical situation is a concept that can help you in two ways: 1) to understand how others compose rhetorically, and 2) to plan and execute your own compositions. The following activity will help you practice how a real podcaster might explore their rhetorical situation to prepare them for soundwriting, and then in chapter four, we'll provide an activity that will guide you in how to analyze *your own* rhetorical situation (in Try-It 4.1).

Start by choosing a particular episode of a popular podcast to analyze. You can choose however you'd like: by browsing some of the podcast genres described in Tip 1.3, by listening to one of the podcasts or episodes described in Tip 2.4 in chapter two, by asking a friend what they've listened to lately, or just by opening a podcast app and choosing somewhat at random. Anything will work.

Then, after listening to the episode or reading a transcript (or both!), answer the following questions, each of which focuses on a different part of the rhetorical situation:

1. **Purpose**: Why do you think this podcast episode was created? Are there obvious purposes that you're sure of that are layered with subtler purposes that you're less certain of? List them all.

2. **Audience**: Does this podcast's description or website describe its intended audience? Does it make choices that seem to suggest it's aimed toward a particular demographic? Can you imagine any actual audiences who might hear it and dislike something they heard?

3. **Context**: Does this episode seem to purposefully or accidentally be part of a larger context—maybe something that was being talked about nationally or in the podcaster's social or cultural context at the time of its release? Does it refer to places or times that are an important part of how the episode will be heard and understood?

4. **Genre**: What kind of podcast episode is this? Does it share genre conventions with other podcasts like it? What makes it similar or different to episodes of other shows?

BEING A SOUNDWRITER

Understanding soundwriting as rhetoric is a focused approach to composing audio projects. But let us also offer you a broader approach, one that provides you with guidance on *how to be* a soundwriter as opposed to *how to understand* soundwriting. In other words, this section describes the attitudes and mindsets that will help you along the compositional journey of your audio project.

Figure 1.9
Sound and
soundwriting
can become
part of you.

We're inspired here by the concept of "habits of mind," a phrase we learned from a report called *Framework for Success in Postsecondary Writing*. This report was generated by leaders in university-level writing instruction and is endorsed by the main scholarly organizations in the field of teaching writing. And even though it's primarily endorsing an approach to teaching alphabetic writing, we find its ideas apply to teaching and learning soundwriting as well, especially in its description of the habits of mind.

Here's how the report introduces the idea: "Habits of mind—ways of approaching learning that are both intellectual and practical—are crucial for all college-level learners. Beyond knowing particular facts or completing mandatory readings, students who develop these habits of mind approach learning from an active stance" (*Framework* 4). Like our approach in this chapter, the authors of the *Framework* support students having specific "experiences with writing, reading, and critical analysis" (6), but they also emphasize that first developing the right mindset will make those specific experiences more successful. It boils down to that sweet phrase they use: "an active stance."

Building on the eight habits of mind described in the *Framework* document, we'd like to propose three more habits for successful rhetorical soundwriting, the traits that we find ourselves returning to again and again as we discuss our own work with each other. These overlap with the *Framework*'s eight habits and aren't intended to replace or change that list; instead, they're simply our attempt to simplify and sharpen the habits of mind that we see as particularly useful and crucial for work in audio.

Courage. Being courageous is perhaps the most important habit of mind to possess when approaching soundwriting. Often, especially when composing in a new mode, fear is paralyzing. New soundwriters might be haunted by insecurities or feelings that just because they are inexperienced they are incapable. This fear—which we know from experience—stifles creativity and invention. So before you even begin soundwriting, let the fear go. Be willing to make mistakes. Be willing to persist. Be willing to take risks. Keep writing, planning, recording, and editing even if you don't know where you're going. Don't be afraid of new genres. Don't be afraid of using technologies you might not have a lot of experience with. Don't be afraid of your own voice. Don't be afraid to ditch an idea or start over or try an idea that you think won't ultimately work. Be courageous.

Play. People define *play* differently in different contexts, sometimes thinking of it as a frame of mind, or as the thing that happens when we engage in games, or as a spirit of fun that is part of an experience. Whatever it is, rhetoric scholar Joshua Daniel-Wariya emphasizes that play happens "at all levels of composing, including invention, production, consumption, distribution, and access" (33)—that is, composers of writing and soundwriting can draw on play the entire time they're composing.

Figure 1.10
A drum circle embodies the habit of play, exercised within the context of the genre of music being played.

Why cultivate a habit of playfulness when soundwriting, specifically? We find that soundwriting offers composers so many possibilities that we sometimes need to be reminded that our first idea isn't necessarily the most successful, lively, surprising, or powerful; instead, we need to play around as a way to challenge ourselves to be better, and to surprise *ourselves* at what we can accomplish. Further, courage begets play and vice versa: the willingness to take risks invites play as play offers the opportunity to build courage.

Reflection. Reflection is sometimes called "metacognition," which could perhaps best be understood as a kind of "thinking about your own thinking." We believe that you learn best when you regularly articulate to yourself what you're doing as you compose and why you're doing it, a habit that then helps you replicate or change your process when revising or in the future. Writing scholar Kathleen Blake Yancey argues that the word *reflection* covers a multifaceted collection of acts: those that happen within ourselves while we're composing, as we build a growing sense of who we are and how we compose, and as we articulate to others how we understand our composing processes (13–14). We agree; our soundwriting projects couldn't have been successful without ongoing reflection on what and why we were composing—and writing the narratives you'll read as interludes between each chapter of this textbook helped us solidify what we know and believe about our composing even more! As

Tanya put it in an earlier article (Rodrigue et al.), reflection helped a group of her soundwriting students "solidify their understanding of their rhetorical strategies and well as the rhetorical knowledge, genre knowledge, and awareness they developed over the course of the project."

Even better, there is evidence that reflection can be especially meaningful when it's done in non-alphabetic texts, like soundwriting. Consider this example: writing scholar Lindsey Harding shares that when her students pushed themselves to reflect on their work in a form beyond the traditional essay form (in her class, by using the visual and spatial modes), their reflections were richer and more meaningful. To us, her experience suggests that productive reflection often results from activities that break us out of what we're used to, helping us understand ourselves in ways we didn't expect.

> **Learn More**
> See the Process Notes and Talking to Others sections in chapter four for more advice on reflecting as a form of brainstorming. See the Peer Review section in chapter five for advice on reflecting with others after you've completed a draft.

These three habits of the soundwriting mind—courage, play, and reflection—might seem at first to contradict how we advised you to attend to the four factors of the rhetorical situation described above—purpose, audience, context, and genre. After all, attending to the rhetorical situation often requires intense attention to *every possible way* you can imagine an audience engaging with and understanding your words, as you predict how your soundwriting will be experienced and compose with those factors in mind. The habits of mind take a different approach, encouraging you to loosen up your shoulders, breathe deep, and acknowledge that you can't predict everything.

We agree that there's a tension here, but not a problematic one. The successful soundwriter both plans and plays, predicts the future and lets the future go. As you soundwrite, move back and forth between a rhetorical focus on your audience and a winking, courageous willingness to dive into the unknown.

WHAT'S NEXT?

With all that groundwork laid, let's start understanding and making soundwriting.

Listen up as we walk you through a full range of strategies to help you plan, organize, and share soundwriting projects from beginning to end, in the most effective way possible for your many, ever-changing contexts. This book will walk you through listening techniques that will help you soundwrite effectively in your context (chapter two), sonic tools like voice, silence, sound effects, and music that soundwriters can employ in different ways for different purposes (chapter three), ideas for planning projects and gathering sounds for whatever purpose you have in mind (chapter four), and putting it all together in your audio editing software before you revise and share your creations (chapter five). Throughout, we'll focus on flexible strategies that can be applied to whatever soundwriting you can imagine.

Key Chapter Takeaways

- Sound plays an active role in human lives and shapes life experiences.
- Sound can be understood as vibrations sent via waves in the air, water, material objects, or the earth surrounding us.
- People express themselves using different vehicles of communication, which are referred to as modes. Linguistic modes reference words, either written or spoken. Nonlinguistic modes reference communication that doesn't use words such as visuals, gestures, and sound.
- Each mode has unique affordances or capabilities in its ability to be used for communication. Each mode has unique constraints or in other words features that prevent or resist certain communicative experiences.
- People often use a combination of multiple modes to communicate. Such communication is described as multimodal communication.
- The word *soundwriting* refers both to the product and process of composing with sound. Soundwriting as a product describes compositions experienced sonically that rely on sonic affordances such as voice, sound effects, music, and silence, and they are often crafted using audio editing software and meant to be engaged with on a sound-playing device. Soundwriting as a process is making something new from the manipulation of recorded sound.
- The "writing" in soundwriting references the similarities both share in the composing process: brainstorming, researching, outlining, reading, drafting, revising, and sharing.
- Soundwriting can be understood through the lens of rhetoric. Rhetoric is the art and practice of effective communication.
- Soundwriters can craft effective communication by identifying, considering, and attending to the multiple factors of their communication setting—their purpose, audience, context, and genre. These factors are referred to as the rhetorical situation.
- Soundwriters who adopt a mindset that invites courage, play, and reflection during the soundwriting process will have more success in learning about and producing effective soundwriting.

Discussion Questions

1. What role does sound play in your life? What kinds of sounds are important to you and why? What kinds of sounds are not important to you and why?
2. What are some ways that you use sound to communicate? What are some

ways other people or material objects use sound to communicate with each other and you?

3. What are some instances when you consciously considered your purpose and audience when communicating or crafting a piece of communication? What led you to do so and what kinds of things did you consider?

4. Can you think of a time when you listened to something—a song, a podcast, a conversation, city sounds, or nature sounds, for example—and were surprised or confused by what you heard because it wasn't what you expected? How did that make you feel? How did it alter your experience?

Works Cited

Ball, Cheryl E., et al. *Writer/Designer*. 3rd ed., Bedford/St. Martin's, 2021.

Bragg, William. *The World of Sound*. G. Bell and Sons, 1921. *HaithiTrust*, https://catalog. hathitrust.org/Record/001988437.

Buchanan, Larry, et al. "Black Lives Matter May Be the Largest Movement in U.S. History." *The New York Times*, 3 July 2020, www.nytimes.com/interactive/2020/07/03/us/ george-floyd-protests-crowd-size.html.

Burrows, David. *Time and the Warm Body: A Musical Perspective on the Construction of Time*. Brill, 2007.

Danforth, Courtney S., and Kyle D. Stedman. "Introduction." *Soundwriting Pedagogies*, edited by Courtney S. Danforth et al., Computers and Composition Digital Press/Utah State UP, 2018, ccdigitalpress.org/book/soundwriting/introduction/index.html.

Daniel-Wariya, Joshua. "A Language of Play: New Media's Possibility Spaces." *Computers and Composition*, vol. 40, 2016, pp. 32–47.

Detweiler, Eric. "The Bandwidth of Podcasting." *Tuning in to Soundwriting*, edited by Kyle D. Stedman et al., enculturation/Intermezzo, 2021, intermezzo.enculturation.net/ 14-stedman-et-al/detweiler.html.

Devitt, Amy. "Transferability and Genres." *The Locations of Composition*, edited by Christopher J. Keller and Christian R. Weisser, SUNY P, 2007, pp. 215–27.

Framework for Success in Postsecondary Writing. National Writing Project, 2011, archive.nwp. org/cs/public/download/nwp_file/15188/Framework_For_Success_in_Postsecondary_ Writing.pdf?x-r=pcfile_d.

Glossary of Multimodal Terms. National Centre for Research Methods, 2012, multimodality glossary.wordpress.com.

Harding, Lindsey. "Writing beyond the Page: Reflective Essay as Box Composition." *Teaching English in the Two-Year College*, vol. 41, no. 3, 2014, pp. 239–55.

Hunte, Tracie, producer. "Nina." *Radiolab*, WNYC Studios, 6 June 2020, www.wnycstudios. org/podcasts/radiolab/articles/nina.

Kapchan, Deborah. "Body." *Keywords in Sound*, edited by David Novak and Matt Sakakeeny, Duke UP, 2015, pp. 33–44.

Kress, Gunther. "What Is a Mode?" *The Routledge Handbook of Multimodal Analysis*, edited by Carey Jewitt, Routledge, 2009, pp. 54–67.

Kress, Gunther, and Theo van Leeuwen. *Multimodal Discourse: The Modes and Media of Contemporary Communication*. Bloomsbury, 2001.

Lipson, Carol S., and Roberta A. Binkley. "Introduction." *Rhetoric Before and Beyond the Greeks*, edited by Carol S. Lipson and Roberta A. Binkley, State U of New York P, 2004, pp. 1–24.

"Podcasts Downloads on iTunes." *Apple*, podcasts.apple.com/us/genre/podcasts/id26. Accessed 28 June 2021.

Rodrigue, Tanya K., et al. "Navigating the Soundscape, Composing with Audio." *Kairos: A Journal of Rhetoric, Technology, and Pedagogy*, vol. 21, no. 1, 2016, kairos.technorhetoric.net/21.1/praxis/rodrigue/index.html.

Shapiro, Julie. "Podcasting Is...." Symposium on Sound, Rhetoric, and Writing, 7 Sept. 2018, Belmont University, Nashville, TN. Keynote Address.

"What's the Science of Sound?" *NASA*, www.nasa.gov/specials/X59/science-of-sound.html.

Williams, Saul. "The Future of Language." *Sound Unbound: Sampling Digital Music and Culture*, edited by Paul D. Miller aka DJ Spooky that Subliminal Kid, MIT P, 2008, pp. 21–24.

Yancey, Kathleen Blake. *Reflection in the Writing Classroom*. Utah State UP, 1998.

Interlude A

Remixing a Written Memoir into Soundwriting: How Kyle Composed "Pincushion"[1]

Introduction to the Interludes

You'll find that between each chapter, we pause to share personal stories about our individual soundwriting experiences. Here's some of what you can expect to read in these four interludes:

- **Details that often go unshared**: We think that soundwriting (or any writing) can seem intimidating to newcomers when all they see is finished, polished products. The reality is that behind most published work is a messy, complex composing process—and learning about the processes of others can help you learn more about soundwriting and inspire your own work.

- **Experiences with different genres**: There are countless soundwriting genres and subgenres. There are ones we can easily name, like a sports podcast, and ones that are not so easy to name, like an audio story that kind of sounds like an oral history but also kind of sounds like a documentary. We purposefully wrote interludes about composing in different and hybrid genres to communicate how knowing and not knowing your genre might play a role in your composing process. You'll read about the common and unique ways we took genre into consideration when soundwriting and how we worked to both incorporate and disrupt genre conventions to meet the goals of our individual soundwriting projects. At the end of each interlude, we provide some guidance for how you could approach soundwriting in common and blended genres.

- **Honesty, not perfection**: We've both published audio work that we love and work that has embarrassing problems, gaps, or technical issues that we wouldn't have made today. These pieces are by no means perfect, and that's exactly why we're including them in this book. We hope that by not hiding our blemishes, you'll be encouraged to experiment, take risks, have fun, and not hold yourself to impossible standards. It's okay to not produce perfect, polished work, and in fact, it's the messy, imperfect work that helps us grow most as soundwriters.

- **Lessons we learned**: The process of crafting audio projects inevitably teaches soundwriters something new or different about soundwriting. And this new knowledge

---

1 The finished version of this audio memoir is available online: Stedman, Kyle. "Pincushion." *Memoir Magazine*, 28 Oct. 2019, memoirmag.com/10-minute-listen/pincushion-by-kyle-stedman/.

inevitably helps soundwriters strengthen and improve their craft. We've learned a lot from our own soundwriting experiences, and we want to share what we've learned in case it helps you as much as it has helped us. So at the end of each interlude, you'll see a quick summary of our lessons learned.

Figure A.1   The published version of Kyle's audio memoir.

INTRODUCTION: DRAFTING FOR A DIFFERENT MODE

In 2019, I published an audio memoir—a focused story about a particular theme in my life—called "Pincushion." It was published in an online literary magazine where the audience can choose to listen to me read the essay with sound effects and music or just read the words alone. But "Pincushion" didn't start as a soundwriting piece. Originally, I hoped to publish it as a piece of written creative nonfiction in a print-focused literary magazine—but it didn't turn out that way, and now I'm glad it didn't. This is the story of how work in one mode can shift into work in another mode, hopefully inspiring you to integrate sound into some of your own written drafts of creative writing, whether it's fiction, nonfiction, or poetry.

It's also the story of discovering that the affordances of audio could help me achieve my rhetorical goals. That is, I always wanted "Pincushion" to invite readers into the emotional experience of my fourth- and fifth-grade conflicts; you could say my rhetorical purpose was to pull readers in, connect them to my story, and remind them of their own stories. Yet I found that revising for audio helped me take that purpose to the next level, as listeners now hear representations of what my younger life sounded like along with sounds that reflected my emotional state as a child.

Many of the steps I took when drafting the alphabetic version of the essay are similar to steps I would have taken if I'd known from the start I was producing an audio essay. For instance, I knew the bare bones of the story I wanted to tell but wasn't sure what details to include, so I did a lot of freewriting, jotting down everything I could remember about the time I lied to my friend's dad as well as memories about that friend, who I called Timothy, and about my fourth-grade enemy, who I called Dustin.

> **Learn More**
> See chapter four for advice on freewriting.

This freewriting helped me remember the sights, sounds, feelings, and even smells of those years—all the sensory details that memoirist Mary Karr calls "carnal details." I also revised the text over and over just as I would any audio piece, asking friends (and students in my creative writing classes!) for advice about the language and organization of my many drafts.

> **Learn More**
> See chapter five for advice on peer review.

REVISING THE SCRIPT FOR AUDIO

The idea to turn this into a soundwriting project came when I saw the annual call for submissions to the Miller Audio Prize, a contest hosted by the literary journal *The Missouri Review*. I saw the contest details and remembered my draft of "Pincushion," filed away in a Google Doc in my creative writing folder. *Could I record myself reading this and turn it into a soundwriting piece?* I asked myself. With no better ideas, I had to find out.

Right away, I knew there would be a problem: my current draft was 3,503 words and took much longer to read than the 15-minute max for contest submissions. In fact, the final, 15-minute audio piece I finally submitted to the contest was performed from a 2,500-word script, so I was originally 1,000 words too long. But the problems went deeper: when I read my sentences out loud, they were unnecessarily long and confusing; they just *didn't work* as a script.

Here's an example of how the essay originally began and how I revised it: my original first sentence was, "Timothy's dad squinted, sized me up for a moment before speaking." It's not the worst sentence in the world, but it didn't have as much impact as the first sentence of a script, and it's unnecessarily long and grammatically a little fishy. It just didn't sound natural when I read it out loud, especially with that weird comma separating two verbs. Instead, I revised it simply to "Timothy's dad was a big guy." (The essay is partly about how masculinity is wrapped up in ideas of body size, so it also focused the audience on a topic I wanted them to be thinking about.) With that idea in mind of simplifying sentences, I suddenly realized I could cut *so much*, both in terms of streamlining sentences and deleting entire sections.

Learn More

See the Scripting section in chapter four for more examples of transforming "writing for reading" and "writing for listening."

Pincushion (version 3)reading script
Kyle Stedman
3,503 words

Timothy's dad squinted, sized me up forwas a moment before speaking. "I just saw Timothy's fourth-grade class photo. Upstairs, a few minutes ago." He paused to clear his throat, a ratchety, sickly sound that seemed out of place for this large man. "big guy.And do you know what I saw?"

I shook my head. We were sitting across from each other at thehis living room table, cluttered with old newspapers and magazines. His table. I felt very aware of who owned this house, this stuff.

He had walked into the living room a few minutes earlier, tellingjust told my friend Timothy to turn off the Nintendo game we had been playing and ride his bike around the block a couple of times so he could talk to me. Dutifully, uncomplaining, he had gotten up and left. I was surprised he hadn't made more of a stink, the way I would have with my dadTimothy's dad kept track of his kids' exercise, tallying it on a chalkboard and rewarding them for it later. I thought it was kind of weird.

Figure A.2   Revisions from the written to the spoken version of the script.

Honestly, my 1,000-word-shorter version is better even when read on the screen; the constraints of the contest forced me to make hard decisions that ultimately improved the piece.

RECORDING THE NARRATION

Now that I had a script, it was time to record. I set up a microphone in my walk-in closet, because I knew from experience that the carpet and soft walls of clothes would reduce odd echoes and tinniness from my recording. I opened the free audio editing software Audacity and read a few test sentences. Then I listened to that test recording a couple of times, checking that my seating arrangement and the mic's input level seemed right—at a level that would pick up a lot of the depth and complexity of my voice sound, but without being so loud that it would create clipping—moments of audio distortion that come from recording a too-loud signal—and without catching any plosives, those moments when letters like P blow air directly into the mic. I also remembered to push my laptop as far away from the mic as possible, even though I still needed to read from the screen, so its fan sounds wouldn't be picked up by the mic, a mistake I've made way too many times.

Learn More

See the Recording Your Own Voice section in chapter four for more advice.

Once everything was set up, I just read my script—but I read it self-critically. Any time I even slightly suspected that I hadn't given my best reading, I just paused for a second and started the sentence over. I didn't pause the recording or touch anything on the computer; I just trusted that I would edit out mistakes later. Sometimes I would say the same sentence 3 or 4 times, trying out different voice qualities: faster, slower, funnier, more serious, and so on. When I was done, I saved the project in Audacity to my computer's hard drive, and then I immediately uploaded everything to Google Drive, so I wouldn't lose it if something happened to my computer.

That day, I needed a break, so I stopped for the day; I find that my "recording" mindset is usually different from my "editing" mindset, so it's good to take a break between them—ideally at least a day. Then I started editing my vocal performance by opening Audacity and saving a new project file, so I would have the raw version of my multiple performances if I wanted any of them later. I started by running the compression effect over the entire audio file, which evens out the volume, bringing the quiet parts louder and the loud parts quieter. Because I recorded in a quiet spot, I didn't need to do any noise reduction, but I often have to do that right away, too. Then I simply listened to the reading with the script open in another window and chose between which performance of each sentence I liked, deleting the sentences and phrases that didn't sound as good. (I could delete with abandon, knowing I had another file with the whole performance, just in case; nothing I could do could ruin the project.) I also deleted things that were obviously wrong: extra pauses, coughs, my cat pushing her way into the room and making a scraping sound, and so on. By the end, I had

> **Learn More**
> See Editing in chapter five for lots more advice.

a strong vocals-only performance that *sounded* like a great single take, even though I knew how much work went into making it sound that good.

I should say here that what "sounds good" is always a judgment call, one that can be hard to judge on our own. Listening back to "Pincushion" now, I hear how I was trying to read a bit slowly on purpose because I mention slow talking in the story, but in some sentences I think I overdid it; I cringe a bit. If I had had more time, I would have asked friends for advice early on, at this stage. But I was in a rush, so I didn't. Oh well.

CHOOSING AUDIO ASSETS THROUGH PLAY

At this point, I wasn't sure how much music and sound effects I should add; I was worried of going overboard and seeming cheesy with effects for *everything*, but I also wanted to take full advantage of the aural mode's affordances, like drawing listeners into scenes and emphasizing emotional impact. Part of my problem was that I was working in a genre I didn't know a lot about; I hadn't heard many audio memoirs that used extra audio assets, so I didn't have a lot of models to help me make a strong decision. Still, I figured I could start big and cut things later. And for me, the fun action of playing around with audio often leads to surprising discoveries that fit my rhetorical situation even more than I expected.

I turned to Freesound, the site that supports my soundwriting more than any other. Leaving it open in a browser tab, I started listening to my project for spots where I might want to add sounds. When I found a possible spot for a sound effect—like the door slam mentioned early on—I searched Freesound for "door slam," listened to a few contenders, checked to make sure they had the right Creative Commons licenses, downloaded the best one, and dragged the file into Audacity to import it into my project and then line it up with my narration. Because I knew I'd want to cite my sources

later (both to follow ethical soundwriting practice in general and to fulfill the legal requirements of the Creative Commons licenses of the sounds I downloaded), I copied links of any sounds I used straight into my reading script, making it easy later to find exactly what I used in which spot of the project. Yes, I could have recorded these sounds myself to avoid needing to give credit to anyone else—for instance, by setting up a microphone and slamming a door a few times—but that would have taken more time, so I just relied on Freesound.

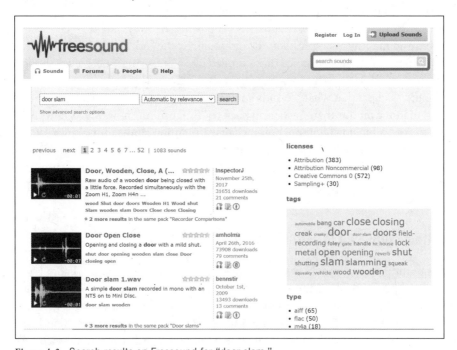

Figure A.3 Search results on Freesound for "door slam."

I also knew that my opening scene (where I lied to my friend's father) should have a growing sense of danger and urgency, so I thought I'd try out some mildly threatening music. For that, I went to Soundcloud, where I have a playlist of tracks that are licensed with a Creative Commons Attribution license, which only requires that I name the artist responsible for the music, no matter what kind of audio project I use it in. I clicked through my playlist and luckily found something fairly early on that I liked. (Well, I *pretty much* liked it. I wasn't *sure* it was the right track, and I'm honestly still not; it's perhaps *too* moody and scary for this scene. But as I wrote above, I was in a rush, so I just grabbed it and moved on.) I dragged the music track into my project and started it at the moment when I thought it would start doing its work, subtly hinting at the danger my lying was getting me into.

But when I heard the end of that section—the end of my conversation with Timothy's dad—I didn't think it had enough of a "bang"; sure, there was music, but it wasn't music that built up toward a climax. Put in rhetorical terms, you could say that I wanted audio assets to help me achieve my purpose of emotionally connecting to my audience. So I found a *wobble-wobble* sound I had made and saved for another project, which sounded kind of *wrong* somehow. I dragged it into Audacity, fading it in to make it louder and louder as the end of the section approached, and when I listened to it, I knew I was onto something. Now the words at the end of the section (as I told my biggest lie yet) were brasher than ever, more dangerous than ever, gutsier than ever. It embodied the feeling that was at the heart of this piece all along: the weird way that lying brazenly can be both horrible and exciting.

> **Learn More**
> Head to chapter three for more about the rhetorical use of sound effects.

I moved forward, editing in many more sounds as I proceeded. Some were simple sounds used to help create an atmosphere: ambient noises from a cafe and of kids playing on a playground, a basketball (for when I mentioned playing four-square), and a coyote (for when I mentioned that one character was like a hyena; I was hoping no one would know the difference, since it sounded hyena-like to me). Other sounds were less strictly representational and more metaphorical, used to amplify the emotional tone of a moment. For instance, at the climax of the piece, when the listeners finally learn that I really did do the thing I was lying to Timothy's dad about, I found a recording of a gong, which I digitally lengthened considerably, creating an eerie, stretched-out sound that still felt physical and metallic, and I layered it with a slowed-down, pitch-shifted recording of a tape recorder noisily rewinding. I didn't know what would happen as I started, but my playful attitude led me to content that I was really proud of.

Now I had a full Audacity file with multiple layered tracks, which I kept organized by putting my narration in the top track and then keeping most sound effects in two tracks below that, with music at the bottom. I knew I couldn't trust my initial reactions on the day I finished my first round of audio editing, so I saved the project file, uploaded everything to Google Drive for backup, and came back the next day.

FINAL REVISIONS AND SHARING

When I listened the next day, I found myself tweaking two main things: timing and volume levels. With timing, I knew I had to be careful, because changes I made to one track had the potential to adjust everything that happened later in the track, messing up all my *later* timings. So I carefully used Audacity's "sync-lock" option to make sure that a timing change on any one track would leave every track "locked" together in time. I mainly adjusted transitions between sentences and sections, inserting a teensy bit of silence or music to give listeners a chance to let things soak in.

I also was carefully picky with my volume levels, always with an ear toward keeping my narration the cleanest, loudest thing in the mix, while also letting other sounds rise and fall in noticeable ways—nothing should be *too* quiet!—both beneath and between my words. I use Audacity's Envelope Tool quite often, fiddling manually with the levels of different parts of each clip, but I also use super-short fades in and out to help make everything sound as smooth and professional as possible. I usually like to listen to the whole project in multiple spaces, when I have time, to make sure it's as good as possible, though I don't think I remembered to do this with "Pincushion."

When I knew I was done, I exported the file as an MP3 at the highest MP3 quality possible, 320 kbps, and uploaded it to Google Drive so I wouldn't lose it. I also uploaded the MP3 to the contest's upload page using Submittable, a common website for creative writing submissions. They didn't ask for anything but the audio file, but I made sure to let the contest organizers know that I had a full transcript and credits to all sounds available upon request; I knew that if I won, they would need that info to give full legal credit to the owners of the sounds I used, following the requirements of the Creative Commons licenses of those assets.

"Pincushion" is a personal essay produced by me, Kyle Stedman. All sounds and music heard are licensed by Creative Commons. In order, you heard (often with some kind of effect added):

- Huminaatio, "Putting & pulling cartridges from Famicom": https://freesound.org/people/Huminaatio/sounds/159342/
- InspectorJ, "Door, Wooden, Close, A (H1).wav": https://freesound.org/people/InspectorJ/sounds/411791/
- exDigita, "Mellow keyboard take": https://soundcloud.com/exdigita/mellow-keyboard-take
- Staile, "clear_throat.aiff": https://freesound.org/people/Staile/sounds/26336/
- bigpickle51, "Stereo Jet Landing Sample 2.wav": https://freesound.org/people/bigpickle51/sounds/262755/

Figure A.4 The first few assets listed at the end of the published version of "Pincushion."

I didn't win the prize—but now I had this audio memoir sitting there just waiting to be shared, and I wanted it to have a bigger audience. So I started looking around for online literary magazines that publish audio memoirs and finally found *Memoir Magazine*, a publication that I liked more and more as I read what they had published in the past. They hadn't published much audio before me (I only found two pieces), but since they said they welcomed it, I thought they might like to hear some more. So I submitted "Pincushion," again, using Submittable, the creative writing industry standard. Fairly soon, I received an email saying that they wanted to publish it, which felt great; plus, it saved me some time, since I was already starting my list of where to send it next. It took a few months before it actually went up on the site, but it was worth the wait to see it there.

> **Learn More**
> See Sharing Your Work in chapter five for more advice on submitting soundwriting to literary magazines.

One thing I'm disappointed about: at its publication site, the audience can listen to my MP3 or read the print version of the memoir, and they can see my list of assets at the bottom of the screen, but the transcript isn't rich. That is, it only lists my narration alone, instead of giving a full description of all the audio heard for someone reading who wants the closest replication of the full audio experience. If I were submitting it again, I'd push for that kind of transcript.

> **Learn More**
> See the Transcribing section in chapter five for more on composing transcripts.

Interlude Takeaways

Don't miss these lessons you can learn from my story:

- Don't delete your old drafts of writing! Some of them might be perfect for a powerful soundwriting piece.
- When revising written sentences to be read aloud, you'll often need to shorten and simplify complex sentences.
- Record narration in a quiet space with soft walls, and be sure to test the sound and placement of your mic before going too far.
- Don't try to do everything in one day. At a minimum, separate your recording and editing sessions.
- Remember that you can modify audio clips and sound effects that you create or download. Play around with different effects in your audio editor to help you discover new sounds that go beyond what you imagined.
- Be prepared to share your compositions with listeners beyond those you initially had in mind.

Genre Conventions: Audio Memoir

Though book-length memoirs and short personal essays about one's life are hugely popular in the creative writing world, most publications of creative nonfiction use words alone, not sound. Even when a journal publishes audio work, there isn't currently a standard: some share audio versions of work they already published in print as read by actors, some invite you to read your own memoir but without adding any extra audio assets like music or effects, and some will publish audio with those assets included. There are also many podcasts focusing on creative nonfiction—though only some of them feature actual authors reading their memoirs—and plenty of personal podcasts that share the qualities of my audio memoir, even if they don't call themselves "memoirs."

With all that, the genre conventions of audio memoir are hard to describe as a whole; it's perhaps better to focus on the stated guidelines for an individual publication. Still, I'll do my best to give some overall advice, since that's how all genres work, with some central qualities and plenty of outliers.

- **Where It's Heard**: *The Missouri Review* is a good place to start; check out past winners of The Miller Audio Prize and hear more in the Miller Aud-Cast podcast. *The Drum* publishes audio in all genres of creative writing (usually read by the author), including memoir. You can hear some audio memoirs read by actors in *Streetlight Magazine*'s podcast, occasional memoir pieces on *The Creative Nonfiction Podcast*, and occasional audio pieces at *Memoir Magazine*. To hear more audio memoirs, browse literary magazines at *Poets & Writers*' website, where you can search for the word *audio*. Plenty of podcasts seem to me to be "memoirs," whether or not they call themselves that—for example, *How to Be a Girl*, *Millennial*, and *Not by Accident*.

> **Learn More**
> See the companion site for links to these publications and more.

- **Length**: There's no set length, but keep in mind that people often listen to audio while doing other things; longer pieces could scare off some listeners (though hour-long podcasts are regularly consumed by some listeners). The Miller Audio Prize caps submissions at fifteen minutes long, while *The Drum* asks for written submissions of 5,000 words or fewer (which could take more or less time to read, depending on your pace).
- **Content**: A memoir is more than just a recitation of things that happened in your life; it's a selected, focused lens into a particular true story to make a larger, more universal point to an audience.
- **Structure**: Memoirs can tell a chronological story of your life, tell multiple stories out of order, or intersperse moments of scene with reflective descriptive moments.

- **Language**: Memoirs use descriptive, powerful language that's full of images and fresh phrases. They may (even if you don't remember exactly what someone said) or may not include dialogue
- **Opening and Closing**: Memoirs (whether written or aural) use powerful first and last lines that leave an impression and always end paragraphs, sections, and the entire piece with memorable "mic drop" moments.
- **Script**: Audio memoirists should definitely read from a script, since the refined, carefully crafted language is part of why someone would want to hear it. They will typically "let the script lead."
- **Sonic Rhetorical Strategies**: Some in the creative writing world will see anything besides a speaking voice as unnecessary or distracting from the power of your words (which is probably the more common view); others will embrace the full use of audio to tell your personal stories.

Ultimately, the best audio memoirs are audio versions of the best written memoirs. I suggest reading the memoirs and the writing advice at the online magazine *Brevity* and studying the suggestions in Mary Karr's *The Art of Memoir* and Brenda Miller and Suzanne Paola's *Tell It Slant: Creating, Refining, and Publishing Creative Nonfiction*.

Works Cited

Karr, Mary. *The Art of Memoir*. Harper Perennial, 2016.

Miller, Brenda, and Suzanne Paola. *Tell It Slant: Creating, Refining, and Publishing Creative Nonfiction*. 3rd ed., McGraw-Hill, 2019.

Stedman, Kyle. "Pincushion." *Memoir Magazine*, 28 Oct. 2019, memoirmag.com/10-minute-listen/pincushion-by-kyle-stedman/.

Chapter Two

LISTEN LIKE A SOUNDWRITER

INTRODUCTION

When podcasting erupted on the scene years ago, we did a lot of listening. Tanya devoured all kinds of nonfiction podcasts and was particularly intrigued by sound-rich programs like *Radiolab* and investigative journalism like *S-Town*. Kyle was one of many who was hooked by the complexity of *Serial*, which led him to start listening to his favorite NPR radio shows in his podcast app, and then the shows on the Radiotopia network, and then shows by other rhetoric scholars and teachers, and then more. We immersed ourselves in these stories; we tried on different perspectives, visualized places we had never been or seen, and got to know our favorite sonic storytellers and their characters.

That listening became a crucial part of our own journeys toward becoming sound-writers. Our listening drew us to notice the rhetorical strategies inherent to sound-writing—voice, sound effects, silence, and music—and their rhetorical functions (which we'll discuss in detail in the next chapter). We started developing our own vocabulary of soundwriting choices, and we consciously practiced identifying and analyzing these strategies while listening to other people's soundwriting. In other words, our own effectiveness as soundwriters began when we listened. After all, the best creative people in any genre immerse themselves in communities of others who practice their art or craft. Writers read other writing; musicians listen to other music; painters study other paintings; engineers pore over other designs; doctors and nurses consult with other doctors and nurses. Why would soundwriting be any different?

We listen to audio works to identify sonic rhetorical strategies, but we still also find ourselves transported into the immersive experience of soundwriting—*feeling, seeing*, and *being* in the experience. When we're immersed in soundwriting, we pay careful attention to our emotions, the visuals we see in our minds, and our reactions. We often experience what NPR professionals call "driveway moments"— occasions when a "story keeps you pinned in your car, in the parking lot, in the driveway or at the side of the road—as you wait to hear how the story will end" (Kern xi–xii). In other words, even though we sometimes listen analytically, we sometimes just listen for the pleasure of listening, to experience the bread-and-butter moments of audio storytelling, the stuff that keeps listeners engaged and wanting more. What's more, we want to be able to replicate immersive moments in our own soundwriting—which leads us back to understanding and naming how soundwriters make these moves.

Figure 2.1
Sometimes we need to touch what we're listening to, feeling its vibrations throughout our bodies.

What we were doing was *listening like soundwriters*. And now, after lots of practice, we unconsciously listen to soundwriting in this way, toggling between immersing ourselves in soundwriting—taking on the role of a listener—and naming and analyzing strategies and their rhetorical effects—taking on the role of an analyzer. Listening like a soundwriter includes both halves, and doing so continuously develops our rhetorical abilities to make good soundwriting. It will help you, too.

Here's a quick glimpse into what listening like a soundwriter can be like. Tanya recently began listening to *Blindspot: Tulsa Burning*, a six-episode podcast about the massacre of a Black neighborhood 100 years ago. The narrator, KalaLea, begins the podcast with this narration: "When I was about 7 years old, our house was robbed" (KalaLea). Tanya immediately recognized the use of personal anecdote, which is a common, effective way to begin an audio story because of its ability to humanize the narrator, foster a personal connection between the listener and the narrator, and ultimately position the narrator as a trustworthy storyteller. Tanya noticed that music began to play at the end of the first sentence and continued while KalaLea spoke. The music bed (music that plays beneath narration) evoked fear, anxiety, and suspense; Tanya felt it in her gut and knew the music foreshadowed a difficult situation. As the story unfolded, Tanya's focus shifted from the music to the narration. The narration transported her to KalaLea's home: Tanya saw a ransacked living room in her mind's eye, and she tried to step into KalaLea's shoes—to feel her astonishment, fear, and pain. Later Tanya thought about how KalaLea's vocal qualities and her delivery, as well as the descriptive language she used, played a role in these immersive moments—the moments that kept Tanya "pinned in her car." Ultimately, Tanya's movement between immersive listening and listening for rhetorical choices further strengthened her understanding of rhetorical moves in this piece of soundwriting, just as it does when she listens to any piece of soundwriting, ultimately improving her own soundwriting abilities.

This chapter teaches you how to listen like a soundwriter. Our listening-like-a-soundwriter (LLS) approach emphasizes careful auditory attention both to the immersive power of sound and how it rhetorically functions. Soundwriters who use the LLS approach to listen to others' work become more attuned to how soundwriting makes them feel, how it's constructed, and how they can make choices that impact their own soundwriting audience. In other words, they listen to become better soundwriters.

This practice will not only help you become an effective soundwriter, it will also enable you to build and develop what rhetoric scholars Michelle Comstock and Mary E. Hocks call "sonic literacy." They define this as "the ability to identify, define, situate, construct, manipulate, and communicate our personal and cultural soundscapes"—in short, the ability to be both savvy listeners and makers of sound.

In this chapter, you will learn listening strategies and develop a mindset to use in your quest to become a strong soundwriter.

LISTENING MYTHS

Let's start by acknowledging and debunking a few myths about listening before we dive into the depths of the LLS practice.

Myth 1: Listening Is the Same as Hearing.

Figure 2.2
Listening is a conscious decision to attend to all sonic vibrations with our entire body.

Listening and hearing are conflated all the time, but we think they're different in important ways.

Communication scholars Milena Droumeva and David Murphy define hearing as "our physical ability to perceive vibrations through the air and identify their frequency, envelope, spectrum, and directivity." In other words, for people who do not have hearing impairments, hearing is the physiological process of receiving sound through the ears. You don't have to do anything to hear; it just happens. It's a sense, just like seeing or feeling, yet unlike other senses, it's always turned on.

Listening is different. Droumeva and Murphy define listening as "a cognitive, socially constructed, and habitually acquired process that allows us to discriminate, both consciously and unintentionally, what it is that we pay attention to." The "attention" part of this definition is important: it's the heart of the process and practice of listening. We listen when we focus our minds on particular parts of what we're hearing. The attention we give or don't give sound ultimately leads to listeners "doing" something with that sound: understanding it, making meaning of it, ignoring it, embracing it, visualizing it, or feeling it. Unlike hearing, listening is a conscious act that takes effort and concentration and practice to get good at.

And that leads to our second myth.

Myth 2: We Can Listen Just Fine without Practice or Instruction.

Figure 2.3
We can learn to listen in groups, yet this kind of instruction is rare in schools.

Even though listening is important, it's not something we just do naturally. Listening, according to communication specialist Julian Treasure, is the "forgotten" and "silent skill," one that is hardly taught or even acknowledged as being important (qtd. in Brady-Myerov 27). Educator and former radio journalist Monica Brady-Myerov explains, "it was generally assumed that because students come to kindergarten hearing, they can listen, and that school instruction should focus on teaching them how to read, write, and calculate" (79). As a result, listening instruction barely exists, and when it does occur, it's primarily in elementary school and the "focus is often on listening to others and listening to instructions" (25).

Yet surely we need to listen to more than just instructions. Listening, in our opinion, should be more like a sport or a skill, something you practice regularly and improve incrementally. That's the purpose of this chapter: to give you a framework and exercises to help you practice listening beyond the meager instruction you may have gotten in elementary school. And while we can't provide you with support in learning all of the different kinds of listening—active, critical, strategic, mindful—we can provide you with a practice that benefits you as a soundwriter.

Myth 3: Listening Can Only Be Done with the Ears.

Figure 2.4
Sound waves affect far more than just our ears.

It seems to make sense that listening is immediately associated with the ear since the ear is the organ associated with hearing. Yet let us help you understand why hearing and listening can both go beyond the ears. Close your eyes. Imagine you're in a subway station. You hear the shhhhhhh, rumble, and squeals of a train approaching. You feel the vibration under your feet and in your gut. You see a person's hair whip across their face and watch the water in a puddle vibrate as the train passes by and comes to a screeching halt.

Listening can entail hearing, feeling, and seeing; it is a full-body experience.

Rhetoric scholar Steph Ceraso refers to this kind of full-body listening as multimodal listening, which she defines as "the practice of attending to the sensory, contextual, and material aspects of a sonic event" (6)—in other words, paying attention to something completely, with all the parts of your body. It's different from what she calls "ear-ing," listening to sound waves through the ears alone. Ceraso's concept of multimodal listening was partly inspired by Evelyn Glennie, a deaf musician, who has spoken about her experiences with listening in several interviews. In one TED talk, Glennie recaps a discussion she had as a 12-year-old with her music teacher:

My teacher said, "Well, how are we going to do this? You know, music is about listening." And I said, "Yes, I agree with that, so what's the problem?" And he said, "Well, how are you going to hear this? How are you going to hear that?" And I said, "Well, how do you hear it?" He said, "Well, I think I hear it through here" [pointing at her ears]. And I said, "Well, I think I do too, but I also hear it through my hands, through my arms, cheekbones, my scalp, my tummy, my chest, my legs and so on."

Glennie also likens hearing to touch: "You feel it through your body, and sometimes it almost hits your face" (qtd. in Treasure 97). Helen Keller made a similar connection in a letter she wrote to the Symphony Society of New York after hearing a radio presentation of Beethoven's Ninth Symphony in 1924. Even though she was both deaf and blind, she describes holding her hand to the speaker, writing, "What was my amazement to discover that I could feel, not only the vibrations, but also the impassioned rhythm, the throb and urge of the music! ... The great chorus throbbed against my fingers with poignant pause and flow" (271).

The feeling of sound and the way it touches our bodies doesn't just happen to people who can't hear with their ears: it happens to all of us. Why? Because sounds are vibrations, and if those vibrations are strong enough, they can be felt in different parts of the body. And when we pay attention to that physical kind of hearing, we are then able to engage and do something with the sounds we hear and feel.

LISTEN LIKE A SOUNDWRITER

The LLS practice is an adaptation of a common reading approach taught in writing classes called "read like a writer" (RLW). This reading practice, described by scholar Charles Moran in the 1980s, involves identifying and analyzing the choices writers make in a way that helps readers write their own texts. When you read like a writer, you carefully think about how and why writers make choices, as well as the available choices not used in a text. Moran explains the value of the RLW practice: "When we read like writers we understand and participate in the writing. We see the choices the writer has made, and we see how the writer has coped with the consequences of those" (61). In other words, readers read to understand how a text was constructed so they can construct something similar. Author David Jauss encourages students to think about this practice like a carpenter. He says, "You must look at a book the way a carpenter looks at a house someone else built, examining the details in order to see how it was made" (64). Mike Bunn, an education and writing pedagogy scholar, claims this reading practice is "one of the very best ways to learn how to write well" (75); students recognize how and why choices are made and can make decisions as to whether they want to use similar choices in their own writing.

We're not the first to apply Moran's RLW practice to sound; composition scholar Amy Cicchino's "sound-mapping" activity asks students to carefully analyze a piece of audio by identifying the different parts of a podcast episode they listen to together in class. They map these parts onto a graphic organizer and later think about their purposes in the episode. It's not surprising that others have connected RLW to sound,

Learn More
Check out our companion site for Cicchino's downloadable graphic organizer.

since, as we said above, everyone who creates in any mode needs to study the way others make compositions in that genre. Really, the heart of our LLS practice is similar to Moran's and Cicchino's RLW practices: the identification and analysis of writerly choices and their effects on an audience.

Try-It 2.1 Using "Sound-Mapping" to Identify Rhetorical Choices

In "Sound-Mapping: Seeing the Rhetorical Choices in Podcasts," writing studies scholar Amy Cicchino offers an activity that guides listeners in visually mapping out the parts of an audio project on a graphic organizer. Sound-mapping, which Cicchino likens to audio storyboarding or an alphabetic outline, enables listeners to identify and later rhetorically analyze the different parts of a piece of soundwriting. It also works to familiarize listeners and future soundwriters with the "look of audio design program interfaces"—that is, with different audio assets layered vertically and with time moving forward horizontally. The following activity is adapted from Cicchino's article; try it out with a group of fellow soundwriters following the steps below.

1. As a group, listen to a sound-rich podcast trailer (with at least three sonic rhetorical strategies used, like sound effects, music, and voice) from a podcast that focuses on one event, person, or experience (such as *Bear Brook* or *S-Town*; both have transcripts). Listen to it several times, sometimes immersing yourself in it and sometimes listening more critically.

2. After listening, discuss the rhetorical situation with your group: the purpose, audience, genre, and context of the trailer, as far as you can tell.

3. Listen to the trailer again. On your own page, draw a box similar to the graphic organizer below. (You can download an editable version of this organizer on our companion website.) Individually, identify the sound sources in the left column (create as many rows as necessary) with descriptive language—perhaps the name of a speaker or a type of sound. Then in the right column, mark when you hear each sound with a line. You may want to use different color markers for each source to create a stronger visual differentiation among them. See Cicchino's completed graphic organizer for the beginning of "Thank You for Noticing," an episode from the podcast *Reply All*, at the bottom of this try-it.

	Time: 0:00 0:10 0:20 0:30 0:40 0:50 1:00…
Source 1:	
Source 2:	

4. Now, get into small groups (2–4 people). In your group, discuss one or two sound sources carefully, identifying their rhetorical function and thinking about the extent to which they are effective in achieving the overall goal of the piece of soundwriting. Be sure to note other ways the soundwriters could have created these rhetorical effects in a different or more effective way.

5. Come together as a large group so each small group can report the highlights of their discussion. Discuss your experiences by making a visual sound-map together on a large board, focusing on how this mapping might help you make choices in your own soundwriting.

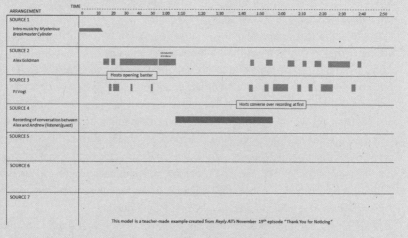

Figure 2.5 Cicchino's sound-map from an episode of *Reply All*.

There's a bit more to our version of the LLS practice because of what we know about the lack of listening instruction in our country, the complexity of sound and our relationship to it, the immersive and emotional affordances of sound, and the difficulty of "allocating our attention," as sound studies scholar Tom Rice says, to different things in different ways (100).

We think of the **LLS practice** as having two fluid stages: a preparation stage and a practice stage. The ongoing preparation stage calls for listeners to attune their ears and bodies to the sounds around them. Such attunement heightens one's awareness of sound and prepares them for the work of the practice stage. The practice stage invites listeners to focus on a text by immersing themselves in it and identifying rhetorical choices and their effects, just as Tanya did when listening to *Blindspot: Tulsa Burning*.

Preparation Stage: Attuning Your Ears and Body to the World

Before you can truly listen to a particular piece of soundwriting like a soundwriter, you should begin developing listening skills in general, through regular practice. This means training the ear and body to notice and pay close attention to sounds and our auditory environments, particularly sounds that aren't heard or felt. This stage isn't bound by time or ever really completed; it is a continuous practice to use in your daily life.

When training your ear and body, pay close attention to:

- Sounds you often tune out, like birds chirping, neighbors chatting, or airplanes flying overhead.
- Barely noticeable sounds, like a whispering breeze, the subtle buzz of electricity in an overhead light, or the hum of a quiet fan.
- Deep sounds that you sense in your chest, hands, or feet, rather than your ears, like a distant machine or nearby ocean.
- Visual sounds that you know are there by their effect on things you see, like vibrations in water or branches moving in the wind.
- Soundscapes, or the collection of sounds in a space that work together to create an environment. Think of a summer day city soundscape: scurrying feet, laughter, conversation, crawling cars in traffic, and music flowing from apartment windows, all blended and experienced as a whole.
- Sounds' origins, like the identifiably different chirp of a cardinal and a finch, the different horn sounds of a Jeep and a Jetta, or the different quality of rustling leaves when made by a snake or a squirrel.
- Qualities of sound, like pitch, volume, speed, and rhythm, for example.
- Changes in sounds, especially how sounds change as you move through different environments.

The attuning of the ear and the body will help soundwriters more easily identify sounds and think about how they might be used in a piece of soundwriting—but we think you'll also find a pre-cognitive sort of pleasure in focused listening alone, even before your mind begins thinking about what it can teach you. After practicing for a while, you'll unconsciously hear and feel sounds that you never did before. It will become a natural way of living and being in the world.

Figure 2.6
On a soundwalk, groups walk through different soundscapes to attune themselves to the sounds of the world.

Try-It 2.2 **Attuning the Ear through Soundwalks**

Of the many ways to listen actively to our environments, soundwalks are some of the most popular, ever since they were described in detail by R. Murray Schafer's research group at The World Soundscape Project in the 1970s. Soundwalks often include a group of people walking silently in sonically interesting spaces with their minds attuned to sound and its vibrations. Various kinds of soundwalks exist: those led by a leader, those that contrast urban and natural environments, those where blindfolds are used to focus attention away from the eyes, those where the participants take notes, those that end with a conversation, and those that blend pre-recorded sounds with the natural sounds in the environment.

The good news is that you can blend any or all of these options in whatever way makes sense to you and your soundwalking group. The key is to try it, and ideally not alone; there's something about having others nearby who are focused on the same listening task to encourage your mind from getting too far off-task. Try to find places with lots of contrast between the natural and human-made and between loud and quiet, and feel free to hypothesize about what you might learn—but also be ready to be surprised by what your listening reveals and what ideas and connections you start to make.

Practice Stage: Focus on Soundwriting through Immersion and Rhetorical Analysis

Once you begin developing a practice of attuning yourself to the auditory world, you're ready to apply your listening skills to soundwriting. That is, you can choose a particular radio show, podcast episode, audio drama, or sonic art piece and listen to it fully, as someone who is practicing the sonic literacies that will help you create something like it in the future. (For suggestions of soundwriting that are particularly amenable to practicing your LLS skills, see Tip 2.4 below.)

This means listening to the soundwriting in two ways: listening to be immersed and listening to identify rhetorical choices and their effects. Let us explain.

Listening to be immersed is allowing or encouraging yourself to be transported into a piece of soundwriting, to experience the journey the soundwriter has designed for listeners. As Tanya's experience listening to *Blindspot: Tulsa Burning* illustrates, we find ourselves immersed in what we're listening to all the time. Indeed that's the nature of good soundwriting: it beckons with an intimacy and humanity that makes it hard to pull away. And that immersion in sound is good! Let yourself be swept away, allowing the sonic experience crafted for you to work its wonders.

Figure 2.7
When we're immersed
in sound, it surrounds
every part of us.

You might be thinking: *Isn't this the same as the preparation stage you described above?* Not quite. We see the preparation stage as an ongoing way of attuning yourself to the world, always turning your attention to listening as a habit of life. But when we talk about listening to be immersed, here in the practice stage, we're talking about listening to particular pieces of soundwriting—listening to crafted, designed audio compositions—in a way that allows them to wash over you and affect your body and emotions.

Figure 2.8   The two stages of listening like a soundwriter.

Visualizing and *participating in* the creation of soundwriting is one way listeners get swept away when engaged with soundwriting. Visualization helps a listener create their own experience, as the mental images they form are unique to them. Tanya, for example, conjured up a specific image of KalaLea's ransacked home: she saw a brown carpet, beige walls, a staircase to the left of the living room, a coffee table upside down, a half-eaten waffle on the floor, and various bits of paper and glass on the floor. She really doesn't know why she saw these exact mental images but, like with all listeners, they somehow can be traced back to her own life experiences.

Tanya made what communication professor Emma Rodero would call her "own production" (qtd. in Wen). These immersive moments that evoke visuals are said to be how soundwriters keep listeners' attention, so when you listen to be immersed, pay careful attention to what you see in your mind's eye and ways that you make the experience your own. Doing so will help you better understand how to trigger listeners' imaginations and emotions in your own soundwriting.

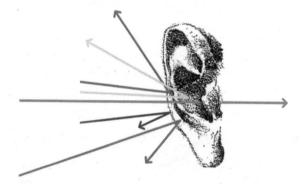

Figure 2.9
Mindful listening focuses the attention on only a chosen selection of what is heard.

TIP

2.1 One Kind of Immersed Listening: Mindful Listening

A "mindful listening" practice will enable you to immerse yourself in soundwriting, either in audio or transcript form. This kind of listening is defined as "paying attention in a particular way: on purpose, in the present, and nonjudgmentally" (Kabat-Zinn 4). Mindful listeners focus on what they are hearing and feeling at the present moment and acknowledge and dismiss the internal thoughts or mind chatter, sometimes called "monkey mind," that prevent them from being in the present. A mindful listener shifts their perspective from "observer" to "participant," detaching from the self and literally immersing themselves in the experience, making the soundwriting their own. Here are some tips for how to practice mindful listening and guidelines for using it to listen to rhetorical choices:

- Minimize distractions and get comfortable.
- Play a piece of soundwriting that you want to listen to in a new way, perhaps something that's from the perspective of someone with a different lived experience than you in some way.
- Take notes while listening, to document what you see, feel, and how you react.
- Be open to trying on different points of views and experiences, even if they are vastly different from how you see the world or make you feel uncomfortable or unfamiliar.
- Read and reread your notes after listening, reliving how you dwelled in the sonic event. Then seek to determine how the soundwriter created immersive moments using your vocabulary bank or language that best fits your understanding of the move.

Listening to rhetorical choices involves identifying and analyzing rhetorical choices and their effects as well as exploring immersive moments to determine what indeed makes them immersive.

In some ways, this part of the LLS practice is like the next step of Try-It 1.3, "Analyzing the Rhetorical Situation of a Podcast Episode." In that exercise, you analyzed the purpose, audience, context, and genre of a particular podcast episode. LLS asks you to make your listening one step more granular by identifying the specific moves the soundwriter used to be effective in that rhetorical situation.

You can probably identify a lot of rhetorical strategies in any piece of soundwriting on your own or within a community of soundwriters, simply by asking yourself: *What do I notice in this piece?* Most of the things you notice—like the relative volume of different layered parts of the audio, the speed of the different segments, the sound effects used, and the emotions you can hear in a narrator's voice—are choices that the soundwriter employed to create a certain effect on their listener. After noticing and naming choices, you then might ask yourself: *How did they do that?* You may need further reflection to identify the choice's rhetorical function, so you could then ask: *What did this choice do to help the soundwriter achieve their purpose?* (See Tip 2.2 for an example of how to use these questions to identify rhetorical choices.) By listening to others' soundwriting, especially when you're listening with other people who may notice different choices, you can build a rich vocabulary to draw on later for purposes of both analysis and your own compositions.

TIP

2.2 How and Why Did They Do That?

Part of listening like a soundwriter is identifying the choices made by creators and determining their rhetorical effects. You can analyze those choices with the language of rhetorical analysis (the text's purpose, audience, genre, and context), but you can also use two simple questions: "How did they do that?" and "Why did they do that?" Here's an example:

- You're watching a TV show about Vikings, and every time the scene changes, you hear a sort of *whoosh* and *clang* that sounds very...Viking-y. *How did they do that?* you should ask yourself. Could you search online for the sound-design tricks of people who work on TV documentaries? Or just rewind and listen to try to hear what the different elements of the sound are, in hopes that you could replicate it from scratch? Then you might ask yourself: What were they trying to achieve with those sound effects? How does adding sound to a visual transition add to the energy and drama of a documentary show?

- You're reading a transcript of an episode of the fictional podcast *Mabel* and notice these sounds between the introductory paragraph and the beginning of a dialogue: "[CHAOS; ROARING; SCREAMING; MUSIC HOWLING; GRINDING AS THOUGH OF ENORMOUS GEARS; GLITCHING]" (De La Rosa and Martin 1). You wonder: What kind of scene do these sounds suggest? How does this set a scene for the dialogue? What is the purpose of using this chaotic language as a transition? Where did they find these sounds and how did they put them together to create a scene?

- You're listening to a song that you've heard on your roommate's computer a couple of times, but this is the first time you've listened to it with headphones. So this is the first time you notice the fun, interesting percussion, which almost sounds like a bunch of cans and wooden objects are being hit, not drums. *How did they do that?* You listen again, paying attention to which ear you hear each sound in, trying to imagine what might make those sounds. *And why did they make the percussion sound that way?* Maybe it adds a physical, unprocessed, live feeling to the music that echoes how other instruments were recorded and even echoes some of the themes in the vocals.

- You're listening to an emotional, pivotal moment in a podcast. You're listening in your car as you drive, but it's so powerful you pull over and just listen for a few minutes. When it's over, you stop and breathe for a second—you're not crying, they're crying—before you ask, *How did they do that?* You rewind and listen to that last bit again, noticing the pieces that were added together to make it so effective: the slow, emotion-filled delivery of the narrator; the perfectly timed, quiet music that swelled in just the right moments; the long pause before the interviewee said just what you hoped he wouldn't have to say; the sound of space where the interview was held, with crowds and traffic in the background making it seem even more real and down-to-earth; the change in music to signify a change in mood. All of these moves contributed to this powerful emotional impact you experienced while listening.

You might not always know the answer to "How did they do that?" or "Why did they do that?" but it's always worthwhile to ask.

Sometimes it's hard to know how to describe the rhetorical choices made by a soundwriter, especially if you feel new to sound; our students often say to us, "I'm not a musician! How am I supposed to know what words to use to describe what I'm hearing?" You might find yourself in need of a vocabulary—which you might find you can develop simply by listening carefully and using your own words, or by relying on a pre-existing vocabulary bank to guide you in your identification and analysis of sound strategies. For example, you might head to chapter three and use the sonic rhetorical terms we describe—voice, silence, sound effects, and music—to guide you in listening and then analyzing sonic choices. You may even combine that list with terms commonly used in other disciplines. For example, your vocabulary bank can be filled with strategies used in alphabetic writing that you notice are also used in soundwriting, like structure, organization, imagery, and transitions, or musical analysis terms like tone, pitch, timbre, and dynamics. A vocabulary bank provides you with language to name rhetorical choices in soundwriting that you might not yet have the knowledge or experience to name. It's also helpful as a guide when you are seeking to understand how a particular strategy—like voice or music—rhetorically functions within a piece of soundwriting. Such isolated identification and rhetorical analysis is helpful for really understanding how a strategy might work on its own or in conjunction with other strategies to achieve a rhetorical purpose.

TIP 2.3 Possible Terms for a Sonic Vocabulary Bank

As you listen like a soundwriter, you'll find there are many different vocabularies you could rely on as you describe the complex interplay of sounds you're hearing. This table is designed to offer a few of those different vocabularies, which you'll find fit better or worse in certain academic disciplines and professions.

How sounds work in a context (words a rhetorician or literary scholar might use)	How sounds can be described in isolation (words a musician or audio engineer might use)	How sounds can be described together (words a podcaster or radio journalist might use)
• How sounds work in their rhetorical situation o Purpose o Audience o Context o Genre • How sounds appeal to audiences[1] o Ethos o Pathos o Logos o Kairos • How sounds reflect the canons of rhetoric o Invention o Arrangement o Style o Delivery	• Pitch (how high or low a sound is, like higher or lower notes on a piano) • Dynamics (how loud or quiet a sound is) • Timbre (the quality of a sound itself, like the difference between the sound of a piano, organ, or trumpet) • Tempo (how quickly or slowly something repeats or acts in relation to other sounds) • Stereophonic space (which speaker or side of the headphones the sound is closer to—left or right)	• Sound that is layered vertically and happening at the same time o Voice o Music o Sound Effects o Silence • Words to describe horizontal changes (in chronological sequence): o Fade in o Fade out o Reverb o Echo o Transitions o Segments

1 For definitions of the rhetorical terms in this column, see Gideon Burton's comprehensive site *Silva Rhetoricae: The Forest of Rhetoric*, which gives both simple definitions and many examples.

Another way to identify rhetorical choices is to return to the immersive moments you experienced in a piece of soundwriting and carefully think about how those moments might have been crafted, as in Tip 2.2. Again, you may find yourself relying on existing vocabularies or creating your own phrases to explain what you're hearing.

Listening to soundwriting to develop your own vocabulary bank or using an established vocabulary bank aren't either/or options. Soundwriters may use both methods to create a vocabulary they can use for analyzing other peoples' soundwriting and later for composing their own soundwriting.

Remember, when you're listening like a soundwriter, you're moving your attention back and forth: immersion and analysis; feeling and thinking; being and knowing.

In Tanya's description of her listening process, you'll notice she moved her attention, for example, between naming and identifying the rhetorical function of music, visualizing the scene of the robbery, and later reflecting on how the soundwriting evoked these visualizations. It takes a lot of practice to listen in this fluid way: to slide across the attention spectrum to notice and analyze how a piece of soundwriting is constructed.

Try-It   2.3 Practicing LLS in a Group

It's helpful to practice the two ways of listening like a soundwriter—listening to be immersed and listening to rhetorical choices—in groups. Below is an activity that's perfect for a classroom, designed to further clarify the importance of both kinds of listening and their value in supporting developing soundwriters.

1. People are divided into two groups: the "listening to be immersed" group and the "listening to rhetorical choices" group.

2. Together they listen to Molly Menschel's "Just Another Fish Story" or another piece from Tip 2.4. The listening to be immersed group allows itself to be swept away by what it hears, visualizing the content and using mindful listening to engage with the story, carefully taking notes about their immersive experience as listeners. The listening to rhetorical choices group uses a critical listening approach, drawing on the community's vocabulary to identify the rhetorical choices used and how they might function. Each group should try their best to note the timestamps of their observations.

3. After listening to the story, the individuals in each group get together to discuss the rhetorical choices they observed and their experiences in using their assigned way of listening to engage with the story. The groups report back highlights of their discussion to the whole class.

4. The groups then listen to the story again, but this time they switch roles: the listening to be immersed group becomes the listening to rhetorical choices group and vice versa.

5. After this listening session, each person responds to the following questions in a five-minute freewrite (without stopping): What was your experience listening in this new way, and how did it differ from your previous listening experience? In what ways did these kinds of listening help you learn about the choices soundwriters can make in their audio projects?

6. In a large group discussion, people volunteer to read or summarize their freewrites. Group conversation ensues.

Try-It   2.4 **Collaboratively Writing "Thick Descriptions"**

In "Tuning the Sonic Playing Field: Teaching Ways of Knowing Sound," rhetoric scholar Kati Fargo Ahern describes the value of collaboratively writing "thick descriptions" to identify sounds and later determine their rhetorical effects. A "thick description" is exactly what it sounds like: a detailed written description of sounds in a piece of soundwriting. For example, Ahern's students wrote the following description for The Shins' song "Pink Bullets": "The song starts with two guitars and a single, male voice. The song has a slow beat. If it were a walk, I'd call it a mosey. The beat has a medium-paced, plodding tempo, setting the mood of a more thoughtful sound. The beat is slow but strong, established by the strumming and then slapping of the guitar" (83). Note how they include physical descriptions of the sounds played along with some interpretive observations as well.

This exercise can remind us that listeners engage with soundwriting in different ways because of various factors, such as our values, culture, race, ethnicity, and listening habits and practices. Ahern claims that a collaborative thick description of a piece of soundwriting highlights these differences and honors these different listening experiences while simultaneously identifying the different rhetorical choices that individuals were able to identify.

The following collaborative activity will guide you in writing thick descriptions that can later be used to build a sonic vocabulary for analysis and soundwriting.

1. Choose a sonically rich story (with at least two sonic rhetorical strategies used, such as music and voice) that is under ten minutes (see Tip 2.4 for ideas); the entire group will focus on different sections of this one piece. People are divided into several groups, with two to three members in each group. Each group is assigned a two- to three-minute segment of the story.

2. Group members write thick descriptions individually, using the questions *What do I notice?* and *What does it do?* to guide them in writing their descriptions. Everyone should be sure to describe a) the sounds themselves, b) how the sounds make them feel, and c) what the sounds remind them of. Individuals then share their descriptions with their group.

3. Group members then work collaboratively to draft one thick description of their assigned story segment in the form of a single long paragraph. They may do this in one of two ways. They might take up one person's thick description and add more details to it or they might collaboratively write one thick description based on their individual descriptions.

4. Each group places their collaboratively written thick descriptions of their assigned segment in a shared document in the order that reflects the order of the story.

5. All individuals read the thick descriptions of the entire story.

6. Everyone then works together to pull out terms from the thick descriptions and describe their rhetorical effects. A chart with the term on the left side and the description of its possible rhetorical function on the right side would be helpful for organization purposes.

2.4 Podcasts That Reward LLS

You can practice listening like a soundwriter with practically any soundwriting you can imagine—perhaps by listening to some of the soundwriting genres listed in Tip 1.2 in the previous chapter, or even just by turning to your local public radio station.

Still, we love how so many podcasts are examples of rich soundwriting that reward careful listening. The shows below are great places to start if you're not sure where to find shows that are sonically rich and digitally edited. **The podcasts that provide transcriptions are marked with **.** For more show ideas, you might want to see the list of podcasts on the Credits and References page of rhetoric scholar (and podcaster) Eric Detweiler's article "The Bandwidth of Podcasting."

Find links to all of these shows and episodes on our companion site.

- *99% Invisible* (nonfiction stories that focus on design and architecture)**
- *A History of the World in 100 Objects* (interviews and descriptions of 100 items from the British Museum)
- *Bear Brook***
- *Bodies* (unflinching narratives about how individuals' bodies act)**
- *Code Switch* (nonfiction stories that focus on race)
- *Constellations* (experimental sound art)
- *Dolly Parton's America* (nonfiction stories across nine episodes that focus on country singer Dolly Parton)
- *Ear Hustle* (nonfiction stories related to life in prison)**
- *Everything Is Alive* (fictional interviews with inanimate objects)**
- *Here Be Monsters* (nonfiction stories about "fear, beauty, and the unknown" ["About the Podcast"])
- *The Horror of Dolores Roach* (fiction)
- *How to Be a Girl* (a mother shares her own story about raising a transgender daughter, with animated versions of each episode without closed captions)
- *Lore* (nonfiction scary stories)**
- Malcolm Gladwell's *Revisionist History* (nonfiction stories that explore the past)**

- *Millennial* (a recent college graduate makes an audio documentary about her struggle to find work and meaning)
- *Modern Love* (nonfiction stories that focus on relationships and love)**
- *Nancy* (narrative journalism about the queer experience)**
- *Radio Diaries* (self-documented nonfiction stories)**
- *Radiolab* (nonfiction narrative stories that challenge "listeners' preconceived notions about how the world works" ["About Radiolab"])**
- *Re:Sound* (stories from the Third Coast International Audio Festival)** (some, but not all, episodes have transcripts)
- *Snap Judgment* (nonfiction stories with rich sound design)
- *The Stoop* (nonfiction stories that focus on Black lives)
- *StoryCorps* (unscripted conversations between two people about "what's really important in life: love, loss, family, friendship" ["StoryCorps"])**
- *S-Town* (nonfiction story focused on one man's life experiences)**
- *This American Life* (nonfiction stories focused on a theme that relates to American culture)**
- *Twenty Thousand Hertz* (a show about the sounds we hear around us every day)**
- *UnFictional* (nonfiction stories that cover a range of people and their life experiences)**
- *Welcome to Night Vale* (fiction)**

Here are some of our favorite pieces of soundwriting to use for LLS exercises:

- *99% Invisible*, "Sounds Natural"**
- *Between the Liner Notes*, "The Tuning Wars"
- *Criminal*, "Animal Instincts" (the program invites those who want a transcript to email them)
- Axel Kacoutie's "How to Remember" (Winner of Best Documentary: Gold at 2020 Third Coast International Audio Festival)
- *Love & Radio*, "A Girl of Ivory"**
- Molly Menschel's "Just Another Fish Story" (Best New Artist at 2005 Third Coast International Audio Festival)
- *Radio Diaries*, "Centenarians in Lockdown" (Winner of Best Documentary: Short at 2020 Third Coast International Audio Festival)
- *Radiolab*, "Gonads: Dana"**
- *Radiolab*, "The Rhino Hunter"**
- *The Stoop* and KALW's *All Things Considered*, "The Problem with Sounding White"

- *This American Life*, "Beaching and Moaning" (part of the episode "When the Beasts Come Marching In")**
- *Twenty Thousand Hertz*, "Sonic Branding"**
- *UnFictional*, "Do You Believe in Daphne?"
- Javier Zamora's "The Return" (Winner of Best Documentary in 2019 Third Coast International Audio Festival)

CONCLUSION: LISTENING TO SOUNDS THAT HARM

Listening like a soundwriter prepares you to move into the practical steps in the next few chapters: you'll have a better understanding of why we spend so much time explaining sonic rhetorical strategies and their rhetorical functions in chapter three; you'll be prepared for the brainstorming and gathering activities in chapter four, since you'll have carefully listened to the ideas and sounds like a soundwriter; and you'll be ready to work in your audio editor as described in chapter five, eager to steal—oops, we mean apply—the kinds of rhetorical moves you experienced and noticed as you listened.

Yet before we move on to those chapters, we'd like to acknowledge one other aspect of listening that we didn't address above: the importance of recognizing that sounds and their qualities don't simply exist; they emerge in and respond to culture, history, and society, and develop meaning as a result. Sound can be used to uplift, to resist, to create controversy, to discriminate, to silence, to oppress, to bring people together or tear them apart, to erase individuals and individual or collective experiences, and even to torture. The absence of sound has the same powers. When you listen like a soundwriter, you're likely to notice sounds that are harmful—sounds that work to perpetuate oppression or trigger trauma. Our hope is that soundwriters who are attuned to harmful sounds will consciously avoid using them and perhaps even think about ways soundwriting can be used to expose, disrupt, and dismantle systems of oppression.

Let us give you an example of a sound that harms, and more specifically, a sound that perpetuates oppression. In *The Sonic Color Line*, Jennifer Lynn Stoever, a sound studies scholar, argues that sound can perpetuate racism. Young Black men have become associated with the "sound of hip-hop pumped at top volume through car speakers" (50), she writes, and noise ordinances—laws about what can be played in which spaces at what volumes—are the racist responses that follow. One such ordinance in Rochester, New York, states that it seeks to "tame the boom car monster" (50)—the "monster" seemingly being young Black men.

Another example is racist responses to accents and dialects, otherwise known as linguistic profiling or vocal stereotyping. One study reveals that people with an African American dialect and a Mexican-influenced Spanish-English dialect were treated differently than those who spoke what the authors call "Standard English" (Rice, Patricia). The people with such dialects who called in response to job ads or real estate offers were repeatedly hung up on or were not called back. In other words, they were denied opportunities for employment and real estate purchases based on their voice.

The examples of sound as a vehicle of oppression and trigger of trauma are countless. They emerge in everyday life in every outlet from real life to the media: the sonic imitation of a person with a disability, the music of blackface minstrelsy productions, and the sound of looting during protests, for example. Over time, these sounds have been ingrained in dominant culture, normalized, and have been used to oppress people. As listeners and soundwriters (and people in general), it's important that we recognize the meaning sound carries, the harm it can do, and how we might be playing a role in reinforcing stereotypes and promoting inequality and injustice.

That anti-racism work can begin with listening, but it can't end there. Let's turn to the tools you can use to compose sounds that will make change in the world.

Key Chapter Takeaways

- Hearing and listening are not the same. Hearing is a transmission of sound taken in through the ears or body, while listening is the act of paying attention to sound in an effort to "do something" with it, such as engage or not engage.
- The act of listening can be accomplished with the ears as well as the entire body. Listening can be heard, felt, and visualized.
- The ability to listen is not innate: it is a learned process that takes practice to get good at.
- There are many ways to listen. Listening like a soundwriter (LLS) is one way soundwriters can enhance their soundwriting abilities. There are two, fluid stages in the LLS practice: a preparation stage and a practice stage.
- The LLS preparation stage is a regular practice that calls for listeners to attune themselves to sounds around them with the goal of heightening their awareness of sound. Strong awareness enables soundwriters to understand and work with sound carefully and strategically in their own soundwriting.
- The LLS practice stage involves two kinds of listening: listening to be immersed and listening to rhetorical choices. Listening to be immersed invites soundwriters to feel, to see, and to experience soundwriting without

assessment or judgment. Listening to rhetorical choices invites sound-writers to identify and analyze the rhetorical moves made in soundwriting (often recognized during the listening to be immersed practice) and their impact on an audience. The LLS method ultimately invites soundwriters to move back and forth between listening to be immersed and listening to rhetorical choices.

Discussion Questions

1. Can you name an instance when you might have heard, felt, and/or seen sounds that others didn't? How did the recognition of those sounds play a role in how you experienced the world at that moment? Alternately, can you think of an instance where someone else heard, felt, and/or saw sounds that you didn't? What was that experience like for you?
2. What are some strategies and habits that you commonly use when you listen to other people or other sounds in the world? How might the LLS approach be similar to the kinds of listening you've done in the past? How might the LLS approach be different from the kind of listening that you're used to doing?
3. What challenges do you think you might have when using the LLS approach? What might you do to overcome these challenges?

Works Cited

"About the Podcast." *Here Be Monsters*, www.hbmpodcast.com/about.

"About Radiolab." *Radiolab*, WNCY Studios, www.wnycstudios.org/podcasts/radiolab/about.

Ahern, Katherine Fargo. "Tuning the Sonic Playing Field: Teaching Ways of Knowing Sound in First Year Writing." *Computers and Composition*, vol. 30, no. 2, 2013, pp. 75–86.

Brady-Myerov, Monica. *Listen Wise: Teach Students to Be Better Listeners*. Jossey-Bass, 2021.

Bunn, Mike. "How to Read like a Writer." *Writing Spaces: Readings on Writing*, edited by Charles Lowe and Pavel Zemliansky, vol. 2, Parlor, 2011, pp. 71–86.

Burton, Gideon. *Silva Rhetoricae: The Forest of Rhetoric*. Brigham Young University, rhetoric.byu.edu.

Ceraso, Steph. *Sounding Composition: Multimodal Pedagogies for Embodied Listening*. U of Pittsburgh P, 2018.

Cicchino, Amy. "Sound-Mapping: Seeing the Rhetorical Choices in Podcasts." *Crowdsourcing with CCDP*, Computers and Composition Digital Press, 14 Mar. 2020, ccdigitalpress.org/blog/2020/03/14/crowdsourcing-with-ccdp.

Comstock, Michelle, and Mary E. Hocks. "Voice in the Cultural Soundscape: Sonic Literacy in Composition Studies." *Computers and Composition Online*, Fall 2006, cconlinejournal.org/comstock_hocks/index.htm.

De La Rosa, Becca, and Mabel Martin. "La Sua Ultima Trasformazione." *Mabel*, 13 Nov. 2017, mabelpodcast.com/s/MABEL-27.pdf.

Detweiler, Eric. "The Bandwidth of Podcasting." *Tuning in to Soundwriting*, edited by Kyle D. Stedman et al., enculturation/Intermezzo, 2021, intermezzo.enculturation.net/14-stedman-et-al/detweiler.html.

Droumeva, Milena, and David Murphy. "A Pedagogy of Listening: Composing with/in Media Texts." *Soundwriting Pedagogies*, edited by Courtney S. Danforth et al., Computers and Composition Digital Press/Utah State UP, 2018, ccdigitalpress.org/book/soundwriting/droumeva-murphy/index.html.

Glennie, Evelyn. "How to Truly Listen." *TED: Ideas Worth Spreading*, Feb. 2003, www.ted.com/talks/evelyn_glennie_how_to_truly_listen.

Jauss, David. "Articles of Faith." *Creative Writing in America: Theory and Pedagogy*, edited by Joseph M. Moxley, NCTE, 1989, pp. 63–75.

Kabat-Zinn, Jon. *Wherever You Go, There You Are: Mindfulness Meditation in Everyday Life*. Hachette Books, 2009.

KalaLea, producer. "The Past Is Present." *Blindspot: Tulsa Burning*, The HISTORY Channel and WNYC Studios, 27 May 2021, www.wnycstudios.org/podcasts/blindspot/articles/past-is-present.

Keller, Helen. "81. Helen Keller, Letter to the Symphony Society of New York." *Music, Sound, and Technology in America*, edited by Timothy D. Taylor, Mark Katz, and Tony Grajeda, Duke UP, 2012, pp. 271–72.

Kern, Jonathan. *Sound Reporting: The NPR Guide to Audio Journalism and Production*. U of Chicago P, 2008.

Moran, Charles. "Reading like a Writer." *Vital Signs 1*, edited by James L. Collins, Boynton/Cook, 1990, pp. 60–71.

Rice, Patricia. "Linguistic Profiling: The Sound of Your Voice May Determine If You Get That Apartment or Not." *The Source*, Washington University in St. Louis, 2 Feb. 2006, source.wustl.edu/2006/02/linguistic-profiling-the-sound-of-your-voice-may-determine-if-you-get-that-apartment-or-not/.

Rice, Tom. "Listening." *Keywords in Sound*, edited by David Novak and Matt Sakakeeny, Duke UP, 2015, pp. 99–111.

Stoever, Jennifer Lynn. *The Sonic Color Line: Race and the Cultural Politics of Listening*. New York UP, 2016.

"StoryCorps." *NPR*, www.npr.org/podcasts/510200/storycorps.

Treasure, Julian. *How to Be Heard: Secrets for Powerful Speaking and Listening*. Mango, 2017.

Wen, Tiffanie. "Inside the Podcast Brain: Why Do Audio Stories Captivate?" *The Atlantic*, 16 Apr. 2015, www.theatlantic.com/entertainment/archive/2015/04/podcast-brain-why-do-audio-stories-captivate/389925/.

Interlude B

Using Rhetorical and Genre Analysis to Make Soundwriting: How Tanya Composed "Peaceful Warriors"[1]

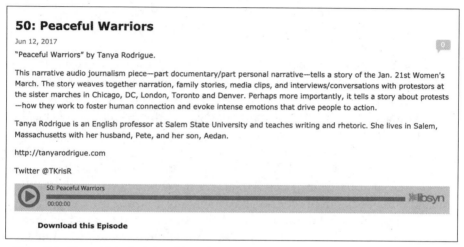

50: Peaceful Warriors

Jun 12, 2017

"Peaceful Warriors" by Tanya Rodrigue.

This narrative audio journalism piece—part documentary/part personal narrative—tells a story of the Jan. 21st Women's March. The story weaves together narration, family stories, media clips, and interviews/conversations with protestors at the sister marches in Chicago, DC, London, Toronto and Denver. Perhaps more importantly, it tells a story about protests —how they work to foster human connection and evoke intense emotions that drive people to action.

Tanya Rodrigue is an English professor at Salem State University and teaches writing and rhetoric. She lives in Salem, Massachusetts with her husband, Pete, and her son, Aedan.

http://tanyarodrigue.com

Twitter @TKrisR

50: Peaceful Warriors

00:00:00

Download this Episode

Figure B.1   The published version of Tanya's story.

INTRODUCTION

This interlude tells the story of how I, a brand new soundwriter with little confidence, nurtured and grew a half-baked idea into a piece of soundwriting. I'll narrate here my journey of struggling to execute that idea without a clear sense of purpose, audience, or genre, and how I eventually came to identify a rhetorical context that guided me in producing a published piece of soundwriting in a hybrid genre. At the end, I describe why, when, and how to disrupt genre conventions and blend genres in soundwriting.

The story begins with a tiny idea responding to a monumental historical moment. It was January 2016. Donald Trump was about to become the 45th President of the United States. People all over the world had organized protests called the "Women's Marches" in response to a Trump election and a multitude of injustices and issues that faced Americans at that time. As soon as the protests were announced, I knew I wanted to create some kind of audio project to capture the historical moment.

---

1   The final version of this piece can be heard at Rodrigue, Tanya. "Peaceful Warriors." *Rocky Mountain Revival*, episode 50, 12 June 2017, rockymtnrevival.libsyn.com/50-peaceful-warriors.

PLANNING THE PROJECT: GATHERING AND WORKING WITH TAPE

My process began with a bare-boned plan that identified my goals: create a documentary using audio recordings from marches across the country (and maybe the world). In order to execute this plan, I needed protest-going volunteers to help me collect tape recorded at the protests. (Tape is shorthand for "recorded audio.") So I sent out a call to friends to ask if anyone would be willing to record their experiences at protests. Friends sent my request to friends and ultimately a dozen people volunteered to help with the project.

> **Learn More**
> See chapter four's Introduction for a more descriptive definition of "tape."

A couple of days before the marches were to be held, I sent out an email to those who agreed to participate. I offered my collaborators some guidance on how to gather recordings but ultimately encouraged them to record what they could or wanted to—anything that captured some aspect of the day. After the protests, I ended up receiving audio files from ten people in cities around the world including Boston, London, Toronto, DC, Chicago, and Denver. Collectively, I had about ten hours of tape, and the tape was all different in nature—brief interviews with other protest-goers; volunteers' descriptions of what they saw and/or how they felt; chanting; singing; and speeches from activists and community leaders.

I listened to all of the recordings and digitally grouped and organized them in folders with descriptive titles. When I looked at all of the recordings, I was completely overwhelmed. Where would I begin? How should I actually start the process of turning these recordings into soundwriting? How should I organize the project? How

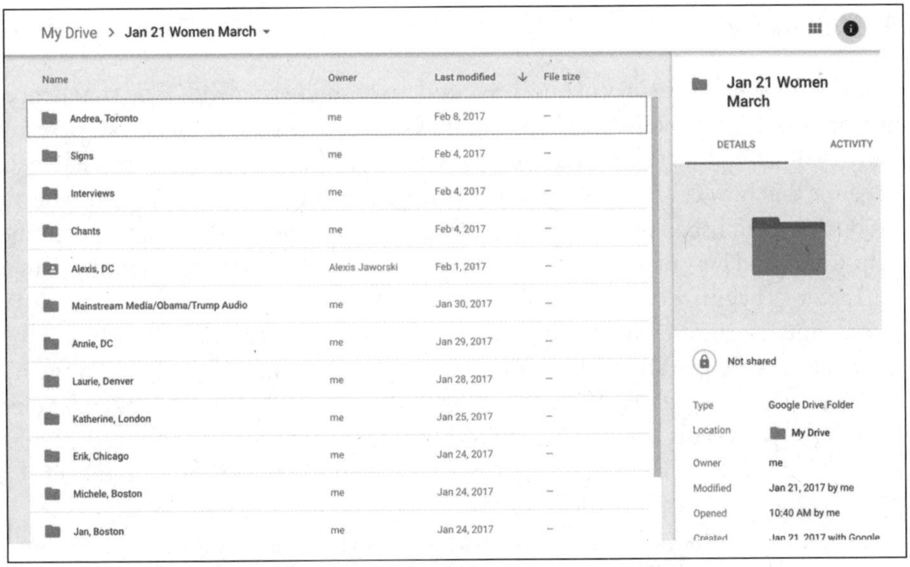

Figure B.2   Tanya's folder structure in Google Drive.

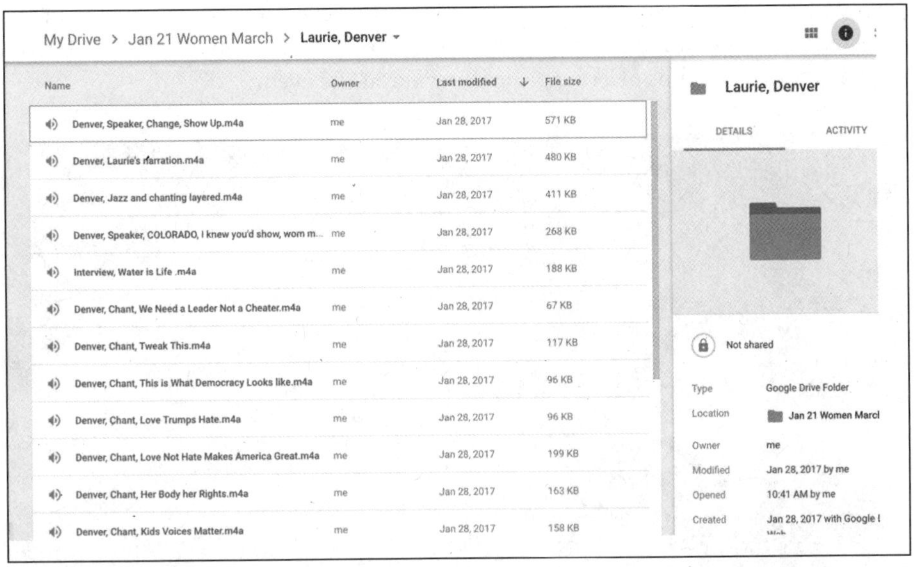

Name	Owner	Last modified ↓	File size	Laurie, Denver
🔊 Denver, Speaker, Change, Show Up.m4a	me	Jan 28, 2017	571 KB	DETAILS ACTIVITY
🔊 Denver, Laurie's narration.m4a	me	Jan 28, 2017	480 KB	
🔊 Denver, Jazz and chanting layered.m4a	me	Jan 28, 2017	411 KB	
🔊 Denver, Speaker, COLORADO, I knew you'd show, wom m...	me	Jan 28, 2017	268 KB	
🔊 Interview, Water is Life .m4a	me	Jan 28, 2017	188 KB	
🔊 Denver, Chant, We Need a Leader Not a Cheater.m4a	me	Jan 28, 2017	67 KB	🔒 Not shared
🔊 Denver, Chant, Tweak This.m4a	me	Jan 28, 2017	117 KB	
🔊 Denver, Chant, This is What Democracy Looks like.m4a	me	Jan 28, 2017	96 KB	Type Google Drive Folder
🔊 Denver, Chant, Love Trumps Hate.m4a	me	Jan 28, 2017	96 KB	Location 📁 Jan 21 Women March
🔊 Denver, Chant, Love Not Hate Makes America Great.m4a	me	Jan 28, 2017	199 KB	Owner me
🔊 Denver, Chant, Her Body her Rights.m4a	me	Jan 28, 2017	163 KB	Modified Jan 28, 2017 by me
🔊 Denver, Chant, Kids Voices Matter.m4a	me	Jan 28, 2017	158 KB	Opened 10:41 AM by me

My Drive > Jan 21 Women March > **Laurie, Denver ▾**

Figure B.3   File names Tanya gave to her audio assets.

many recordings would I use? How would I choose these recordings? What other sounds might I incorporate? Would I use narration? What other sounds did I need?

I reflected on my initial plan: to create a documentary using audio recordings from the Women's Marches. When I devised this goal, I didn't think carefully about what constitutes an audio documentary—I just knew that a documentary reports an experience and just assumed that a protest invited the genre. Before my academic life, I was a news reporter, and I was thinking like a news reporter when I immediately thought I would compose a documentary. I remember my husband, who is also a former news reporter, saying, "You better do something with this project fast because it's going to be old news in a day." I remember thinking: fast? I can't do anything fast! I ignored the suggestion and safely pursued my plan to approach the project from a traditional journalistic lens, an approach I was comfortable with and had done many times. I decided to wade through the tape and report the experience of the day in what I hoped would be an interesting and unique way.

I decided to first look for patterns across the recordings. I identified similarities across the interviews and created categories based on these similarities. I transcribed the interviews pretty much word for word, literally cut up the alphabetic transcriptions, arranged the content in various ways, and then used the paper slips of transcription to guide me in cutting up the audio content in the audio editor. I played and experimented with employing different sonic rhetorical choices that conveyed different messages, evoked different emotions, and achieved different goals. After playing, and playing some more, I ended up creating a ten-minute remix of the interviews without any narration. I did the same thing with media coverage from that day, as well as clips of Trump speaking about the event.

Figure B.4   Tanya's workspace, showing how she cut up and rearranged the script.

So now I had a remix. Could a remix be an audio documentary? Could an audio documentary be a remix? Maybe. Maybe not. I wasn't quite sure. I also wasn't sure about why I proceeded in the way I did: cut up audio and mix it together. I later reflected and realized I didn't really have a good reason at all. I think I was just excited about the affordances of writing with sound and wanted to do some cool experimentation that I couldn't do in alphabetic writing!

In the days that followed the protests, my husband was absolutely right. The media barraged the public with stories about the Women's Marches in newspapers, newscasts, and on the radio. Protest-goers in published stories and reports said nearly the same exact things as the protest-goers said in my remix. My plan to document the day and produce something interesting and unique failed: it was indeed old news, at least it was in the way I decided to report the experience. I needed a new plan that would guide me in achieving a new purpose in possibly a different genre. I also needed an approach to work with the significant amount of tape from the protests.

MAKING A NEW PLAN: BUILDING CONFIDENCE AND A GUIDE FOR COMPOSING MY PROJECT

I did a lot of work to compose a new plan. I conducted research to help me think more carefully about the genre of the audio documentary. I had high hopes that this story may be played on the radio or in a podcast, so I determined I needed a more solid understanding of what constitutes a good radio story. I read and reread every source I could get my hands on, including lots of articles from Transom.org. I listened to podcasts about the art and craft of audio storytelling, like Rob Rosenthal's podcast *HowSound*. I learned a lot from this independent exploration of audio storytelling: the various ways to structure a story, start a story, end a story, and different ways to keep listeners engaged. I also learned about different ways to work with tape to create a script: "letting the script lead"—writing a script and using collected sound to enhance the script—or "letting the tape lead"—choosing compelling moments from recordings and writing a script around those moments. I had a lot of information swimming around my head and all of it was useful but I was missing a key component of the plan: the story's purpose.

> **Learn More**
> See the Scripting section in chapter four for more on "letting the script lead" and "letting the tape lead."

I struggled for weeks to identify a purpose for the story. I distinctly remember one conversation with a friend where I kept saying, "I don't know what I want this audio project to do." She asked me one simple question: "Why did you want to make it in the first place?" Well, that was an easy question to answer. I told her I had never been involved in a large-scale protest and have always wanted to participate in one to help make change. It was really as simple as that.

The story's purpose finally became clear: to use the Women's Marches as a way to help explain protests in general—what they do and how they work. I wrote down everything I knew about protests and every personal story I had associated with them. I did a lot of research on protests. I used my guiding question—what do protests do and do they work?—to help me choose moments from the tape and craft a story. I ended up using a ton of recordings to create a half-hour piece of soundwriting that was part personal narrative, part documentary, and part scholarship with narration.

I was done, or so I thought. I listened and relistened. Then I decided ...

I hated it.

I made big claims about protests that I didn't even believe myself. Yet I wasn't ready to give up. I knew I needed support and feedback from an experienced audio storyteller. I asked around and a friend put me in contact with a radio producer in Colorado who ended up giving me strong feedback. I thought carefully about how I would approach revising the project, and I decided to document my revision process. I recorded myself before or during or after each session in hopes that just talking aloud would help me revise the project. Through

> **Learn More**
> You can hear bits and pieces of my audio process notes in my book chapter, "Speech, Invention, and Reflection: The Composing Process of Soundwriting."

what I came to call audio process notes, brief recordings of me talking through my ideas, I realized that I needed to do much more than simply work with the radio producer's comments. The biggest problems I had with this project were that one, I lacked confidence, and two, I needed to establish a more concrete rhetorical situation to guide my process.

<aside>
Learn More

See the Process Notes section in chapter four for more on audio process notes.
</aside>

The first thing I did was recognize and name my insecurities and fears. As an academic, I was so accustomed to writing scholarly alphabetic texts that a project in an unfamiliar mode and in a foreign genre (one that I couldn't even quite pin down!) was scary. What if I couldn't compose a piece of good soundwriting? What if I was terrible at doing it? What if it never got played on the radio? I confronted these insecurities and fears and significantly lowered my expectations. After all, I was a novice soundwriter. I could have never realistically produced something like I heard on the radio or an established podcast, and if I failed, oh well. I'd just keep trying.

The second thing I did was establish my rhetorical context—more specifically, I identified an audience, purpose, context, and genre. I searched for a podcast that played compelling stories of real-life experiences, and I imagined that I would compose a story that could potentially be played on this podcast for its listeners. I then conducted a genre analysis on podcast episodes, studying the common features and conventions with efforts to really understand the expectations of the genre and in turn the expectations of the audience. The genre of that particular podcast would fall under narrative journalism, a term I really didn't quite understand until much later.

<aside>
Learn More

See Try-It 4.3 in chapter four for guidance on how to conduct a genre analysis.
</aside>

Now equipped with a guide to help me approach the project, I then thought about how I would work with my tape. I remembered what I had learned about the difference between "letting the script lead" and "letting the tape lead." I decided I would try to "let the tape lead" but instead of identifying commonalities in the recordings like I did in the first version of the story, I would listen for moments that were interesting, unique, troubling, unexpected, or just plain weird.

Interestingly, nearly every clip I chose was different from the clips I had chosen for the first version of the story. After I chose my clips, I reflected: What story did these clips tell about the day of the Women's Marches? They told a story of people who felt relieved and happy to be together during a time when many Americans felt hopeless and helpless. After some research, I discovered that this feeling is actually a psychological phenomenon called "collective effervescence." I decided to use this concept as a framework for the story and to claim the marches were indeed an instance of this phenomenon.

With this idea in mind, I began crafting a new audio story. The story, I decided, would have some common features and conventions as stories in the podcast I used to identify my rhetorical situation. It would also have some unique features, mainly the integration of my personal experiences with protests in general and at the march as well as an unfolding of my understanding of what this day was and meant to people—a perspective that I felt had not yet been discussed in the mass coverage of the event. The genre, you could say, was a blend of personal narrative and narrative journalism.

Feeling great and confident, I pitched my idea to the podcast I had identified for my rhetorical context. The pitch was very quickly rejected. The producer said the piece wouldn't work because it focused more on a topic (the marches) than a story, and they specifically wanted a character-driven story with a plot and momentum as opposed to a snapshot of a particular time and scene, like the Women's Marches. Since the march was exhaustively covered in the mainstream media, as I already knew, the producer also said the reason for *why* I was telling this story wasn't compelling enough to get people to want to listen to yet ANOTHER piece about the Women's March.

Eek!

But what did I expect? I was brand new to audio storytelling! It was the first time I had written a pitch, and it was my first time composing an audio story, let alone an audio story that blended genres. I decided to forge ahead with the project despite the fact I never thought the piece would see the light of day. Rather than podcast listeners, I imagined myself, my children, and my family, now and in the future, as listeners. I imagined listening for the purpose of remembering the day or learning about the event or witnessing how my mother has influenced my perception of the world. I decided I could still create something meaningful and interesting...to me, at least...and still draw on and practice (and disrupt!) some of the genre conventions of narrative journalism.

> **Learn More**
> See the end of interlude D for more on narrative journalism genre conventions.

I ended up creating a nearly 30-minute piece of soundwriting. I amped up my role in the story, drawing a lot from my experience and my personal life with sound-rich descriptive anecdotes, scenes of my childhood, and an interview with my mom. If any character could be identified as the central character (which is arguable), it was me. (The use of "I" pushed me further and further away from common practices in narrative journalism, since this rhetorical move is rarely used in that genre. Check out Rosenthal's "When the Story Is about You" for more on the subject.) But I also integrated traditional audio journalistic rhetorical moves, such as incorporating interviews from other people and using narration with the interview quotes to move the story forward (check out Rosenthal's "Writing Out of Tape" for more on how narration and quotes work together). So in the end, my piece would fall into this weird, messy hybrid genre of personal narrative, audio memoir, narrative journalism, and audio scholarship.

After I completed the story, I decided I'd try to pitch it again. Since I knew it wouldn't fit a mainstream podcast, I searched the internet for a podcast that was more open to non-traditional ways of telling stories or even invited genre experimentation. I found

Rocky Mountain Revival, a podcast that plays the work of novice audio producers in all different kinds of genres. Perfect. I was indeed a novice! And because of that, I knew the podcast listeners wouldn't have strong expectations of what the story would be or how it would be told. I pitched the project, which I titled "Peaceful Warriors," and it was accepted for publication. It can now be heard in the *Rocky Mountain Revival* podcast archives.

The process of creating this project was long and arduous yet incredibly rewarding. I learned a lot about audio storytelling and composing processes that I continuously draw on when I soundwrite.

Interlude Takeaways

Don't miss these lessons you can learn from my experience crafting "Peaceful Warriors":

- Be sure your first project is manageable in scope and size with a limited number of recordings to work with in an audio editing program.
- Make a plan and be okay with altering your plan during the composing process.
- Provide yourself with lots of opportunity for play and experimentation with sound and with genre.
- Be able to identify your rhetorical context. Use rhetorical exercises—audience analysis, genre analysis, and rhetorical analysis—to gather information that will guide you in making choices in your soundwriting.
- Reflect on your ideas and process throughout the composing process, being thoughtful and strategic about why you're doing what you're doing and how particular moves can help you achieve your goals.
- Get as much feedback as possible—from classmates, friends, family—at every step along the way. Be thoughtful about working with revision comments.
- Recognize that you are a beginning soundwriter and set your expectations accordingly.

Breaking the Rules: Disrupting Conventions and Blending Genres

In this book, we offer up genre analysis as a way to help you build a guide for composing audio projects in a specific genre, like narrative journalism, audio memoirs, audio tours, soundscapes, and audio remixes. This is sound advice. Genre analysis helps you identify genre conventions and use them in your own work to fulfill your audience's expectations. Your listeners immediately have an idea about *what* they're going to listen to and *how* they should listen.

But sometimes genres are hard to pinpoint or don't yet have a name. Sometimes they beg for disruption and play. And sometimes, they can work together in ways that more appropriately fit a composer's goals, like the genres in Tanya's "Peaceful Warriors." A lot of the time, this kind of genre blending and disrupting yields the most creative and inventive audio projects. Yet knowing when to do it, why to do it, how to do it, and its consequences is important. Here's some advice:

Why to Do It: There are lots of reasons you would want to disrupt traditional genre conventions: to better achieve your purpose, connect with your listener in different ways, to exercise your creativity, to show off your talents, to solve an unexpected problem, to differentiate your work from others, to experiment with the affordances of sound. For example, Leila Day, from the podcast *The Stoop*, says she breaks with traditional journalism by using personal stories and "I" in her narrative journalism so her audience has a stronger connection to the story. She says a listener is more invested in the story if they have a stronger connection to the person making it. She also claims the use of "I" "humanizes the experience of being a journalist" (Rosenthal, "When the Story").

When to Do It: There's a time and a place for creating work that blends and disrupts genres. If you are in a class with a specific assignment, your assignment might direct you to compose in a particular genre. Talk to your instructor about the flexibility you have in disrupting genre conventions and blending genres. If you're not in a class or have a very flexible assignment, you'll have all the opportunity in the world to create writing that best enables you to achieve your purposes and goals. You may consider sharing your work on social media or maybe even starting your own podcast to feature it. With that said, if you plan to pitch it to a publication, you'll need to make sure the genre experimentation you do matches the podcast's goals and purposes.

How to Do It: There are times when you'll disrupt or blend genres to create something and have no idea that you were even doing so until after it's done. Your rhetorical context or even your inclinations may just direct you to draw on various kinds of genre conventions. It might just make sense to you. Yet there are other times when this might be purposeful. It's hard to give concrete advice for exactly how to disrupt or blend genres because it's so dependent on the project, its rhetorical context, and the genre or genres in question, yet we can say this: it's all about your rhetorical situation. You might try this strategy: identify what you want or are trying to do, the various ways you can do it using different genre conventions, the extent to which the moves could help you achieve your purpose, and how your audience might react. For example, Tanya needed to describe what led up to the Women's Marches (i.e.,

Donald Trump's presidential win). She could have simply reported the happenings per narrative journalism conventions: "Donald Trump won the presidency." Yet she wanted to evoke emotions in the listener, perhaps reminding listeners of the same emotions they felt election night. She also wanted to convey the kind of emotions that catapulted many to attend protests, searching for some kind of respite from the chaos and turmoil. She wanted them to connect with her as a person and as a storyteller, but she also wanted them to be immersed in a sonically rich experience. Tanya chose personal narrative to do this work because she thought it would be more effective in achieving her goals.

What Are the Consequences: There are favorable and not-so-favorable consequences to every decision you make in soundwriting. The favorable consequence of disrupting or blending genres is that you wow or surprise your listener in a good way, keeping them engaged or creating something really memorable. The not-so-favorable consequence, particularly when blending genres, is that your listener may have trouble following the piece because they don't have any expectations or a mental guide to help them do so. Worst yet, a person may tune out quickly or might not even choose to listen to your piece at all. For example, say a person is searching PRX (the Public Radio Exchange), looking for something new and interesting to listen to. They see a piece called "Rock Out" and it's marked as in the "interstitial" genre (i.e., a non-genre genre). Maybe they'll take a listen because they think the piece is about rock 'n' roll (or maybe rock climbing?), but maybe not...likely not. People are busy and the world is inundated with content, but that's not to say there isn't an audience for wild work. There is, but it's likely smaller than other kinds of audio work. So take this into consideration when making choices about disrupting and/or blending genres.

Works Cited

Rodrigue, Tanya K. "Peaceful Warriors." *Rocky Mountain Revival*, episode 50, 12 June 2017, rockymtnrevival.libsyn.com/50-peaceful-warriors.

———. "Speech, Invention, and Reflection: The Composing Process of Soundwriting." *Amplifying Soundwriting: Integrating Sound into Rhetoric and Writing*, edited by Michael J. Faris et al., WAC Clearinghouse, forthcoming.

Rosenthal, Rob. "When the Story Is about You but Not about You." *Transom*, 7 Jan. 2020, transom.org/2020/when-the-story-is-about-you-but-not-about-you/.

———. "Writing Out of Tape." *Transom*, 10 Oct. 2015. transom.org/2015/writing-out-of-tape/.

Chapter Three

A TOOLBOX OF CHOICES

INTRODUCTION

In 2019, *The New York Times* announced the winners of its Second Annual Student Podcast Contest. In their introduction, the authors write, "These podcasts pulled us in right from the start and kept our attention to the end. They brought their topics to life with music, environmental noise, media clips and the human voice. They were entertaining, informative and emotionally gripping" (The Learning Network).

Notice how the *Times* describes both the effects of the podcasts and the choices the student composers made to make those effects happen: sure, the podcasts were "entertaining, informative and emotionally gripping," but how? What did the students do to ensure that those rhetorical effects would come alive for their listeners? Simple: they powerfully combined "music, environmental noise, media clips and the human voice." This chapter is all about why and how you can use those sonic strategies to impact listeners in your own soundwriting projects.

Now at this point, after reading chapters one and two, you already know that soundwriters (well, really *all* writers) make choices. They make choices that enable them to create desired effects on their listeners and achieve their purposes and goals. You also know, from reading about and practicing the listening-like-a-soundwriter (LLS) approach, that soundwriters make an array of choices to craft soundwriting. You've named those choices, and you've done some investigative work and reflection to explore their rhetorical nature. This work has prepared you to become a successful soundwriter yourself.

We want to prepare you even more! And that's where this chapter comes in. Here, we offer what we call a robust sonic toolbox that will help you think more about the choices you have as a soundwriter and how to go about both making and executing these choices in a piece of soundwriting.

Figure 3.1
Use the right tool—and the right sonic tool—to get the job done.

We stole the toolbox metaphor from horror novelist Stephen King because it makes so much sense in this context. In *On Writing,* King suggests that alphabetic writers should imagine vocabulary, grammar, sentences, and paragraphs as tools in a box (114): writers should learn about these tools and how they work, thinking of them as the various instruments they can pick and choose from to compose good writing. We like this metaphor because it reminds us of the rhetorical nature of writing—that is, the fact that not all tools available to use are always useful for a particular purpose; you need to choose the *right* tools to get the job done.

While King offers a toolbox for alphabetic writing, we offer a toolbox for soundwriting. While a sonic toolbox can be comprised of many tools, the tools in this toolbox are the most commonly used instruments to craft soundwriting: voice, music, sound effects, and silence. And like the tools in King's toolbox, these sonic instruments are often used together. Below, we dive deep into each of these sonic tools, always explaining both what they can do and how you might use them in soundwriting. After reading this chapter, you will be better equipped to make choices that will help you achieve your desired effects when you soundwrite. You might think of this chapter as an introduction to the sonic strategies that will bloom into full, detailed actions in chapters four and five. This chapter is like flying over a landscape and noticing how the forests, rivers, buildings, and streets are laid out and intersect with each other; the next two chapters are like landing and using the knowledge you got from your flight to start making things.

VOICE

Figure 3.2
Many soundwriting projects rely on the power of voice.

Think about your cell phone. How do you decide what you want your voicemail message to sound like? You have all kinds of options. You might use your voice—maybe your "professional" voice or your "friendly" voice—with a generic message, or maybe something a little more creative or light-hearted. You might hate the sound of your voice and ask your best friend to record the message for you, and you might even direct her to sound a certain way—"serious" or "fun." You could even turn to the internet and rip a voicemail greeting from your favorite actor or singer—maybe you want Beyoncé to sing a greeting to people when you can't take their call. Or maybe you just opt for the default "robot-voice."

Depending on who you are, this choice may be really important. Why? Because to a certain extent, the voice you use and the words it carries reflect your identity, and you want to project yourself in a specific way, convey a certain tone, and make your listener feel a certain way. If your voicemail makes a joke, you're giving your listener insight into your style of humor and even your approach to everyday things like voicemail. But if you're on the job market, you use your voice to portray yourself as a professional, letting your possible future employer know you're competent and confident.

The point? Voice matters. And when you soundwrite, you'll often have options, just as you do with your voicemail message, about which voice you will use and how that voice can work to help you achieve your desired effects. This section explains some of the ways voice can be used powerfully as well as how you can execute your choices in your soundwriting projects.

Understanding Voice

The voice emerges from a body (with the exception of machine-generated voices): it can either be sound expressed verbally—in words, sentences, or song—or sound expressed nonverbally—in grunts, cries, laughs, sobs, or sighs. Just like a fingerprint, each voice is unique and can be characterized by various vocal qualities such as pitch range (high or low), pronunciation (accents and tone), loudness (booming or soft), tension (tight or strained), roughness (raspy and throaty), and tempo (the rate and pace of speech or sound). Some of these qualities are difficult to change, like pitch, while others can easily be manipulated by a speaker, such as volume and tension. The distinctness of each voice and its vocal qualities are a result of body makeup—the size and shape of body parts that play a role in voice-making and voice delivery—as well as sociological factors like culture, education, class, birthplace, residence, and gender. We all have particular accents because of our past or present geographical locations, for example.

While all voices are different and each body projects speech and sound in different ways, they do share a commonality: they have impressive power.

Think about it: voice functions as a tool of communication in projecting words and sounds that embody meaning and emotion. Voice also mediates human relationships, playing a big role in how people connect: by facilitating communication, signaling a particular body (from which the voice is being projected), and creating certain effects for listeners. It is one of the most effective sonic strategies in pulling listeners in and keeping them engaged in a piece of soundwriting.

Here's a little exercise to help you further understand the way voice can mediate relationships. Close your eyes and think of the person you love the most. Imagine that person telling you how much they like you—"You're the best!" or "I'm so proud of who you've become." It feels good, right? There are likely several reasons why you feel good: the words the voice carries are encouraging and positive, and you imagined they came from an actual person, someone who is very important in your life. The qualities of the voice might also play a role in your reaction. Maybe the voice sounds calming and friendly, or, at the very least, familiar and comforting because of its associations to this person you love.

Research confirms the importance of these warm feelings. It shows that voice can evoke emotion and alter one's mood or perception. It can even change the chemicals in the brain. Multiple studies, for example, have revealed that a mother's voice can immediately soothe her child when they are in distress; the voice triggers a child's brain to reduce a stress chemical and release oxytocin, the "feel-good" chemical (Criss).

While voice in general can produce effects on others, so can particular vocal qualities. While there is no one-size-fits-all effect on listeners, psychologists and linguists have identified common ways vocal qualities are associated with human traits and emotions, which we'll describe in detail below. Knowing these common associations in US culture is helpful when thinking about how to employ voice in soundwriting since you can, to some extent, control the "person" you project or how your audience might respond to a voice or particular vocal qualities.

While most of the time we think of voice coming from a body, it's also helpful to think of voice as something that exists beyond or without a body, something that in its own right can produce a desired effect. Erin Anderson, a professor at the University of Pittsburgh, describes voice as a "malleable material" to compose with, something to transform and use in a different way than its original state ("Toward a Resonant"). Her understanding of voice, which she calls vocality, is especially helpful when thinking about the various ways voice can be made, manipulated, and altered in audio editing software.

Below, we'll explain how to employ voice as a composing "material" that comes from a "lived" or "has-lived" body, as well as a "bodiless" voice, to produce desired effects on your listener in soundwriting.

Using Voice as a Tool

Evoke People and Characters

Voice is powerful in its ability to foster human connection in soundwriting, especially since it can instantly evoke the characteristics of actual people. Listeners hearing a human voice can visualize the person using that voice. Maybe the voice is reminiscent of their mom or best friend; maybe it's friendly or pitiful—but regardless, there's a mental connection between the listener and the voice being heard. And unlike in alphabetic writing where a person's voice is captured in quotation marks, voices in soundwriting immediately bring people to life in a way that's markedly different from the other voices surrounding them. Here's an example: say you're interviewing a bunch of college students for an audio documentary about how shared complaints about campus food led to new friendships. You interview the students and incorporate the interviews into your soundwriting. When you finish and play it for a friend, they first hear a deep voice with a New York accent say, "The pork chops taste like rubber and the peas are mushy like paste." Immediately after, a high-pitched voice with a quick tempo comes in: "I thought my mother's cooking was bad. Now I'm happy to go home and eat her tuna casserole." Two voices bring forth two humans with lived experiences that the listener can relate to in some way, especially if they've had shared experiences with others with similar voice qualities. And just like drawing on sources in an alphabetic essay, soundwriters can use voices that signal real people to make various rhetorical moves, like providing an authentic testimony of an event in an oral history or presenting different perspectives in an archival audio remix.

And don't forget that your documentary about campus food might highlight one voice more than any others: your own, as narrator. As you deliver the words listeners will hear with the audio quotations, the choices you make while speaking will go a long way toward telling listeners about your attitude toward the subject. For instance, a simple line of narration like "The students had a lot to say" could be read with a passion that aligns with the views in the quotations about to come, or it could be read with a tone of sarcasm that suggests

> **Learn More**
> See the Recording Your Own Voice section in chapter four for advice on recording narration.

readers should take the quotations with a grain of salt. Kyle faces this issue of narration regularly in his podcast *Bad Ideas about Writing*, where he reads chapters aloud from an open-source book. When reading a topic that he feels passionately about, his vocal qualities change: he speeds up, gets louder, and uses more dynamic changes in pitch, signaling that he believes this topic is really important. So when recording your own voice, don't forget that *you're* one of the characters you're evoking in your listener's imagination, not just the people you interview.

You may also use a voice to speak *as* or *for* another person. This can happen in the most literal sense when someone voices a fictional character, records a script they didn't write, or when an interpreter or computer vocalizes the words conceived by someone else. You can also have other voices speak for you in a more metaphorical way, such as when you compose a story that doesn't have a narrator. Let's return to the example about the school food story from above. Say you're no longer keen on the idea of employing your own narration; you decide that you're going to tell this story entirely from the student interviews. So you pick and choose moments of the interview that work together to say something you think is important about the role of food in friendship-making. You activate savvy editing skills to piece together these multiple voices, perhaps stringing them back to back and giving prominence to those voices you agree with most. Or perhaps you get fancy and weave together words and short phrases from different people to tell what seems like one coherent story. Voila—a story is born. And that story is built on the power of voice, even if your own voice is never heard.

You may also use voice to *build a character* from your imagination, constructing a new "person" by manipulating the recorded voices of others. Take, for example, an audio story called "Our Time Is Up," composed by Erin Anderson, the professor we mentioned above. Anderson used speech from oral history recordings (including her own grandfather) to create two fictional characters who never existed in real life, even though all of their words were spoken by real people—just not spoken in the order listeners ultimately hear them. That is, using audio editing software, Anderson cut up, rearranged, and patched together snippets of these recordings to create a fictional scenario wherein the fictional couple Jake and Helen McCleary sit in multiple therapy sessions to discuss their flailing marriage. That's the power of audio editing: voices no longer have to say exactly what they originally said—a power that soundwriters should take seriously and use ethically.

Voice also has the power to suggest what a speaker might be like or look like. As a result, a listener may use their imagination to build their own characters, and these characters are often entwined with the emotions listeners feel about those kinds of people. While the character one builds is fairly subjective, research suggests there are particular voice qualities that are associated with character traits and emotions. For example, studies have concluded high-pitched female voices signal young, attractive women, while loud, low-pitch voices signal a confident, strong person (Levitt and

Lucas). Unfortunately, these studies as well as stereotypes that have emerged over time reinforce some problematic associations that we don't advocate you perpetuate in your own soundwriting. Yet we do want to let you know that listeners will draw some of these conclusions about bodies connected to the voices they hear whether we like it or not. We encourage you to do the important work of dismantling those stereotypes in your own soundwriting by giving all kinds of voices the qualities that might not have first come to mind to listeners.

Convey and Evoke Emotions

While voice may convey a certain trait of a character, it also conveys *feelings*—and feelings may work to evoke emotion in the listener, help a listener further characterize or visualize a body, or establish atmosphere and tone in the project itself (or do all of these at once). Now, there is not a master list for soundwriters that identifies which vocal qualities evoke what feelings, since every person understands and responds to vocal qualities in different ways based on factors like gender, culture, and life experience. Yet we can look to research to help us think more carefully about what feelings and emotions are infused in particular vocal qualities.

Let's start with linguist Theo van Leeuwen. He identifies several vocal qualities and their associated feelings:

- a tense voice signals tension, fear, or sarcasm
- a breathy voice signals intimacy and sensuality
- a loud and low-pitched voice signals dominance and power
- a soft voice signals intimacy, confidentiality, or something secretive
- a high-pitched voice is associated with submissiveness or the feeling of being less significant
- a trembling voice might signal fear, love, or emotional detachment

Research in psychology also reveals findings about the relationship of vocal qualities and associated feelings. A study we referenced above (Levitt and Lucas) suggests that high-pitched voices can come off as annoying, unpleasant, or anxiety-producing, while low-pitched voices can be soothing and grounding. These same findings have become commonplace associations and stereotypes along with many others, just like the associations between voice and bodies we discuss above. While your listener may certainly hear particular kinds of voices and feel their commonly associated emotions, we do want to warn you again to approach using voice to convey emotion with care; you don't want your soundwriting to do any harm.

When choosing among different voices or vocal takes, there is clearly lots to consider, as you decide what vocal qualities you want to emphasize for your rhetorical purposes. Yet there are times when you *can* control voice and the way it conveys and evokes emotion and times when you *can't*. Let's start with an example of the sound-writer having control. Tanya once composed an audio documentary called, "A Plea for Earlids" (Rodrigue), on a rare ear condition that makes sound unbearable, and part of her composing process was to interview several people, asking everyone the same questions. Two of the interviewees responded in a similar fashion about their experiences, and either interview clip would have worked in the context of the project—that is, they both answered with information that Tanya wanted her listeners to know. Tanya had an opportunity to choose which voice she thought would work best within her rhetorical context: she could choose a low-pitched, shaky-but-confident voice with rapid pacing, or she could choose a medium-pitched, confident voice with moderate pacing. She chose number two for a couple of reasons. Tanya thought that the voice's pitch and pacing would appeal to a wide audience and the voice would be easier to edit. The other reason may seem superficial and arbitrary, but it's honest: Tanya just personally *liked* the voice; it felt familiar, like the voice of a good friend or a kind person, and she hoped some of her listeners would feel the same. After all, voice is powerful in its ability to foster human connection and, by extension, listener engagement. This is all to say that soundwriting with the voices of others sometimes means trusting these gut impressions and sometimes means questioning how our own privilege and positionality may have led us to that judgment.

Yet there are also times when you have little or no control over voice. Say you're composing an audio project with a serious topic. You interview a researcher who studies climate change and their responses make up the bulk of the project. You think the researcher's high-pitched, loud voice may sound "annoying," and you think there's a chance some listeners may stop listening simply because they don't like the voice. In this case, you don't have much choice, unless you interview someone else or manipulate the pitch and volume in audio editing software. The latter option may cross some ethical lines: the voice is attached to a living body who happens to be an expert in the topic under discussion. With that in mind, it's best not to manipulate this voice's sound too much, regardless of how you think a listener might respond; you want the speaker's voice to still sound like *them*.

Signal Time and Place

Voice, and particular vocal qualities, can also work to indicate a period of time and place, either in isolation or along with other sounds. While the effective use of voice to indicate time and place is dependent on your audience, there are some voices that have the power to immediately evoke time and place on their own or accompanied with other sounds.

An easy and powerful way to denote place is to use a voice with a particular accent or dialect, one that may either be immediately recognizable to your audience or one that you may identify in the audio project. For example, "Chicken Pills," an episode from the podcast *The Kitchen Sisters Presents*, tells a story about how women in Jamaica work to uphold traditional standards of beauty in their culture. The episode begins with a woman speaking in a Jamaican accent, saying, "Some girls, to be more attractive to the male, they get themselves into this new soft chicken pills." The accent immediately denotes a location—Jamaica—and the Jamaican music further solidifies the location of the story.

Voice, either an accent or particular vocal qualities, can also function to convey a particular generation, decade, or span of time. For example, one of the most well-known accents from the 1930s and 1940s is the Transatlantic or Mid-Atlantic accent, or what some people might describe as the "old-time announcer accent." This kind of voice blends standard American English and Britain's Received Pronunciation (Taylor) and may signal an early-to-mid twentieth-century setting to some listeners.

Voice Section Takeaways

Choices: What Voice Can Do	Execution: How to Employ Voice
Evoke people and characters	Use voice with various vocal qualities, either real or machine-generated, in an audio project, paying attention to how vocal qualities might contribute to a person's character formation. Use voice and voice qualities that challenge research, assumptions, and/or stereotypes associated with them.
Convey and evoke emotion	Use voice and vocal qualities associated with particular character traits, identities, or emotions. Use words and context to infuse particular emotions in a voice.
Signal time and place	Identify possible accents or dialects that may be associated with a particular place; use voices that employ these accents or dialects. Identify possible voices and vocal qualities that may signal a particular time period; use voices that employ these vocal qualities.

Try-It 3.1 Playing with Voice with a Recording Device

This activity encourages play with vocal qualities and invites vocal analysis. You'll need a word processor or pen and paper in addition to a voice recording device. You can do the activity by yourself or work with a group of people.

1. Write a paragraph describing a happy memory.
2. Record yourself reading this paragraph three different times, each time changing the tone, pace, pitch, or volume of your voice. You might want to imagine that your attitude toward the story changes—maybe in one you're sincere, while in another you're sarcastic or bored, or with some other tone. Listen to your recordings.
3. Now respond to this question: How does the shift in your own voice impact how another listener might hear or experience this story?
4. This activity can be collaborative with simple adjustments. For step two, ask three people to read and record the same paragraph, and for step three, respond to these questions: How would you describe the vocal qualities of each speaker? How might these vocal qualities engage a listener in different ways?

Try-It 3.2 Playing with Voice in the Audio Editor

This activity encourages play with audio clips for the purpose of exploring how different voices can be used together to create various rhetorical effects. You will need a program that can download sound from the internet as well as audio editing software.

1. Search online for two people talking about the same subject, download the clips, and import them into your audio editing program. (If you can't think of a topic, try a recent news event.)
2. Isolate one or two sentences from each clip by deleting everything except those two sentences. This editing move is called "trimming."
3. Then position these two clips next to each other and respond to the following questions: How do these clips work together to say something about the subject matter? What rhetorical effects might they have when strung back to back?

Learn More
Chapter four has more advice on downloading sound from the internet, and chapter five will teach you about trimming audio in audio editing software.

Learn More
See the Editing Basics section in chapter five for how to get started in an audio editor.

4. Now try overlapping the end of one clip and the beginning of the other clip and respond to this question: What might be different about the rhetorical effect of this editing move?

5. Now, try cutting up each clip into sections and weaving the different sections of the different clips together. Then respond to these questions: What kind of rhetorical effect might this move make that is different from the above moves? What might be the purpose and rhetorical effects of this move?

This activity can also be done with a transcript. Complete the above steps using cut-up pieces of a transcript and imagine infusing them with different vocal qualities. For step two, excerpt two sentences from the transcripts.

MUSIC

Figure 3.3
Music's rhythmic, emotional power can amp up your soundwriting.

An easy way to experience the power of music is to try this experiment. First, open a recording of any politician giving a speech on any topic—maybe something you find on YouTube or a news website. Then, in another window on your computer, play instrumental music at the same time as the speech, so you can hear both the talking and the music at the same time. Now change the tune, again and again. Try playing music from different genres and with different moods—something orchestral from a movie score, something with a groovy beat, something you fall asleep to. And as you switch from musical piece to musical piece, we think you'll immediately sense the power of music to affect the impact of the speech and the speaker: suddenly, the politician will seem grand, or hopelessly comedic, or subtly threatening, or cheerfully optimistic.

Here's our point: just like voice, music is *powerful*. When words or visuals are paired with music, the music lends an energy to the whole that is hard to describe but even harder to forget.

Understanding Music

Music can give us the ability to express things that are hard or impossible to say otherwise. African American composer and performer Duke Ellington once wrote, "The music of my race is more than just the American idiom. It is the result of our transplantation to American soil and was our reaction in plantation days to the life we lived. What we could not say openly we expressed in our music" (qtd. in Banfield xii). To Ellington, the music of Black America contains the seed of the experience of slavery, when music could offer a subversive way to express what couldn't be expressed openly. Philosopher Susanne Langer makes a similar point about music's power to express complex realities when she writes, "Because the forms of human feeling are much more congruent with musical forms than with the forms of language, music can *reveal* the nature of feelings with a detail and truth that language cannot approach" (235). To Ellington and Langer, music is an essential tool for human communication, since language alone isn't good enough at mirroring the flowing, pulsing nature of human emotion and connection.

But when music expresses emotions, it's not always a pleasant experience. Music philosopher David Burrows reminds us of this when he writes, "[b]ecause a listener cannot always know what caused a sound, or exactly where it is coming from, and because sound cannot always be shut down, it can have a disturbing, even a fearful side when compared to sight" (70). Music can be played in a way that is hard for listeners to escape, latching into their minds and affecting them in ways they might not have expected. The most benign example would be what neurologist Oliver Sacks calls an earworm—music that gets stuck in your head, like it or not, but eventually fades away (44). The most extreme example is music used for torture, like when the Barney theme song was continuously played to torment prisoners during the Iraqi war (Gallagher).

Another musicologist, Arnold Perris, demonstrates the power of music when he describes how it affects us: "We use music to change our behavior. We may play a recording or turn the radio dial to match or change our present mood. We go to a concert expecting to be aroused to excitement and pleasure by the music, by the performers' skills, and by their enthusiasm, as well as by that of the other members of the audience" (6). Music changes how we experience the world.

Taken together, these thinkers emphasize music's power to express and to make change. So in your own soundwriting projects, use music with those same goals: to express what's hard or impossible to express otherwise, and to change your listeners in some way.

In practice, those changes we aim for might be grand and life-changing, or they might be fairly basic: we might simply want to change the pace of how quickly information is communicated and processed, or change the subtle emotional tone of a message. But big or small, music is powerful.

Using Music as a Tool

Convey and Evoke Emotion

It seems like philosophers and musicians have been trying to name the relationship between music and emotion since music began. Does music *make* listeners feel emotion, or does music *transmit* emotion, or does it help us *understand* emotion, or something else entirely? It's even more complicated when we consider the nature vs. nurture debate: Is music's connection to emotion tied intrinsically to the way human brains work, or do our emotional reactions have more to do with the music we grew up hearing?

Those are big questions, but we think that when it comes to your own soundwriting projects, you can use emotion powerfully without necessarily knowing the answers. In other words, we bet you can affect our emotions with music just by following your instincts. In fact, you don't need to know any formal musical terminology to understand how music works emotionally, as long as you pay attention to what evokes emotion in yourself.

> **Learn More**
>
> See Tip 2.3 in chapter two for some terms that can be used to analyze music.

The simplest way to evoke emotion is to layer music under speech in a way that matches and amplifies the words being said (sometimes called a "music bed"). Maybe you interviewed a father who was separated from his child, so you layer it with slow music in a minor key on a single instrument (like a piano or cello) that just feels right. Or maybe you recorded yourself telling a fun story about sneaking into a neighbor's pool as a child, so you layered it with music that feels upbeat, peppy, rhythmic, and positive. In both cases, the music will encourage the listener to empathize emotionally with the speaker, helping create a connection grounded in feeling. The music acts like an amplifier of what's already there in other parts of your project.

While some music is commonly associated with particular emotions, which we talk about more below, emotional connections aren't an exact science. The solo piano that Kyle thinks adds a serious gravity to a section might sound like too much of a downer to Tanya; that is, we might interpret the same instrumental music in different ways. So, perhaps more than when using other rhetorical strategies, musical choices are always something you should get feedback about. But we think that the more you experiment with finding the perfect music—the pieces that sound right to you and to your listeners—the more you'll enjoy the hunt.

Make and Create Associations

Music has a particular power to connect ideas, people, and emotions. It's as if the right piece of music can immediately draw our minds to other places and times we've heard it before—like the TV cereal ad we saw as a child, or the pumped-up music played before every basketball game, or the song your parents played every time they cleaned the house. It's like our memories are filled with closed doors that we assumed were locked, until we hear the right music to unlock them and fling them open.

Composers of classical music and film scores know this power of musical connection intimately. In the nineteenth century, German composer Richard Wagner was famous for associating each character in his operas with a particular, short melody (which he called a "leitmotif"), which allowed him to musically remind the audience of characters even when they weren't on stage. That association of characters and ideas with music continues today—try watching any of the *Star Wars* films and listening to how composer John Williams introduces a particular melody every time the scene focuses on Leia, Yoda, Kylo Ren, or Rey.

Of course, you can't predict the musical experiences of all of your listeners, so you can't use music associatively in a definitive way; our musical associations are contextual and cultural, just like everything else we've been taught. But still, you can use the associative power of music in your own soundwriting projects in at least two ways. First, rely on the associations you expect many of your listeners to have, such as by playing sweeping symphonic music when you want to subtly make your listeners feel like they're watching a movie. Don't forget that those associations can be time-based as well: the protest songs of the 1960s will immediately bring listeners' minds to that decade, for instance. And second, you can create new associations in your projects—such as by playing a certain piece of music every time a particular idea, person, or conflict is introduced.

Organize the Project

One way writing words seems to be superior to writing sounds is the ease of organizing words on the page, as opposed to the comparative difficulty of organizing sounds for the ear. As we described in chapter one with the example of a lengthy novel, the linguistic mode has powerful affordances when it comes to organization. Readers can skim up and down a text and immediately grasp how the material is organized: into sentences that are then chunked into paragraphs, sections, and chapters. Those visual and spatial decisions help frame the content, letting you know what to expect, how many main ideas there are, and what genre you're reading.

But a soundwriting piece is often experienced quite differently. Sure, listeners can often preview on their screen how long a single audio file is, and in some projects the audience might be able to skim to see how many audio clips there are, how long they are, and where they fit into a multimodal whole. But still, the soundwriter is often faced with a simple truth: if you don't include audible cues about how your material is organized, your listeners might feel lost.

Thank goodness for music. A theme song played at the beginning of every podcast episode can tell readers, "Here's my show! It has an attitude and energy that's echoed by this song!" The same goes for ending music, which can tell listeners, "Okay, we've reached the end! You'll hear this every time an episode is over, signaling that we're about to move into the credits!" (As an aside, this reminds us of another reason you might want to use music: to brand your audio projects, letting listeners know that they're always hearing something you made, with your musical stamp on it.)

Even more importantly: you could use music to signal to listeners that you're transitioning to another section of your piece. You might use the same piano music at the beginning of every main section, so we always know where the content is going to change somewhat—or you could do the same thing with different music, which would say to listeners, "Okay, that last section felt more light-hearted, but we're getting into something much darker and serious now."

Musical cues say, "We're entering into a new sonic 'paragraph.' Listen up and you'll see why it's a development of the ideas that came before it."

Pace the Project

Related to the above sections on affecting emotions and organizing material is the power of music to set the pace of a project. Sometimes, it just doesn't feel right for words to move too quickly or too slowly; sometimes, you need to let something sink in, or you need ideas to push forward, making your ideas seem urgent, terrifying, or ready to break free. That's something that words on a page aren't very good at, since readers can choose their own pace when reading. But when you soundwrite, you're in control of the speed at which listeners experience your work.

And luckily for us, music often comes with a pace of its own. Much contemporary music is organized into predictable rhythms that come at definable speeds (sometimes organized by BPMs, or beats-per-minute). That means that if you choose to use music with a beat, you can have a somewhat predictable idea of whether it will make the accompanying ideas feel lazier or more frantic, based on how large its BPM number is.

But we can also use music (with or without a beat) to fill silences, especially when we want listeners to have time to consider the ideas we've just presented. In that way, music allows us to slow down the pace of our project. For instance, imagine that you're playing an interview clip from someone who just shared a difficult story of a traumatic experience. It might feel rude to simply barge in with your own narration or explanation before letting the interviewee's story stand on its own—but if you just leave a few seconds of complete silence, with no audible information at all, it could sound to listeners like a production mistake. (You don't want listeners to turn their volume up, up, and up again to see if they're missing something, only to be BLASTED TO BITS when content comes back.) So music is there for us—in this case, quiet, thoughtful music, right?—to fill the gap and let the idea sink in.

Music Section Takeaways

Choices: What Music Can Do	Execution: How to Use Music
Convey and evoke emotion	Find music that matches and amplifies the emotional tone of words being said, and layer them together.
Make and create associations	Choose music and styles of music that you think your listeners will associate with the idea or mood you're going for. Create new associations, always playing a certain piece of music every time a particular idea or character is introduced or mentioned.
Organize the project	Play music between different sections of your project, helping listeners "see" how your ideas fit together. If you have multiple projects that fit together (like multiple episodes of a single podcast), brand your project by using the same music at the beginning and ending of each segment.
Pace the project	Choose fast or slow music to emphasize the excitement and importance of the content it's paired with. Fill silences with fast or slow music to match the emotional tone of the surrounding content.

Try-It   3.3 Playing with Music on the Computer

This activity gives you a chance to experience the various rhetorical functions and effects of music. You will need a computer connected to the internet.

1. Search the internet to find a television commercial set to music. Watch and listen to the commercial, and after watching, respond to this question: What is the rhetorical function of this music and how might it impact the listener?
2. Now, go to a website that hosts music like Spotify, YouTube, or Bensound, or open a folder on your computer where you store music files. Find a song that is opposite in nature to the song in the commercial. For example, if the original

music is an upbeat, techno music, find music that is slow and melancholy. Cue up the song.

3. Now play the commercial with the original sound muted along with the new song playing in another window at the same time. Respond to this question: What is the rhetorical function of the music now, and how might it impact the listener in a different way than the original music?

4. Now try step three one more time with a different song—perhaps a song in a different genre with different instruments than the previous two.

5. Lastly, respond to this question: Why do you think the commercial's creators chose the music they did originally? To what extent did it enable them to achieve their purpose and goal with regard to their target audience? Do you think a different song might have worked better to help them achieve their goals and impact their audience?

Try-It   3.4 **Playing with Music, Friends, and Words**

This activity invites you to play with background music to think about its rhetorical function when paired with words. You'll need a couple of friends and an internet-connected device for this activity. Here are the steps:

> **Learn More**
>
> For a more robust activity involving identifying sounds, see Try-It 2.4: Collaboratively Writing "Thick Descriptions."

1. Find a podcast with a person speaking at the same time as music is played. (See Tip 2.4 in chapter two for a list of podcasts and podcast episodes that could work for this activity.)

2. Play the same clip for at least three different people and ask them to write words to describe the music—and be sure not to tell them anything about the broader context of the episode. Be sure to get them to describe both the qualities of the music itself (perhaps fast, filled with short notes, guitar-centered, drum-heavy, major key, changes quickly, etc.) and the emotions they associate with the music (perhaps "like someone is about to go on a date" or "it's like the bad guy is planning evil with his minions").

3. Either alone or in conversation with your friends, jot down some notes about the extent to which these words match the content and emotion of the story that the music is paired with.

4. Now, go to a website where you can search music by tags (like FreeSound, the Free Music Archive, or Bensound), and try searching for some of the words people used to describe the music in the podcast.

5. Once you pull up music connected to some of these words, respond to these questions: Could any of this music you found work better for the story than the music the producers chose? Explain why or why not. What rhetorical effects might it have?

SOUND EFFECTS

Figure 3.4
A student at Vancouver Film
School creates sound effects
in a Foley studio.

Here's a selection of the script from the first *Star Wars* film (1977), as found at the
Internet Movie Script Database:

> **INT. DETENTION AREA**
> Elevator doors open. A tall, grim looking Officer approaches the trio.
>
>
>
> **OFFICER**
> Where are you taking this...thing?
>
>
>
> Chewie growls a bit at the remark but Han nudges him to shut up.
>
>
>
> **LUKE**
> Prisoner transfer from Block one-one-three-eight.
>
>
>
>
>
> **OFFICER**
> I wasn't notified. I'll have to clear it.
>
>
>
> The officer goes back to his console and begins to punch in the infor-
> mation. There are only three other troopers in the area. Luke and
> Han survey the situation, checking all of the alarms, laser gates, and

camera eyes. Han unfastens one of Chewbacca's electronic cuffs and shrugs to Luke.

Suddenly Chewbacca throws up his hands and lets out with one of his ear-piercing howls. He grabs Han's laser rifle.

HAN

Look out! He's loose! ("Star Wars")

Of course, a script is just a pale shadow of the real experience of seeing—and hearing!—a film. For instance, if you read along to this script while listening to the scene in the finished version of *Star Wars*, you'll hear John Williams's musical score along with a complex "symphony" of sound effects: elevator doors opening and closing, footsteps, the rising and falling mechanical ambience of the detention area, the subtle click when someone handles a blaster, and of course all the sounds of the fight that immediately follows this scene: a punch, a body hitting the ground, blaster fire, glass shattering, buttons pushed on the console, Chewbacca's growls, and an insistent beep from the console. (To watch and hear this scene in context, look for it about an hour and fourteen minutes into the film.)

But think how odd, how unrealistic the scene would seem without those sound effects. Even if the dialogue and music remained, we would notice the lack of door sounds, or footsteps, or blaster sounds. It would feel incomplete, noticeably unreal.

Adding these sounds is the work of Foley artists—the people who create the sounds that make a film sound real. They add all the things that we take for granted (unless we go out of our way to watch a clip with them removed): the sounds of footsteps, doors closing, crowds murmuring outside the window, punches, gunshots, or the subtle rustling of clothes as people embrace or hold hands.

But how does the work of Foley artists inspire what we can do in our own soundwriting projects as we work with sound effects—both sounds we fake for effect and record in real contexts?

Understanding Sound Effects

We define sound effects as any non-musical, non-voiced sounds—all the stuff that doesn't fit in the sections on Voice and Music above. This includes sounds you download, record on your own to sound like something it's not (like coconut shells to sound like a horse clomping), or record yourself on location—what many refer to as "ambient sound" (or ambi for short, a term often used in the radio industry) or "scene tape." And in soundwriting projects, you might find yourself using recordings you gathered from a location or using effects in the same way as Foley artists: by replicating the experience of being in a real space through the use of carefully chosen sounds. You can also use sound effects in other ways, too, in ways that are similar to how you use voice and music: to grab listeners emotionally and evoke a particular time and space, hooking them in the way you want them to be hooked, working your rhetorical magic.

Sound designer Randy Thom, who designed the wand and dragon sounds in *Harry Potter and the Goblet of Fire*, says a film that "really works" is "almost alive, a complex web of elements which are interconnected, almost like living tissues." When you're adding sound effects to your project, think of these sounds as being part of the same living body as the rest of the project, with all of its voices, music, and silences. To extend Thom's metaphor, effects can "flesh out" the experience your soundwriting piece gives the audience, even if you're working without the added affordances that visuals give a filmmaker. In practice, those effects can make your project sound real, magically transporting your listeners into the space that you're trying to evoke, whether it's a campus cafeteria or dorm room or a fictional detention cell or Quidditch ground. As communication scholar Emma Rodero writes, sound effects are there "to create an audio reconstruction of reality, imitating reality's actual sounds so as to create in the listener's mind a specific image of the phenomenon that it is intended to represent" (5).

Some soundwriters especially love working with sound effects because of the chance they give you to creatively play around with various editing effects, in a way that you can't always do with voice or music. For instance, voice and music are often incorporated in a way that sounds recognizably similar to the original, raw audio before it was in the project; sure, it's edited, but you still can say, "Oh, that's Bob," or "Oh, that's the hip-hop beat I downloaded from Freesound." But with non-musical effects, you have the chance to try more tricks in search of the mood you want: creating the soundscape of a damp cave by blending multiple drip sounds with footsteps and splashes, and adding tons of reverb and echo to the whole thing; or building to a dramatic climax by slowing down the recording of a plane engine and blending it with a tape recorder sound that you've reversed, all layered and fading in to a mechanical nightmare moment in sound. Your creative editing has a chance to shine when you play with effects.

> **Learn More**
> See the Adding Effects section in chapter five for a few suggestions about how to edit audio clips in these ways.

Here's a real example of that complex layering of effects: in the book *Out on the Wire*, cartoonist Jessica Abel interviews Jad Abumrad, who was then co-host of the popular radio show and podcast *Radiolab*. Abumrad explains that in one show, he wanted the sound to represent the experience of test pilots passing out and regaining consciousness while getting used to the feeling of extreme flight pressures by spinning around in a centrifuge. Here's some of how Abumrad describes his goals and choices as he designed the sounds he layered into an interview with pilot Tim Sestak:

I wanted to create the sound of a void. But it's not an entirely pleasant void. This is an adult who has some weird shred of awareness, like, this isn't right.

But it's calm and womb-like, and that's the starting point... And you hear this whoosh of energy and it lands. And so now the sound is dense. You hear the beeps, you hear all the computer sounds, you hear a kind of roar from the speed at which he is moving. It's all there.... Finally he grabs the controls, and boom. "I'm Tim Sestak." And at that final punctuational moment, you take all the sound away. (Abel 155–58)

Practicing your skill at composing sound effects gives you the power to do what Abumrad describes here: to simulate the sound of a void that's both unpleasant and womb-like, to help your listeners hear whooshes of energy, to fill the soundscape with beeps and computer sounds, all surrounded by a roar—or to create whatever other effect you want to give.

Whether your use of effects is subtle or dramatic, this section will help you determine how non-musical, non-voiced sound can enhance your soundwriting.

Using Sound Effects as a Tool

Signal Time and Place

You're telling an audio story set in a crowded cafe... or in an abandoned house with creaky stairs... or in the downtown streets of Mexico City, Addis Ababa, Bangkok, St. Petersburg, small-town Wisconsin... or at a political protest... or in a hospital room... or in the quiet space where your ancestors sat together in the evening, hundreds of years ago.

In any of these stories, you could signal location and place through voice, music, and silence alone. Or, if you're at the site you're evoking, you can simply record the ambient sound around you, capturing some authentic "scene tape." Another option is to work some magic with sound effects, crafting the exact space and sounds you imagine—the people, machines, and natural sounds that characterize any particular soundscape. We think you'll be hooked when you start experimenting with all the different ways you can use sound effects to whisk your listeners away to different times and places, just like the people who made the effects live on the radio dramas in the early twentieth century. But unlike those radio pioneers, you don't have to make and record the sound effects yourself: you can download sound effects from a number of different websites: creaky stairs, strong wind, knife and fork, computer beeping sounds, and anything else you can imagine, which you can then edit and layer into your project in a way that adds to or creates an atmosphere.

Of course, you may at times be taking listeners to times and places you've never been to, such as homes of the past or fantasy worlds from your imagination. So the art of using effects to evoke a time and place is always fundamentally artistic and rhetorical, as you make choices that you think will do the work they're supposed to do, inviting your listeners to stand in the space where you've brought them, with their eyes closed and their imaginations filling in the gaps. You can never escape your rhetorical situation.

Just as when you use music, choosing the right effects can be a complex rhetorical decision-making process, since what sounds right to one person might not sound right to another. We're reminded of nature recorder and sound artist Bernie Krause, who writes about how difficult it is to record the ocean in a way that sounds like the ocean to everyone; he even claims that you need to blend recordings from three different distances "just to begin to approach the experience of being at the shore" (185). So as always, we suggest you play drafts of your work to multiple audiences to make sure you're signaling the time and place that you intend in a way that "begins to approach the experience" you're trying to create for those real listeners.

Convey and Evoke Emotion

Those sonic places where you bring your listeners need not be emotionally neutral, of course. Depending on the story you're telling, you might use effects to evoke certain emotions in your listeners—perhaps subtly, or perhaps in strong, overpowering ways.

Sound effects can even be used to begin changing the emotional tenor of the piece as you move from one section to another. For instance, let's imagine you're making an audio documentary about living in a dorm on your college campus. The first part begins cheerfully, with interview clips from many students telling about how much fun they're having decorating their own rooms and staying up late with friends. These early parts of your documentary might have sounds of positive, bustling joy: clips of TVs on in the background, feet running down the hall, laughter, beds creaking, chairs being pushed in and out, phones ringing and notifying and vibrating constantly. (As we wrote above, we think there are rhetorical situations where it's important to record all this ambience yourself, and others where it's fine to download effects recorded by others.)

But later, let's say that you want to transition into a couple of harder, more emotional interview clips of students sharing how hard it was to leave home for the first time, and you don't want to just jump from the happy stuff to the harder parts. Maybe the bustle simply gets quieter and quieter as you get closer to those difficult interviews, but maybe you could find other effects to fade in as you approach those moments: a solitary pen clicking, or breathing sounds that build up to a sigh, or even weather sounds like rain and wind, all of which could say to listeners, "This part is going to feel different; pay attention."

Because sound effects can have so much emotional power, it's important to recognize when the use of them might be emotionally triggering for a listener. For example, the use of sound effects to recreate a domestic abuse situation or a violent encounter may be traumatizing for listeners, so keep this in mind when making decisions about how and when to use them (if at all), including how to warn listeners about what they're about to hear.

Design an Experience

Most of our examples above are about using sound effects that replicate recognizable sounds in the real world: creaky stairs that sound recognizably like creaky stairs, or clicking pens that sound recognizably like clicking pens. But what about the use of sound effects in ways where the sounds played aren't necessarily recognizable? We're thinking of examples like we described at the top of this section, where Abumrad used a combination of sound effects to create a fictionalized version of an experience.

In short: you can manipulate sound effects so they create an experience that you or your listeners might have never had.

You might enjoy thinking of this process as being similar to composing electronic music, but with recorded sound effects as your "instruments." It can be fun and surprising to download or record a sound and then run it through various effects in your audio editor—especially effects that dramatically affect the sound's duration or pitch, or effects that play the sound in reverse or add reverb or echo. Layering multiple copies of a sound can also be powerful (and powerfully weird), especially when each layered copy starts at a slightly different time and has other subtle differences edited into it (like which ear it sounds closer to in stereophonic space, or how long it lasts, or how deep or high the sound is). This can lead your listeners to say, "And in the background, there was this thing that sounded familiar, but also unfamiliar, and it made me feel unsettled, or empowered, or like I was flying."

We've both enjoyed using this kind of sound effect in our own projects. For example, in Kyle's audio memoir "Pincushion" (described in interlude A), he told the story of when he pulled the fire alarm in fifth grade, and he wanted to end the piece with the sound of fire engines and a feeling of being unsettled; in short, he didn't want the story to feel like it had been resolved too tidily. Sonically, this led him to take a single recording of a fire engine and layer it multiple times, with varying amounts of reverb added. The end effect is a creepy sound that is recognizable for what it is, but also with an unnatural tone; listeners are supposed to hear it and say, "Ouch—something isn't quite right there."

In "A Plea for Earlids," Tanya used sound effects to create the everyday experience of someone who lives with a debilitating ear disorder: loud disturbing sounds from the inside of one's body (think breathing and hearing yourself speak) colliding with chaotic and multilayered sounds of the outside world. Yes, someone with this disorder would recognize this experience, but most listeners would not. In fact, most people can't even fathom or imagine what it's like to endure this kind of sonic torture. Now, Tanya wanted to create this experience but knew she could only do so for a short period of time before a listener would find it unbearable and tune out. She had to make careful rhetorical decisions about the kinds of effects to use, the duration of the effects, and how and where to layer them. Tanya chose a multitude of body and world sounds—the sound of breathing, blinking, a heartbeat, a crowd, and a siren, along with voice. She began with one sound effect and slowly layered them until the sounds rose to a crescendo. At the height of the crescendo, the listener hears two seconds of what it sounds like to live with this condition. The layered sound effects were meant to make the listener feel anxious, and by the crescendo, completely overwhelmed—just as many people with this condition feel like on a daily basis.

Translate Ideas into Sound

As with any communication, it's easy for soundwriters to forget that their audience might need help understanding complex ideas. That's why writers sometimes insert visuals into their writing, and why speakers use slideshows: the writer or speaker thought, "Ooh, if I just use words alone to describe this, people might not quite understand my point. I'd better use another mode of communication to help them get it."

Soundwriters have a number of tricks to help listeners "get it," even when they're not using any visual aids (beyond a transcript, of course). Some of those tricks are more related to voice and silence than effects: repeating information multiple times so listeners won't miss it if they tune out for a second, pacing things so information has a chance to sink in, and so on.

But what if sound effects were used as sonic "visual aids"? The possibilities are endless and depend on your context, but here are two examples:

1. Kyle was once soundwriting a podcast episode about copyright (Stedman). He was trying to explain the complicated relationship between content in the public domain and content that was copyrighted, and he was struggling to use audio alone to make sense of it—he kept wanting to draw pictures! So eventually he turned to the piano, playing a wide, open chord with lots of space between the notes to represent the freedom of the public domain, and then playing a tight, close chord, with the notes butting right up next to each other, to represent the control and regulation of copyright. It was a sonic metaphor used to help listeners understand his complex point.

> **Learn More**
>
> You can learn more about copyright's effect on your own soundwriting in the Collecting and Downloading Sound section in chapter four.

2. In another project, Kyle was working with Courtney S. Danforth to tell the story of inventor of the telephone Alexander Graham Bell, his father Alexander Melville Bell, and his grandfather, Alexander Bell (Danforth and Stedman). All those *Alexanders* quickly became confusing, especially out loud without any visual aids to help clarify who was meant. So they devised a simple system to help listeners keep them straight: when they mentioned the middle Alexander, they played the sound of a bell (naturally), but whenever they mentioned the older Alexander, they played a two-note bell chime, with the second note lower than the first. Then, the younger Alexander got his own two-note chime, with the second note played *higher* than the first. The result, they hoped, was that people knew instantly and audibly which person they were talking about,

because they could literally hear the difference; each member of the family got his own little chime.

These examples aren't quite the same: the first example is using sonic metaphors to help listeners understand the point, while the second is more about teaching listeners to associate certain information with certain sounds. But both of them are using sound in creative ways to help make sense of complex ideas.

Sound Effect Section Takeaways

Choices: What Sound Effects Can Do	Execution: How to Use Sound Effects
Signal time and place	Add sound effects that would be heard in the real time and place that you're evoking.
Convey and evoke emotion	Choose effects that reflect the emotional tone of the story you're telling; don't assume that any sound is emotionally neutral.
Design an experience	Use all the powers of your audio editor's effects to adjust and layer sounds into something completely new.
Translate ideas into sound	Convey complex ideas with sonic metaphors and by building sonic associations that will take the place of visual aids.

Try-It   3.5 Playing with Sound Effects in the Audio Editor

This activity invites you to practice using sound effects to signal a time and a place. You'll need a computer connected to the internet and a website or program that hosts sound effects.

1. Do an internet search to find the lyrics for the nursery rhyme "Old MacDonald Had a Farm."
2. Rework the lyrics or part of the lyrics into a piece of writing that is better suited to be read aloud as a story instead of sung. Record yourself narrating

the transformed nursery rhyme. Upload your narration into an audio editing program.

Learn More
See Scripting in chapter four for more on how to write in a way most conducive for listening.

3. Visit freesound.org and find various sound effects that could work together to create the "sounds of a farm" in present day (or what you imagine a farm would or could sound like). Import the sound effects into your audio editing program.

4. Take up those sound effects and combine them (either back to back or layer them) to create a sonic farm for your listener to imagine or be transported to.

5. Now, layer your narration with sound effects to create your own rendition of "Old MacDonald Had a Farm."

Try-It 3.6 **Playing with Sound Effects on the Page**

This activity encourages play with sound effects for the purpose of identifying, imagining, and reimagining how sound effects rhetorically function in a piece of soundwriting. You will need to access a transcript of a piece of soundwriting—a *Radiolab* episode transcript would work well. Follow the steps below:

1. Read through the transcript, taking note of the various kinds of sound effects used and what their rhetorical function may be.

2. Work with a partner to imagine other sound effects that might work to accomplish the same rhetorical goal as the original (perhaps to create the same setting) or a different rhetorical goal (perhaps to situate the listener in a different place).

3. Now, discuss the extent to which the new set of sound effects may or may not be effective in achieving the intended purpose of this piece of soundwriting.

SILENCE

Figure 3.5
"[S]ilence can be as powerful as speech...silence and silencing deliver meaning" (Glenn xi).

Imagine these scenarios:

1. You're on summer break. You haven't seen or heard from your best friend in a while, so you text her: "Haven't heard from you in a couple of days, is everything okay?" You see your message has been read. Your friend never responds.
2. You're in school. A tragedy has happened. Your teacher asks you to take a moment of silence. You close your eyes and silently express gratitude that your family wasn't involved.
3. You're scrolling through Katy Perry's Instagram page. You see a photo from her NOH8 photoshoot—a campaign that was launched in response to California's passing of Proposition 8, a law that banned same-sex marriage. You stop to reflect on why she has duct tape across her mouth and what that might mean.

Many people think of silence as the absence of sound; it seems to be empty and void, a sea of nothingness like a black hole. Yet silence itself, as the saying goes, can "speak volumes," or in other words, can carry words, meaning, and emotions in the absence of sound. The above scenarios illustrate just how silence rhetorically functions in everyday life and likely has functioned in your own life. Silence from an unreturned text can feel hurtful, awkward, and maybe confusing. It might mean your friend is angry or apathetic...or maybe just busy. A "moment of silence" after a tragedy invites people to remember, to reflect, to honor, and to pay respect, while the silence (literal and physical) in the NOH8 campaign functioned as a form of protest, an argument about same-sex marriage, and an invitation for viewers to think and act. Silence *is* and silence *does*; it acts on us and we act on it.

Silence is a powerful rhetorical tool for soundwriters, one that is often overlooked and underappreciated. Below, we will help you think about what silence is, what it can do, and the ways you can use it to achieve your desired goals in any audio genre.

Understanding Silence

We love how Paul Goodman, an American writer, philosopher and psychotherapist, describes silence. He writes:

Not speaking and speaking are both human ways of being in the world, and there are kinds and grades of each. There is the dumb silence of slumber or apathy; the sober silence that goes with a solemn animal face; the fertile silence of awareness, pasturing the soul, whence emerge new thoughts; the alive silence of alert perception, ready to say, "This...this..."; the musical silence that accompanies absorbed activity; the silence of listening to another speak, catching the drift and helping him be clear; the noisy silence of resentment and self-recrimination, loud and subvocal speech but sullen to say it; baffled silence; the silence of peaceful accord with other persons or communion with the cosmos. (15)

This quote is striking for two reasons. First, Goodman categorizes the nature of silence and describes it in a way that most people have likely witnessed or can imagine, just as the above scenarios do. Having a sense of all those different kinds of silence is helpful when imagining how and where you might use silence in an audio project. Second, Goodman points out something very important about silence: it is read, understood, or described only when it's situated in relation to a person, an activity or event, the material world, or other sounds. This is especially true in an audio project. Unlike a sound that may immediately denote a meaning, like the sound of a kiss to signal love or affection, silence needs a *partner sound* in order for it to carry meaning or emotion.

When it comes to audio projects, silence and its partner sounds can be defined and thought of in two ways: an **absence** with bookended partner sounds, and a **present absence**, as Writing Studies scholar Heidi McKee calls it, with simultaneous partner sounds. That's a little confusing, right? Let us explain.

First, silence may literally be an absence of sound, and its partner sounds may be an audible sound that bookends that absence. For example, say you're listening to a crime podcast and an interviewee says, "I thought I'd never do it." A brief bout of silence follows. Then a voice comes back: "But I did." The silence creates drama and suspense. The listener is on the edge of their seat, likely asking themselves: Did she do it? What is "it"? That's silence as absence, with the words on either side of the silence as the partner sounds, drawing attention to and emphasizing the importance of the silence.

In contrast, silence may be a sound that once existed along with other sounds, but is taken away from its partners. And in turn, the listener *notices* that sound's absence. Just noticing that nothing is there makes that nothing a presence; it was once there and now it's not. The memory or remnants of the sound lingers: it still acts on other sounds and on the listener, and it has the potential to produce a number of rhetorical effects. Let's infuse the above example from the crime podcast with some present absence. The interviewee says, "I thought I'd never do it." A brief bout of music follows: the tune features a minimalist electric guitar solo, and it feels heavy and sad, but then the song quickly disappears just as the voice comes back. The interviewee says, "But I did." The music is no longer there, but its presence is still felt. The listener gets the sense that whatever story is about to be told is sad and perhaps tragic: whatever the "it" is should be read and understood as such. There was never a moment of actual silence, as in the first example; listeners always heard speaking or music—yet taking away that music beneath "But I did" is a subtraction that seems to mean something. That's silence as present absence, when an element of the audio is silenced in relation to something else that is heard.

Soundwriters use different lengths of silence in audio projects. Silence may appear as an extended absence of sound or as a present absence, when something heard has been removed from the mix. It also may simply be a brief pause that may occur naturally, like natural spaces during speech, or it may be employed strategically, like a second or two of silence inserted in speech to allow the listener more time to digest the information presented. Or, as we mentioned at the end of chapter two, silence may be thought of as something that is unspoken or not attended to—another side of an argument, a different perspective, research, facts, or opinions. Someone may intentionally or unintentionally employ these kinds of silences, producing a rhetorical effect.

Using Silence as a Tool

Organize a Project

Silence, just like voice and music, can work to *structure* and *organize* an audio project. Think about the last research paper you wrote on a computer. In each paragraph, you marked the end of every sentence with a period and used one space between each sentence. After each paragraph, you indicated a new paragraph with an indent or by hitting the enter key a couple of times. Now let's imagine all those spaces as brief pauses, brief moments for the reader to regroup and understand where they are in the larger context of the writing. In an audio project that uses narration, the use of silence will function similarly to those spaces in an alphabetic text. A person will speak, briefly pause, then proceed to the next sentence, thought, or idea. Longer bouts of silence, either as an absence or a present absence—kind of like the indent spaces before a new paragraph begins—can be used to indicate a transition to a new idea or another part of the project.

Here's an example of the use of present absence for a transition: say you're crafting a scene at a nightclub. You layer three sounds: hip-hop music, chatter among club-goers, and the voice of a DJ. As the scene comes to a close, you fade out the chatter and DJ, allowing the music to continue, then fade out a couple of seconds before you begin the next scene with narration. While the chatter and voice of the DJ no longer exist, they've left an imprint on the listener, and the absence immediately signals the soundwriter is transitioning to another part of the project. Even though the silence isn't entirely "silent," since music is still playing, the present absence of the speaking voices that used to be there acts as a kind of silence; an audible cue has disappeared, and the audience will notice and realize it signifies something—just as a visible paragraph break in an essay signals to readers that things are changing.

Emphasize Content

In a typed, alphabetic document, writers have all sorts of tools to mark certain words as more emphatic than others, such as boldface and italics. But how can we "bold" or "underline" something in a soundwriting project, and what does that have to do with the rhetorical function of silence? Think of it this way: silence can emphasize a point, indicating what's important.

For example, say you are composing an audio project about a haunted dorm room at your college. You are the narrator and begin describing the night you camped out in the dorm room and witnessed a haunting for yourself: "This dorm room looked like any other normal dorm room on campus," you say. "There were clothes strewn on the floor, books and papers on the desk, and posters hung on the wall. I thought it was *completely normal.*" You carefully enunciate "completely normal" (the partner sound for silence about to come) for emphasis and then you insert several seconds of silence. Just like when alphabetic text is italicized or bolded, the silence combined with the enunciated words works to emphasize that sentence; like it's telling your listener: "listen carefully, this small detail is important!"

The above example is an example of employing silence as absence. Yet the use of silence as present absence works wonders for bringing attention to a specific part of your audio project. When a listener notices that a sound was present, then no longer exists, they perk up and pay attention to what's coming next. For instance, you could edit everyday dorm room sounds under your initial narration, but then after the words "completely normal," those sounds suddenly cut off. BAM—present absence.

Pace the Project

Just like music, silence is incredibly helpful for pacing an audio project. Thanks to audio editing software, a soundwriter has complete control over where and when to add or delete silence. When an interviewee is talking a mile a minute and you're positive your listener will not understand what they're saying, add some pauses. When an interviewee is speaking like a turtle and it's hurting the pace of the project, delete some pauses. When you want to build drama, evoke emotion in your listener, or shift ideas, add some silence…and maybe add some more.

> **Learn More**
>
> Well, you might not always want to add COMPLETE silence. See the section on Recording Interviews in chapter four for suggestions on how to edit in the ambient, near-silent noise of a room to make your edits feel natural.

That's the thing about soundwriting: a lot of the time soundwriters need to listen and relisten to moments of silence in an effort to determine what *feels* like a good pace and works best for your rhetorical context. We even like to listen to our drafts in different spaces, using different speakers. Kyle remembers one time he almost submitted a piece for publication that he had only listened to through his headphones, so he decided to give it one more listen in a different way: played through his teeny laptop speakers while he paced at the other end of the room. Somehow, this change in listening context made him notice tons of pacing errors: transitions that happened too quickly, sentences that needed more room to breathe, and fades that should have taken longer. When Kyle was in the editing mindset, he wasn't using silence to its full potential, and the pacing of the project would have suffered if he hadn't caught it.

Convey and Evoke Emotion

Similar to music and voice, silence, both as an absence and a present absence, is powerful in its ability to convey emotion and evoke emotions in a listener. As a soundwriter, you may use silence to convey anticipation, confusion, wonder, apathy, interest, fear, sadness, or joy. Silence as absence is particularly effective for creating a mood and establishing a tone in a piece of soundwriting. For example, let's say you're composing an audio project about the relationship culture of college students. You interview two students and incorporate this unedited interview into your audio project. You ask, "So when did you guys get together?" Three seconds of silence. You ask again, "No, really, I'm curious about when you two started dating." Again, three seconds of silence. Um...awkward, right? The silence immediately positions the mood of the situation as uncomfortable and establishes an uneasy tone.

While the assets you work with may already have silence imbued with emotion, like the example above, you as a soundwriter have lots of control over employing silence to make your listener feel emotions like fear or joy. The way silence makes listeners feel is mostly subjective: it depends on the listener's relationship to the subject matter of the audio project, their engagement with the piece, and their personal associations, yet soundwriters can indeed make assumptions about audience reaction based on how that kind of silence has been understood in US culture, like the "awkward silence" or the "dramatic silence."

So let's go back to the example of the haunted dorm room story. Imagine that you end the first dorm-room description scene like this: "And then I saw it." Then you employ silence for four seconds before creepy music begins. That silence is infused with fear, with anticipation, and with anxiety, and those emotions contribute to the construction of a mood and tone. With only four seconds of silence, you have evoked a feeling in your listener largely by the question that hangs heavy in the silence: WHAT did she see? The listener may feel anxious or nervous about what's to come.

Invite Co-Creation

Silence is particularly effective for crafting moments that invite the kind of immersive listening experience we described in chapter two. Yet unlike other rhetorical strategies that guide listeners to visualize and participate in soundwriting (like how KalaLea, in *Blindspot: Tulsa Burning*, used descriptive language that led Tanya to visualize her ransacked house), silence offers the listener the chance to create their *own* experience. It gives them the time and space to reflect, contemplate, ask questions, make connections to their own life, and make their own meaning in a way that's meaningful for them. A painter who experienced temporary hearing loss explains this sentiment well. He says, "Sound imposes a narrative on you and it's always someone else's narrative. My experience of silence was like being awake inside a dream I could direct" (qtd. in Prochnik 13). A quiet place is a welcoming space that offers listeners unique opportunities to design an experience even when they're technically the *listener*, not the soundwriter. That is, listeners can become co-creators of the experience, filling in unspoken gaps in a way that's personal to them alone. Silence and quiet invites this co-creation.

One of the most compelling ways we've heard silence used to invite listener co-creation and meaning-making is in Kate Artz's "The Conversation." (You can hear Artz's piece online as part of the larger article by Rodrigue et al.) Kate's soundwriting is an audio drama that depicts a one-sided phone call. The listener hears only one part of a telephone conversation; the other part is represented through various lengths of silence. Despite not knowing anything about the context of the conversation, the listener does the work of filling in the silence, imagining what the person on the other end of the line is saying. In doing so, the listener literally *creates* the conversation. Kate's complete surrender of rhetorical control yields a unique listener experience and opportunity for soundwriters and listeners to interact and collaborate in an unusual and extraordinary way.

How else might you give your listeners space to co-create along with you? We don't know all the possibilities out there, but the key is to allow yourself, when it fits your purpose, to edit a little more minimally. Add more quiet "paragraph breaks" between sections of your audio essay; resist the urge to fill every moment of your audio drama with sound effects and music; let some ideas be implied but unspoken. When you do, you're telling your listener, "You're a part of this too."

Silence Section Takeaways

Choices: What Silence Can Do	Execution:
Organize the project	Determine the genre of the project and possible organizational structures. Visually chart out the various elements of your story. Identify different sections, scenes, or areas that may need transitions. Aurally indicate different sections, parts, or transitions in your soundwriting.
Emphasize content	Employ silence after an important moment, detail, phrase, or scene.
Pace the project	Add pauses or silence in rapid speech (if the speed does not achieve your rhetorical goals), moments you want to emphasize, or times when you want to connect with your listener. Delete pauses or silence in slow speech (if the slowness does not achieve your rhetorical goals).

Convey and evoke emotion	Use silence as absence or a present absence before or after a compelling moment—something interesting, important, or shocking; after a rich description; after a presentation of a person, place, event, or setting; or a question.
Invite co-creation	Identify moments where you want your listener to feel an emotion, ponder a question, make a connection, visualize, and direct their own experience. Experiment with employing silence at these moments.

Try-It   3.7 Playing with Silence in the Audio Editor

This activity encourages play with silence to help soundwriters determine where and how long to use silence. Often, a soundwriter makes this decision after playing around with various lengths until it *feels* like it works. Try it for yourself by following the steps below:

1. Import a recent political speech into your audio editing software and/or print a transcription of the speech.

2. Identify sections of the speech that you think would benefit from more or less silence, for any reason.

3. For each of those sections in the audio editor, experiment with adding or taking away silence. Be sure to try minor, moderate, and extreme changes to the original. If you're with a printed transcript, cut up the transcript into pieces and use physical spaces between the pieces to experiment with different lengths of silence.

4. For each bout of silence, note if and why you think this length is or could be effective. Ask yourself how the different silences seem to change the meaning or emotional tone of the words.

5. Share your responses with a peer and discuss. Use these two questions to frame your discussion: What was the process you used to determine a good length of silence within this particular context? What did this exercise teach you about how you might make decisions about the length of silence to use in an audio project?

Try-It 3.8 **Playing with Silence with a Recording Device**

This activity invites play with different lengths of silence to identify its various rhetorical effects. It is also meant to help soundwriters acknowledge and identify the similarities and differences between how it *feels* to use silence while recording narration, and how it *feels* to listen to silence in a recording. You'll need a recording device and a computer with a word processing program. Here are the steps:

1. Imagine you're leaving a voice message for your best friend about what you want to do over the weekend. Write this hypothetical voice message in a document file. Record yourself reading the message without any use of silence.

2. Now, return to your document file. Use the spacebar and enter key to insert various amounts of "silence" in different places throughout the message. For instance, a paragraph break with lots of space between it suggests more implied silence than one or two taps of the space bar.

3. Record yourself reading the voice message, allowing the spaces to guide you in determining how long to pause between each word.

4. Listen back to your recordings and note the rhetorical impact of your play with silence. How did the various bouts of silence impact your message? How might your best friend react to these two versions of your message?

5. Now, turn your reflective lens inward and freewrite about how you felt when recording these various lengths of silence and how that may be similar or different to how you felt when listening to those different bouts of silence. What might this teach you about recording narration?

Discussion Questions

1. Of the four sonic rhetorical tools described in this chapter—voice, music, sound effects, and silence—which do you find the most important? Which are you best at using rhetorically, and which do you need the most practice with?

2. All four of the sections in this chapter discuss different ways to convey and evoke emotion in your listeners. Why do you think emotion is discussed so much in this chapter?

3. This chapter is full of examples of how the four sonic rhetorical tools have been or could be used. What did we leave out? What are some examples from podcasts, songs, TV shows, movies, or other audiovisual texts where these four tools have been used powerfully or poorly?

Works Cited

Abel, Jessica. *Out on the Wire: The Storytelling Secrets of the New Masters of Radio.* Broadway, 2015.

Anderson, Erin. "Our Time Is Up." *PRX*, Sarah Awards Winners, 2016, beta.prx.org/stories/193003.

———."Toward a Resonant Material Vocality for Digital Composition." *enculturation: A Journal of Rhetoric, Writing, and Culture*, vol. 18, August 2014, enculturation.net/materialvocality.

Banfield, William C. "Introduction." *Musical Landscapes in Color: Conversations with Black American Composers*, edited by William C. Banfield, Scarecrow, 2003, pp. ix–xvi.

Burrows, David. *Time and the Warm Body: A Musical Perspective on the Construction of Time.* Brill, 2007.

Criss, Doug. "Study: Mom's Voice Works like a Charm on Your Brain." *CNN*, 18 May 2016, www.cnn.com/2016/05/18/health/mom-voice-study-trnd/index.html.

Danforth, Courtney S., and Kyle D. Stedman. "Introduction." *Soundwriting Pedagogies*, edited by Courtney S. Danforth et al., Computers and Composition Digital Press/Utah State UP, 2018, ccdigitalpress.org/book/soundwriting/introduction/index.html.

Gallagher, Danny. "6 Songs Used to Torture & Intimidate." *Mental Floss*, 25 June 2009, www.mentalfloss.com/article/22075/6-songs-used-torture-intimidate.

Glenn, Cheryl. *Unspoken: A Rhetoric of Silence.* Southern Illinois UP, 2004.

Goodman, Paul. *Speaking and Language: Defence of Poetry.* Random House, 1972.

King, Stephen. *On Writing: A Memoir of the Craft.* Pocket, 2000.

The Kitchen Sisters, hosts. "Chicken Pills: A Hidden World of Jamaican Girls." *The Kitchen Sisters Present…*, PRX, 27 Nov. 2017, beta.prx.org/stories/221669

Krause, Bernie. *Into a Wild Sanctuary: A Life in Music & Natural Sound.* Heyday, 1998.

Langer, Susanne K. *Philosophy in a New Key: A Study in the Symbolism of Reason, Rite, and Art.* 3rd ed., Harvard UP, 1957.

The Learning Network. "Winners of Our Second Annual Student Podcast Contest." *The New York Times*, 19 June 2019, www.nytimes.com/2019/06/19/learning/winners-of-our-second-annual-student-podcast-contest.html.

Levitt, Andrea, and Margery Lucas. "Effects of Four Voice Qualities and Formant Dispersion on Perception of a Female Voice." *Psychology of Language and Communication*, vol. 22, 2018, pp. 394–416.

McKee, Heidi. "Sound Matters: Notes toward the Analysis and Design of Sound in Multimodal Webtexts." *Computers and Composition*, vol. 23, 2006, pp. 335–354.

Perris, Arnold. *Music as Propaganda: Art to Persuade, Art to Control.* Greenwood, 1985.

Prochnik, George. *In Pursuit of Silence: Listening for Meaning in a World of Noise.* Anchor, 2011.

Rodero, Emma. "See It on a Radio Story: Sound Effects and Shots to Evoked Imagery and Attention on Audio Fiction." *Communication Research*, vol. 39, no. 4, 2012, pp. 1–22.

Rodrigue, Tanya. "A Plea for Earlids." *PRX*, 2019, exchange.prx.org/pieces/292879-a-plea-for-earlids.

Rodrigue, Tanya K., et al. "Navigating the Soundscape, Composing with Audio." *Kairos: A Journal of Rhetoric, Technology, and Pedagogy*, vol. 21, no. 1, 2016, kairos.technorhetoric.net/21.1/praxis/rodrigue/index.html.

Sacks, Oliver. *Musicophilia: Tales of Music and the Brain*. Vintage, 2008.

"Star Wars Episode IV: A New Hope." *Internet Movie Script Database*, imsdb.com/scripts/Star-Wars-A-New-Hope.html.

Stedman, Kyle. "Using Creative Commons to Make Stuff." *Plugs, Play, Pedagogy*, 20 Oct. 2014, plugsplaypedagogy.podigee.io/3-using-creative-commons.

Taylor, Trey. "The Rise and Fall of Katharine Hepburn's Fake Accent." *The Atlantic*, 8 Aug. 2013, www.theatlantic.com/entertainment/archive/2013/08/the-rise-and-fall-of-katharine-hepburns-fake-accent/278505/.

Thom, Randy. "Designing a Movie for Sound." *FilmSound.Org*, 1999, filmsound.org/articles/designing_for_sound.htm.

van Leeuwen, Theo. *Speech, Music, Sound*. St. Martin's Press, 1999.

Interlude C

Podcasting with a Partner: How Kyle Composed "Grumble, Grumble"[1]

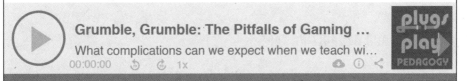

Figure C.1 The published version of Kyle's podcast episode.

INTRODUCTION

In 2014 and 2015, I produced a twelve-episode podcast on teaching writing and rhetoric in the twenty-first century. I was still pretty new to soundwriting, so podcasting every month helped me constantly sharpen my audio production skills and focus regularly on my audience's needs—in my case, faculty and graduate students in my field of writing studies. I'll narrate here the story of a particularly collaborative episode to show how collaborative soundwriting can work and to give a bit of insight into the podcasting world.

Here's how this episode happened: I got an email one day from Dr. Stephanie Vie, who was then a professor of writing and rhetoric at the University of Central Florida. She asked if I'd like to collaborate on an episode about teaching with games—and over the next two months, that email led to twenty-five more emails from Stephanie, multiple video-chats, and so much content that it filled two hour-long podcast episodes. Whew. (She really likes games.) Our ultimate purpose was two-fold: to

---

1 The finished version of this podcast episode can be heard online at Kyle's podcast hosting site: Stedman, Kyle. "Grumble, Grumble: The Pitfalls of Gaming Pedagogy." *Plugs, Play, Pedagogy*, episode 5, 22 Dec. 2014, plugsplaypedagogy.podigee.io/5-grumble-grumble.

　　You can see a video of Kyle's final audio editing process (at high-speed) on YouTube: Stedman, Kyle. "Editing a Podcast: Plugs, Play, Pedagogy Episode 5." *YouTube*, 22 Dec. 2014, youtu.be/YK5kckEVFaA.

encourage listeners to use games in meaningful ways in writing and rhetoric classrooms, but also to warn them of some of the common mistakes that teachers new to gaming commonly make. And of course, there was the sub-purpose of amplifying the work of scholars doing work in gaming and teaching; I wanted my show to give a shout-out to all the smart people out there doing this work.

I don't want to tell the whole story of those two podcast episodes—that would take forever—but I do want to share what I learned about working collaboratively (including the things it's best to do together and the things it's best to do alone). I'll focus especially on the second of the two game-focused episodes, which I called "Grumble, Grumble: The Pitfalls of Gaming Pedagogy," since it focused on the challenges of teaching with games. ("Grumble, grumble" is an inside joke from the first *Legend of Zelda* game; I assumed many in my audience would get the reference.)

GATHERING AND ORGANIZING TAPE

Collaboration worked so well for me and Stephanie as we produced this episode because it let us play to our individual strengths. Stephanie was tapped into a professional network of rhetoric scholars who taught with games, and I had the skills and audience of a podcast. Win-win.

After a lot of emails and planning, we conducted three long interviews over video call (using an open-question strategy) and collected four shorter segments recorded by other scholars, plus some more short segments that Stephanie alone had soundwritten. It was way more content than I could have gotten if I had just cold-called people, begging for their wisdom.

> **Learn More**
> See the Generating Interview Questions section in chapter four.

With all that content, we had a lot to organize, especially if we wanted to achieve our complex purpose of both encouraging and warning teachers about gaming in the classroom. To help us organize, we wrote together in a massive Google Doc that was filled with a lot of things: a list of the segments we'd collected, informal logs

> **Learn More**
> See the Making a Plan section in chapter four for more advice.

of our interview tape (that is, time-stamped notes from the interviews) to remind us of what we talked about, links to different assets we'd downloaded online (like the music we played between segments), and brainstorming notes from each of us about what needed to stay and what needed to go. Eventually, we carved out a space on the Doc with a detailed outline where we drafted what we wanted to keep and how long each segment was (to keep each episode to one hour max). The collaborative nature of a Google Doc allowed us to easily comment on what the other had typed, moving us closer and closer to a final draft.

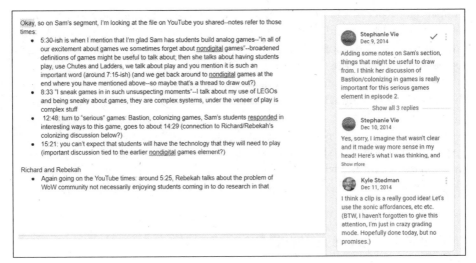

Okay, so on Sam's segment, I'm looking at the file on YouTube you shared--notes refer to those times:

- 5:30-ish is when I mention that I'm glad Sam has students build analog games--"in all of our excitement about games we sometimes forget about nondigital games"--broadened definitions of games might be useful to talk about; then she talks about having students play, use Chutes and Ladders, we talk about play and you mention it is such an important word (around 7:15-ish) (and we get back around to nondigital games at the end where you have mentioned above--so maybe that's a thread to draw out?)
- 8:33 "I sneak games in in such unsuspecting moments"--I talk about my use of LEGOs and being sneaky about games, they are complex systems, under the veneer of play is complex stuff
- 12:48: turn to "serious" games: Bastion, colonizing games, Sam's students responded in interesting ways to this game, goes to about 14:29 (connection to Richard/Rebekah's colonizing discussion below?)
- 15:21: you can't expect that students will have the technology that they will need to play (important discussion tied to the earlier nondigital games element?)

Richard and Rebekah
- Again going on the YouTube times: around 5:25, Rebekah talks about the problem of WoW community not necessarily enjoying students coming in to do research in that

Stephanie Vie ✓
Dec 9, 2014

Adding some notes on Sam's section, things that might be useful to draw from. I think her discussion of Bastion/colonizing in games is really important for this serious games element in episode 2.

——— Show all 3 replies ———

Stephanie Vie
Dec 10, 2014

Yes, sorry, I imagine that wasn't clear and it made way more sense in my head! Here's what I was thinking, and
Show more

Kyle Stedman
Dec 11, 2014

I think a clip is a really good idea! Let's use the sonic affordances, etc etc. (BTW, I haven't forgotten to give this attention, I'm just in crazy grading mode. Hopefully done today, but no promises.)

Figure C.2   Sample notes and comments in Kyle's Google Doc.

This plan was made easier by the transcripts we had of some of the segments and the logs we had made of the interviews, since we could search and skim text instead of opening up a lot of audio as we moved things around in our outline. You could say that we were using the affordances of the written word to help us produce a project with the affordances of audio.

> **Learn More**
> Check out chapter four for more about logging in the Choosing Tape for Your Project section.

COLLABORATIVE, PLAYFUL INVENTION

My collaboration with Stephanie also helped me feel brave enough to try a wild idea that I wasn't sure was any good: I wanted Stephanie and another of our interviewees (Jennifer deWinter) to watch me playing some retro videogames over a video chat and comment in real time on what my playing made them think about, especially as it connected to teaching.

But honestly, I think if I had been working alone, I might not have felt brave enough to try this, since after all, it could have led to a lot of useless tape, if Stephanie and Jennifer didn't think of anything interesting to say. (I know that with the advent of Twitch, watching and commenting on people playing live games is normal now for many people, but in 2014, it felt like new ground to me.) There was something about having a teammate that led me to playfully try ideas that I wasn't sure would work. That kind of bravery and play is important in any composing context, but I wonder if it's especially important when soundwriting, since there are so many ways to play around in audio, allowing us to walk the borderline between audio texts that are more "critical" or more "artistic." In this case, we tried it, and a version of this segment made it into the final episode. It worked!

(Well, almost: my recording of the conversation didn't include the actual sounds of the games I was playing, so I had to go back later and fake it, editing in newly recorded sounds of me playing the same games they had seen me play.)

My point is that the process of generating ideas—the "invention" process, as it's often called by rhetoric scholars—is often most effective when it's playful and when you're working with others, bouncing ideas off each other and encouraging even the oddest digressions.

> **Learn More**
> There's lots more about invention in the beginning of chapter four.

GATHERING ASSETS AND FINISHING THE SCRIPT

We didn't collaborate on every single decision, partly because Stephanie and I lived hundreds of miles away from each other, and partly because some detailed audio editing decisions are easiest and quickest for me to do alone.

For instance, I gathered the musical assets myself, since I know more about videogame music and legally usable remixes than she does. I also scripted the narration that would stitch the segments together, since it was language I'd be reading/performing as the show's host. This scripting was easy, since Stephanie and I had already collaboratively drafted an outline, following a model of "letting the tape lead" us to find connections. And since I was a few episodes into the podcast at this point, I was getting a better sense of how to write scripts that would sound like the version of me I presented as host: a little zanier and more outgoing than I am in person, but still smart and not afraid of a bit of academic terminology here and there, which I knew wouldn't scare off my audience of teachers.

Writing a script also gave me a chance to carefully introduce all the speakers in the episodes in the way they had said they wanted to be introduced, including their exact job titles and plugs for their books; if I had just talked off the cuff without a script, I could easily have made a mistake. I ended the script with a reminder about how to contact me and Stephanie on Twitter, which Creative Commons license I use for my own show (which tells listeners how they may share and remix my audio), which videogame music remixes I used from a site called OverClocked ReMix (since their site explicitly allows this kind of use with attribution), and a friendly gimmick I used at the end of every episode: commenting on the weather in Rockford, Illinois, where I live.

PUTTING IT ALL TOGETHER: EDITING AND SHARING

Really, it's only at this point when I started what some might think of as the heart of the soundwriting: recording my narration and putting all the pieces together in a single file in Audacity. In fact, just for fun, I recorded a screencast of my soundwriting process starting at this stage, which I then sped up and posted on YouTube (Stedman, "Editing"). From that video, you can see that I did almost two hours of work to record the narration and edit all the pieces together (from 9:21–11:10 a.m.), but it would have been much longer if Stephanie and I hadn't done so much work preparing everything before this final push.

What steps does the video show?

- Scrolling through the narration document as I read it straight into Audacity.
- Compressing the audio so the louder and quieter parts of my narration are evened out.
- Importing the first music track that would play beneath my opening narration and adjusting the volume manually using Audacity's Envelope Tool.
- Cleaning up my narration throughout as I went: deleting accidental flubs in the narration, adjusting the amount of time between words and sentences, and little things like that.
- Importing the other segments and musical tracks when appropriate, and adjusting the volume levels to make them all fit together without any one sound overpowering anything else. Because I had already recorded and compressed my narration, which led to a fairly level volume, I adjusted everything else to match that volume level.
- Playing Solitaire and FreeCell when doing a "double-check" listen to some segments. I find that games like that give me something to look at while listening to something at the same time: it works as a focusing tool.
- Downloading a song that I didn't already have on my computer and pasting the link to it in my planning doc so I wouldn't lose track of it.
- Double-checking a transcript from Stephanie while listening to an audio clip, to make sure that the cuts I had made to an interview in a previous editing session matched the transcript. This was a way to ensure that my interview clip was the right clip, beginning to end.
- Navigating my browser to my podcast host (a site called Podigee, which I chose because it was free and I'm cheap).
- Tweeting an excited tweet to let the world know that it was done and would be live soon.

At that point, the episode was nearly complete, but not quite. After exporting the final audio file as a high-quality MP3, I uploaded it to podcast host Podigee, wrote show notes that gave credit to all the people and music involved, and got everything into a clean transcript document—a process that involved pasting all the individual transcripts and my narration script into a single file, standardizing the format, adding relevant links throughout, and giving the whole thing a listen to make sure that what I meant to say is what I *actually* said and that all non-verbal sounds were described. (It's not as good a transcript as I would use today; for instance, it simply mentions when music starts instead of actually describing the music.)

Learn More

Learn tips for composing transcripts in chapter five.

Grumble, Grumble: The Pitfalls of Gaming Pedagogy » Edit

🗓 Change publication   ✕ Unpublish

Media Files   General   ☆ Chapter Marks   Social   More options

General » General information about this episode   Last saved: 5 months ago Save

Title *   Grumble, Grumble: The Pitfalls of Gaming Pedagogy   ⓘ

Subtitle   What complications can we expect when we teach with games? And why are   ⓘ

Description   This is the second in a two-part series of episodes on how games intersect   ⓘ
                           with pedagogies of writing and rhetoric. Its special focus is on the
                           complexities of gaming pedagogies, especially the resistance we can

Show notes   **B** *I* A % 🖼 ≡ ≣ </> 66 Q Preview   ⓘ
Edit with Markdown
                           # Plugs, Play, Pedagogy

Figure C.3 Kyle's podcast host Podigee.

Once I clicked "publish" on Podigee, the podcast was automatically available to anyone who subscribed to my feed. I had manually added my feed to the iTunes store (now Apple Podcasts) and Stitcher, two popular places for people to find podcasts, so anyone searching for it or any of the keywords I chose could find it there. Then it was up to me and Stephanie to spread the word, using our social media accounts and other networks to make sure people could listen to it. And of course, because so many people were involved in these two episodes, that meant that all of *those* people were eager to share it on *their* networks as well.

THE ONGOING FRUIT OF COLLABORATION

Even though this story is mostly done, I want to mention one more thing: the way that sharing our soundwriting can lead to connections in the future. Specifically, in March 2015 (three months after posting the episode), Stephanie and I received an email from another person who podcasts about technology in higher education: Chris Friend with the *HybridPod* podcast. He was interested in soundwriting his own episode about play in the classroom, and he thought our work on games had a lot to say about that topic, so he emailed us to ask if *we* would be on *his* show. We of course agreed, and we set up a time for us to record interviews with Chris, leading to another whole process as Chris composed his own episode, which ended up as the episode "Play in Education," which he published on May 20, 2015. (Somehow, he kept his episode to just 33:30; I'm not very good at keeping things brief.)

And if that's not enough, the connections kept coming. Since 2014, I've regularly seen all the people involved in that episode at academic conferences; now that we know a little bit about each other, it's easier for us to share each other's work, brag about how cool we all are, and even get a bite to eat together to hear how things are going. And in May 2019, Stephanie emailed me and a couple of other academic podcasters to introduce a new friend who was doing good work and would benefit from the scholarly friendships we had all established. My point is that connecting with people always pays off, including years after the fact in ways you can't predict at the time.

Takeaways

Here's what I hope you'll apply to your own soundwriting after reading my story:
- Don't be afraid to reach out to potential collaborators. Smart people like talking about their area of expertise; you can use that to your advantage when soundwriting.
- Stay organized! Make sure all your notes, logs, transcripts, outlines, links, and citations are in writing in a place where you can't lose them.
- Bravely try creative ideas, especially when you're working with someone else.
- Know what parts of your podcast episode are best to script (like the introduction, transitions, and conclusion) and which parts you can improvise (like interviews).
- Before putting all your audio assets together in one file, try to have as much as possible prepared in advance. This lets you focus on putting together the pieces in your first pass of editing.
- Keep up the relationships you form with collaborators and interviewees.

Genre Conventions: Podcasts

When I first tried podcasting back in 2014, I hadn't listened to many podcasts yet—just enough to give me a basic idea of the conventions that were out there. But listening back to my early episodes now can be a cringe-worthy experience for me, especially when it comes to timing (jokes and end credits that go on forever, for example). I made those mistakes because of my unfamiliarity with genre conventions about how much time successful educational podcasts spent on those things.

I want to guide you so you don't have to make some of those mistakes, but with a warning: as you learned in Tip 1.3 in chapter one, there are *a lot* of podcast genres, each with their own set of genre conventions. The conventions listed here are especially applicable to what might be called "carefully edited podcasts"—shows where each segment has been planned and carefully presented for a rhetorical purpose, as opposed to shows where people just turn on the mics and chat with each other.

> **Learn More**
>
> Learn some more of the basics about setting up and distributing podcasts at the end of chapter five.

- **Where it's heard:** Most listeners access podcasts in apps that let them easily search and download the newest episodes to their phones or devices. But podcasts can usually also be heard on the web in a browser; most podcast hosting sites will help listeners find them both ways.
- **Length:** While unedited, conversational podcasts sometimes go on for hours, I think the max length for an edited podcast should be an hour, and many are much shorter. It depends on the conventions in whatever sub-genre of podcasting you're working in, as well as your own rhetorical purpose.
- **Content:** Since podcasts are organized into shows with multiple episodes, a good show has a focused show topic with facets that can easily be explored in different episodes. Many edited podcasts include a blend of narration, interviews, and field audio (something you left your office to record), often blended with music and effects (either ambience you recorded yourself or sounds you downloaded).
- **Structure:** Podcasts have a number of tricks to make sure listeners know what they're listening to and don't feel lost. Early in an episode (perhaps after an attention-grabbing teaser), they often introduce the topic, guest speaker, and theme of the episode. Transitions are marked extremely clearly, using language like, "Now that we've talked about X, let's move on to the second half of the show, which focuses on Y." They often use music at the beginning, ending, and at transitions to help listeners audibly hear where they're at in the episode's structure.
- **Language:** Podcasts use conversational language that sounds natural, since the intimacy and personality of podcasts are part of what draws listeners. Special-

ized language ("jargon") is used to the extent that a podcaster can expect their specialized audience to understand it.

- **Opening and Closing**: Early in every episode, many podcast hosts introduce themselves, the name of the show, and a tagline: a one-sentence overview of the show's topic, repeated in each episode. For instance, my current podcast always includes a line like this in the first ten seconds: "This is *Bad Ideas about Writing*, the podcast that counters major myths about writing instruction. I'm Kyle Stedman from Rockford University." Then at the end, most podcasts give credits and thanks, mentioning by name everyone who helped in any way, including guests, everyone who gathered tape, everyone who helped with the production, peer reviewers, musicians or sound effect creators whose work was heard, and to anyone whose work was relied on for content and inspiration.
- **Script**: Podcasters especially need scripts when they need to get specific details right (like interviewees' names and job titles), when they're afraid of leaving something out, and when there are lots of segments or interviews. The best, most ethical podcasts also prepare a transcript and share a link to it in the "show notes," the written description of the episode that listeners will see in their podcast apps.
- **Sonic Rhetorical Strategies**: The majority of podcasts rely on the power of voice, often with the subtle power of music used to enhance especially powerful or emotional moments. Some use more or less sound effects and recorded ambient noise. And of course, some podcasts feature nature recordings or sound art that breaks the mold of the edited, radio-influenced shows that are guiding most of this information.

For more advice on crafting edited podcasts, we suggest turning to the most up-to-date information online and reading Jessica Abel's excellent comic on radio and podcasting *Out on the Wire*: *The Storytelling Secrets of the New Masters of Radio*.

Works Cited

Abel, Jessica. *Out on the Wire: The Storytelling Secrets of the New Masters of Radio*. Broadway, 2015.

Stedman, Kyle. "Editing a Podcast: Plugs, Play, Pedagogy Episode 5." *YouTube*, 22 Dec. 2014, youtu.be/YK5kckEVFaA.

———. "Grumble, Grumble: The Pitfalls of Gaming Pedagogy." *Plugs, Play, Pedagogy*, episode 5, 22 Dec. 2014, plugsplaypedagogy.podigee.io/5-grumble-grumble.

Chapter Four

PLANNING AND GATHERING SOUNDS

INTRODUCTION

If you're reading this book in order, by this point you've thought about how sound-writing addresses a rhetorical situation, you've listened carefully to the world around you (both with your ears and your body), and you've stuffed your toolboxes with sonic strategies to use in your soundwriting. You're ready to dive in and make some soundwriting happen—and this chapter and the next are designed to support those practical goals. This chapter guides you as you generate ideas, plan a project, and gather audio from interviews, your own recordings, or the internet. Then, chapter five helps you take those plans and recordings into your audio editor, revise, and share your finished soundwriting with the world.

Before we begin, let us define two terms we use a lot in the next two chapters:

- **Tape**: We use the word *tape* when talking about the audio that you gather and work with. We know that word sounds weird; most of you probably haven't created soundwriting with physical spools of magnetic tape in a cassette or reel-to-reel machine since the 1990s or earlier. So don't worry: when we write something like, "Did you get good tape at that interview?" we're actually referring to digital audio recorded with a computer, digital recorder, phone, or other device. "Tape" is just a quick, convenient shorthand for "recorded audio" that's survived the shift from analog to digital production.

- **Assets**: In a soundwriting project, think of an "asset" as any piece of audio that is included in your audio project (even if it's manipulated or layered with other assets). It can exist on its own but is ultimately used as part of a larger whole. Don't mix up an asset with a "source," something that inspires or guides you in some way but doesn't make its way into your soundwriting. For example, an article about microphones is a *source* if you read it and use the advice to help you choose a microphone; if you record yourself reading a clip of the article for a podcast episode about microphones, that recording is now also one of your project's *assets*.

GENERATING IDEAS

Imagine this. You've just been given a soundwriting assignment, or perhaps you have a bud of an idea for an independent audio project...but now what? How do you begin? How do you move from a writing prompt or a tiny idea pebble to a full-blown audio project?

The answer: it depends. The way a composer begins to generate or grow ideas is dependent on numerous factors like the assignment they're responding to or the project they have in mind; their relationship and previous experiences with writing, school, sound, genre, and the topic of the audio project; their learning style; their personality and habits...and we could go on and on.

Some people already know what to do or where to go to generate ideas, and some have a specific method or process for approaching a writing project. For example, Tanya finds her best ideas come when she's alone, driving in her car, or taking a walk. She often talks out loud, recording herself so she can later listen and notice anything good that might have come from her ramblings. Meanwhile, Kyle often finds ideas during the composing process itself—when he's reading, researching, taking notes, and even scripting or editing. He might be in the middle of producing an audio recording when he'll suddenly be struck by the perfect combination of music and effects to go with his narration.

So perhaps the first step in brainstorming a project or firming up half-baked ideas during the composing process is to determine if you already have a brainstorming process or know how to get your mind to a place where ideas emerge, grow, and flourish. If you find it hard to generate ideas, you're in good company, since a major part of classical Greek and Roman rhetors' education was what they called "invention": techniques for finding ideas that fit a particular rhetorical situation. When it comes to today's soundwriting, here are our favorite invention techniques.

Rhetorical Analysis

Remember our discussion of rhetoric and the rhetorical situation in chapter one? We explained the value of identifying and exploring all four factors of a rhetorical situation when analyzing or composing soundwriting. As soundwriters it's helpful to conduct a rhetorical analysis of our own soundwriting situations, asking ourselves questions about our purpose, audience, context, and genre. The responses to these questions provide material that helps soundwriters determine how to best approach an audio project and what ways they might appeal to and impact their target audience.

For example, think of Kyle's process when composing "Pincushion" (as described in interlude A). His rhetorical situation guided the choices he made throughout the process:

- **Genre:** As an audio memoir, he knew there were lots of moves that would feel odd; he didn't, for example, include a sociological analysis of the gendered expectations put on elementary school boys in California in the 1980s, with lots of academic citations. Instead, his genre required accessible language, poetic comparisons, and lots of "mic drop" moments that made the ends of sections feel especially powerful and memorable.
- **Audience:** He composed it for an audience that was interested in hearing about aspects of an author's life packaged in a creative way (especially people who read creative writing publications). That is, he expected that his writing voice and speaking voice could draw them in, hopefully making them feel empathy for him and consider similar experiences in their own lives.
- **Context:** He originally composed it for the context of an audio prize he wanted to win; this led him to be extra-careful to sound professional with his recording quality, vocal delivery, and the timing throughout the piece.
- **Purpose:** He had lots of overlapping purposes: to win the prize money (which he didn't win), but also to establish himself as both a scholar *and* practitioner— a teacher who is out there in public making the kinds of things he teaches, in both creative nonfiction and soundwriting circles. He also had a topical purpose: to get listeners to reflect on how boys can bully each other in overt and subtle ways.

These same categories of rhetorical analysis can inform your own choices when composing—and when you know how you'd fill in those categories, you can use them as a guide to help narrow down your choices. That is, if you're unsure if you should include a particular segment in your project, just ask yourself if it fits your overall purpose, matches the needs of the audience, and fits the expectations for that context and genre.

Try-It **4.1 Rhetorical Analysis as an Invention Tool**

Learn More

See Try-It 1.3 in chapter one for an exercise that guides you in analyzing the rhetorical situation of a podcast episode. This Try-It is more about using rhetorical analysis for your own soundwriting.

The questions below and your responses will guide you in identifying and later analyzing your rhetorical situation. Once you do so, you'll have a better understanding of what you need to consider and do to create effective soundwriting.

- **Purpose:** What do you ultimately hope your soundwriting will achieve, both for your audience and for yourself? How do you want listeners to perceive you after hearing this? Do you have larger, overarching purposes and smaller (even sillier) purposes?
- **Audience:** Who do you want to hear your project? What might your audience need or expect? Do you anticipate any actual audiences hearing your work beyond your intended audiences?
- **Context:** What is the social, cultural, political, and economic context in which you are situated? Where and when will your soundwriting be published or played? How will listeners engage with your soundwriting? Using what technology, surrounded by what other audio, with what kind of framing?
- **Genre:** Is there a particular type of soundwriting piece that you're drawn to? What characteristics have you noticed in the work you've heard that you might be inclined to include in your own work? What kind of project sounds like it might be fun to try out?

After you respond to the above questions, find someone to chat with about your rhetorical situation brainstorm. Talking through these kinds of messy, uncertain questions is sometimes more helpful than the solidified certainty of writing them down.

While a general rhetorical analysis will always help you understand your overall composing situation, you may benefit from examining one or more factors more closely. For instance, try exploring your audience deeper in Try-It 4.2, which will help you better determine how to achieve your purpose and which sonic tools will be most useful.

Try-It **4.2 Understanding Your Intended Audience**

The questions below and your responses will help you generate big-picture knowledge about your intended audience's needs. Don't worry if you can't answer all of them—but don't be too quick to move past the hard ones, either.

- What purpose am I trying to accomplish with my soundwriting? What kind of people care about that purpose already, or might be persuaded to care more when they hear my soundwriting?
- What do I want my audience to do with the information conveyed in my soundwriting?
- What needs and wants does my audience have?
- What do they value or think is important?
- What is my audience less likely to care about?
- How much does my audience know about my topic? Does my audience have more or less knowledge than I do?
- Is my audience familiar with the language and terminology that I'm using in the project?
- What questions do I anticipate the audience might already have?
- What does my audience expect from this genre of composition?

Once you've started thinking about those big-picture needs of your audience, you can start imagining what specific choices you might need to make to affect them most powerfully. Try responding to the questions below to help you do so.

- What genre of soundwriting makes the most sense in communicating to this audience for a particular purpose?
- What content do I need to include? What content can I leave out?
- What do I want my audience to think, learn, or assume about me as a sound-writer and the topic I'm addressing, and how can I make that clear in my writing?
- What kind of organization, format, and/or arrangement would best help my audience understand what I'm trying to communicate?
- What kind of language and tone is most appropriate for this audience?
- Which sonic tools from chapter three might work best for affecting my audience?

In addition to giving advice on audience, chapter one also discusses the value of knowing your intended genre and using that knowledge to build yourself a guide for approaching a soundwriting project. Conducting a genre analysis will help you do so. You'll have a better understanding of the kinds of rhetorical strategies your audience expects and, perhaps surprisingly, a better idea about how you might disrupt genre expectations to impact your listener. The more you study what people expect in a particular genre, the more you might see value in breaking certain genre conventions as part of your rhetorical effect. That's how Kyle felt when he asked his interviewees to discuss the videogames he played live during his "Grumble, Grumble" podcast episode (described in interlude C); he had never heard of anyone doing that before in a podcast, so it felt like a fun subversion of genre that would engage his audience.

> **Learn More**
> See interlude B for advice on when, how, and why to disrupt genre conventions and blend genres in soundwriting.

Try-It 4.3 **Genre Analysis**

This activity will guide you in conducting a genre analysis, which can help you to identify genre conventions, giving you an idea about what your audience expects and ways you might stretch or disrupt these features to achieve your rhetorical goals.

First, gather three pieces of soundwriting in the same genre. If you're not sure where to start, see the list of soundwriting genres and podcast genres in chapter one, Tips 1.2 and 1.3, and the list of compelling podcasts in chapter two, Tip 2.4—and if you choose podcasts, be sure to choose a specific kind of podcast (like a science or true crime podcast). Be sure to look for a podcast with rich, complete transcripts if you plan to engage with it via sound, words, or both.

As you listen to the three examples and/or read the transcript, use these questions to help you generate responses about the qualities that hold this genre together:

- Where is this genre of soundwriting generally heard or played?
- When were these pieces originally heard, published, or performed? Was there anything else in the timing or context that might change how the original intended audience might have experienced them?
- What do we know about people who listen to this genre? What expectations might they have about the contents and moves in this genre?
- Do these three pieces of soundwriting have a common purpose?
- Let's get specific. Across the three pieces, what similarities do you hear with regard to the following (noting that you may not need to use everything on this list; your genre will dictate which ones to focus on):
    - Length
    - Content (what is included in the piece)
    - Language (level of formality, word use, tone)
    - Structure (the kind of organization used)
    - Opening and closing (how the recording's title and creators are introduced, how thanks are given, if those things are skipped)
    - Sonic rhetorical strategies (the use and function of voice, music, sound effects, silence)
    - Script (whether this genre followed a "let the tape lead" or "let the script lead" script, as far as you can guess)
- Did any of the three pieces make a rhetorical move that the others didn't? If so, did that outlier seem more like an accident (i.e., a failure of the sound-writer's genre awareness) or a purposeful move (i.e., a savvy disruption of genre expectations)?

Freewriting

Figure 4.1
Freewriting helps us
discover ideas and
make connections.

Many of you have likely heard the term "freewriting" before in past English or writing classes. Freewriting invites composers to write for a certain period of time—maybe two minutes, maybe twenty minutes—without stopping, rereading, or worrying about grammar and mechanics.

Think of freewriting as a way to let all your words fall out of your mind and onto the paper without any worry, just as you might when speaking without any plans for what you're going to say. In fact, writing studies scholar Peter Elbow explains that freewriting helps us switch from a "mental writing gear" to a "mental speaking gear" (143), as if our brains have different gears, just like in a car. Our mental speaking gear helps us do the verbal blabbering we do naturally when we're excited or passionate or just riffing about something—but we can engage that speaking gear even when we're writing, using our natural ability to produce language out loud even when we turn to written or typed words. You might say that freewriting takes the affordances of speaking in the aural mode (words that flow easily) and blends them with the affordances of the visual mode (getting those words on the page where they can easily be reread, revised, copied, and pasted).

Some might call it a word purge, some might call it word vomit, and some might have less-gross phrases for it—but whatever you call it, freewriting captures ideas free from restrictions or inhibitions or concerns. Tiny jewels of ideas, or maybe even elaborate ones, often emerge in purge. And what's best about freewriting is that a soundwriter can find value in doing it at any stage of the composing process.

Try-It **4.4 Freewriting**

This activity will guide you in composing a freewrite.

1. Close your email, mute your computer, and silence your phone. Then set a timer for five minutes. Get a fresh sheet of paper (if you prefer handwriting) or open a document on your computer—but if you use a computer, consider blocking your view of the document by turning the monitor off or blocking the screen with a piece of paper. Then, depending on where you are in your composing process, try writing for five straight minutes without stopping, following one of these prompts to get you started:

   a. **If you're just starting**: Mentally walk through a recent or typical day, writing down everything that sparks an emotion—all the thoughts, objects, people, messages, encounters, actions, and reactions that made you feel something. Keep writing about more and more sparks of emotion . . . and push yourself just a bit further than feels comfortable. After the five minutes are up, look through your freewriting for ideas that you could translate into some kind of soundwriting project.

   b. **If you're revising your ideas or editing audio**: Write all the things that make you happy or proud about your ideas or draft so far, and write all the things that are most frustrating or hard to solve. You can bounce back and forth between the two types of writing, positive and negative. Just let it all out. Sometimes, expressing our joys in words helps us see new ways to achieve joys in other parts of the project, and sometimes, expressing our frustrations helps us write our way past them.

2. Now, reread your freewriting to look for helpful ideas, or even better, discuss it with a friend, teacher, or someone working at a university writing center. Often, freewriting is just a first step toward ideas that become more fully fleshed out through conversation, or even a second round of more focused freewriting.

A particular, focused kind of freewriting can probe your passions, knowledge, and experiences. Whether you're 18 or 100 years old, you've lived a life full of experiences—everything from going to school to attending a rally for a cause you believe in. You've gained lots of knowledge inside and outside of school, and you've developed interests and curiosities about the world. *Your* experiences are all rich sites of invention for a soundwriting project, and it's worth your time to pause and think about how to make those connections in audio for an audience.

Both of Tanya's projects described in the interludes emerged through retrospection about her life and herself. Her interest in feminism and social movements inevitably led to her creation of "Peaceful Warriors" (see interlude B), and her interest in sound, listening, hearing, and baffling health disorders led to "Play It Loud" (see interlude D). And it's the same for Kyle: of *course* the creative nonfiction professor who is obsessed with nostalgia would compose the memoir "Pincushion," and of *course* that nostalgia would lead him to creatively explore the videogames of his youth in a podcast episode.

Try-It   4.5 **Brainstorming about Your Experiences**

The following questions will guide you in brainstorming. Try using the questions as the starting point for a freewrite, as guidance for audio process notes (more on that below), or just as ideas jotted in a brainstorming document or notebook. They're especially designed for when you want to soundwrite something but don't know what.

- What are your passions and interests? What and who do you care about?
- What are you curious about? What questions do you have about people and the world? What do you want to know more about?
- Who do you admire the most and why?
- What is one of your most memorable experiences? (Think both externally, when something major happened, and internally, when the main change was inside you.)
- What experiences have taught you the most about yourself, other people, or something about the world in general?
- What current issues are most important to you and why?
- What roles and identities do you inhabit when you're at the different places you go throughout your day? What knowledge and skills could you share from those various identities that comprise the whole you?

Process Notes

Writing and reflecting during different stages of the composing process can also be productive for making your work even more rhetorically effective. That's why we love writing *process notes*—brief, informal reflections about your writing experiences at regular intervals while working on a project. Process notes can be in alphabetic or aural form—on paper or in an audio recording. You can even make process notes in a video recording, talking or signing in a selfie video on your phone.

We find audio process notes to be a particularly productive tool because of how closely they resemble freewriting. You can think of them like "free-speaking"—talking through ideas without worrying about grammar or incomplete thoughts. The great thing about talking aloud without restrictions is that you can digress and move from idea to idea without judgment from the self or others. These digressions often lead to "a-ha!" moments or connections between and among ideas.

While making "Peaceful Warriors," Tanya relied heavily on audio process notes for invention. She recorded herself after each work session and used talk—or more accurately, stream-of-consciousness rambling—to work through challenges and problems, and to discover, develop, flesh out and flush out ideas. Later, she listened to the recordings, taking notes and thinking about how she could best move forward with the project. For another example, you can read more about (and listen to!) Tanya's students' process notes in an open access book chapter she wrote called "Speech, Invention, and Reflection: The Composing Process of Soundwriting" (Rodrigue).

Try-It 4.6 **Process Notes**

The following questions and responses can guide you in composing alphabetic or audio process notes. Use them when you're in the *process* of working on something and trying to do your best work possible. As with any freewriting or free-speaking, it's okay if you don't know the answer to some of these questions, but you should never be too quick to skip a question and move on, until you've struggled with it for a bit first.

- Where are you in your soundwriting process? What's been done and what's still left to do?
- What are your biggest accomplishments and failures so far? How do you feel about that?
- What have you learned so far?
- What ideas did you grapple with? Which problems have you solved, and which are you continuing to grapple with? How might you overcome the challenges and struggles?
- What decisions have you made, and what alternatives did you have?
- What questions have emerged lately as you plan and work on your project?
- What is the next step in your composing process? What do you need to do, know, and write?
- Walk through the four elements of the rhetorical situation: how are you feeling about your progress toward achieving your purpose, affecting your audience, situating your work in the time and place of your context, and following the expectations of your genre?

Talking to Others

Figure 4.2
Talking to others helps us crystallize our ideas.

Have you ever talked with a friend about a paper you're writing or talked to a family member about a problem from school you were trying to solve? If so, did you walk away from the conversation with a new perspective, idea, or a solution to the problem—whether or not the other person had much to say? That's the thing about conversations: talking with others is often generative, sometimes because of the other person's insights, and sometimes just because you needed someone to listen to you put the pieces together out loud.

As with process notes, consider talking to someone at regular stages throughout your soundwriting process, and especially when you feel stuck. It could be a five-minute or hour-long discussion, scheduled or impromptu, with friends or at your university's writing center—but however it happens, we're huge believers in the power of conversation. (It's not a coincidence that we're *cowriting* this textbook; our individual ideas are constantly being improved and enlarged through our regular conversations.)

> **Learn More**
> See interludes C and D for more about Kyle's and Tanya's invaluable experiences talking with others.

Listening to the Sounds and Ideas around You

In chapter two, we explained how listening like a soundwriter (LLS) involves both paying attention to the world around you and focusing your attention on rhetorical choices in other examples of soundwriting. Those two angles of listening can also guide you to generate ideas, if you're listening carefully.

A social media post, a poster, a new city, an internet search, a trip on a bus, a random piece of trash on the street—all of those random-seeming aspects of your surroundings can be turned into sparks for your projects; you can "listen" to all of them as part of your invention process. Those random objects or places may help you develop a topic or focus for an audio project you've already started, perhaps by suggesting an audience or an angle that you hadn't considered. They may also help you generate, grow, nurture, or develop new ideas earlier in your composing process.

For example, Kyle once noticed an odd connection: a piece of classical music he was listening to sounded remarkably like a videogame theme he knew well. That small start led him down a rabbit hole that ended up as a semi-scholarly soundwriting piece investigating how and why we notice similarities between different sounds (Stedman). But to get there, he had to be living life in a way that made him think of everything around him as potentially leading him to an interesting composing project. He had to engage in the preparation stage of LLS: listening to the world that was already around him.

The LLS practice stage focuses on listening to particular, designed pieces of soundwriting, which can also inspire you. Indeed, listening to other audio projects helps soundwriters become more aware of available soundwriting choices, the possible effects and consequences of those choices, and the way choices impact or engage an audience. That's why we think you should listen to lots and lots of audio before and during your own soundwriting process. Hearing other people's work can be inspiring and can unexpectedly spark new ideas or help develop existing ideas.

Figure 4.3
Your soundwriting can be inspired by your environment and by what you choose to listen to.

For example, Tanya recently listened to an episode of *Lore*, a "podcast about true life scary stories" ("About the Podcast") and was suddenly struck with an idea for an experimental soundwriting assignment that could help her students learn how to play with sonic rhetorical strategies. That inspiration was accidental, but it can also be planned. Before Kyle teaches a soundwriting class, for instance, he digs into three main podcasts: *Re:Sound*, a podcast that plays audio from the Third Coast International Audio Festival, where he can hear the latest and most interesting audio from around the world; *HowSound*, a podcast from Rob Rosenthal and Transom. org that gives lots of tips and examples of great radio storytelling; and *Twenty Thousand Hertz*, a show from Dallas Taylor that investigates the histories of the sounds we're surrounded by every day. Those three shows are sure to suggest other things he should be listening to in the world and in the podcast landscape, which in turn affects the assignments he gives his students and the soundwriting he creates himself.

4.1 Searching for Interesting Podcasts

One study suggests that there were over two million podcasts in 2021 (Winn). With so much content out there, and more being released all the time, how do you wade through it all to find something inspiring? Here are just a few tips, but we're sure you can think of more:

1. Search the internet for podcast (genre), filling in any genre you like. See the list of podcast genres in chapter one, Tip 1.3 for a few ideas if you're not sure where to start. Or you might identify genres that interest you by thinking about the kinds of movies, television shows, or books you like: true crime, thrillers, comedy, drama, fiction.

2. Or instead of searching by genre, try searching podcast (interest or hobby). Fill in the blank with any interest at all: the name of specific celebrities, travel destinations, sports you follow, science, food, comedy, and so on.

3. Search for lists of "most popular podcasts" or "best podcasts." Magazines, blogs, newspapers, and organizations regularly publish articles identifying the top 20, 50, or even 100 podcasts, and they're always being updated.

4. Search and browse genres in any podcast app or on any podcast website, like Apple Podcasts, Spotify, Stitcher, Google Podcasts, Podcast Addict, or whatever else has come out since we wrote this. If you've subscribed to a few shows already, see what recommendations they give you.

5. Ask your friends! We've seen lots of people ask for podcast recommendations on social media, and there are always lots of opinions.

PLANNING AND PITCHING YOUR IDEAS

Once you've generated ideas through invention, it's time to start putting them together. We see this as a two-part process: making plans for yourself or your team to guide your work, and then presenting public versions of your plan in a pitch to an audience.

Making a Plan

We get it: sometimes you don't want to make a project plan or don't have the time. Sometimes you're out in the world with your digital recorder, grabbing audio at random and then figuring out what to do with it later. This might be a great strategy to use for some projects, but not so much for others. We know from experience that sometimes a careful project plan can make a world of difference: it can save time, help avoid frustration, and help you envision ways to make compelling soundwriting.

A soundwriting project plan is a document that helps you chart out your project and keep you on-task, organized, and able to meet writing deadlines. You might think of it as written documentation that helps you know where you're going through identifying various factors or elements related to your project like purpose, assets, audience, collaborators (see a more complete list in Try-It 4.7), and perhaps even answers to the popular "Five W" (and One H) questions used in journalism:

- Who will contribute to the project and support you in composing it?
- What do you need to know and gather?
- When is it due, and when will you carve out time to do it?
- Where will it be heard, and by whom?
- Why is this project important?
- How will you carry out the various aspects of the plan?

Plans can be written after your invention process—that is, after you've tried some or all of the brainstorming activities described above—but your plans will also likely transform over time, excitingly becoming sites of invention in themselves. They can lead you to think, rethink, and readjust your thinking about content, structure, genre, and project goals.

For example, Tanya continuously referenced and revised her writing plan for "Peaceful Warriors." It became her touchstone, a document she visited during many work sessions to check off goals she accomplished and revisit how she was thinking about her purpose, audience, genre, and narrative. Similarly, Kyle and his co-editor Stephanie used a Google Doc to keep track of their ever-changing plans for the "Grumble, Grumble" podcast episode. They used the document to brainstorm about their ultimate goals for the episode, play with structural ideas, save links to audio assets, write notes about various contributors to the episode, and keep track of deadlines.

Try-It 4.7 Writing a Project Plan

The following questions and responses will serve as a guide for writing a project plan. Try your best to answer all of them, even if you're not exactly sure about some specifics.

- **Rhetorical Context**: What are your purposes and goals for this project? Who is your audience? What is your context? How do these factors play a role in what and how you will compose?

- **Genre**: What genre are you composing in? What are the rhetorical strategies that composers need to use for their soundwriting to be identified as a piece in that genre? What are some of the "optional" rhetorical moves people make in the genre?
- **Structure and Organization**: What structure might you imagine for this audio project? How might you organize your content?
- **Audio Assets**: What kind of audio do you need to collect? Where and how will you collect these audio assets? How and where will you organize these assets?
- **Contributors** (if applicable): Who will play a role in composing your project? What role will they play? How will you contact them? When are they needed in your composing process?
- **Audio Editing Software**: Which software will you use? Who or what will support you in learning the editing moves you'll need to make this project?
- **Reviewers**: Who will provide you with feedback on your project? When will you ask for feedback? When do you need to contact contributors or possible contributors?
- **Deadlines**: What do you need to get done and by what date? What days and times will you devote to this project?
- **Sharing Work**: How will you share or distribute your project? Who will you share it with and why?
- **The Journalist's Questions**: Looking at the Five Ws and One H above, are there any you haven't answered yet in your plan? If so, answer them here.

Pitching Your Idea

You might have heard of a pitch before, since people and professionals write and deliver pitches for different reasons all the time. An entrepreneur, for example, might write a pitch about a project idea and recite that pitch at the beginning of a presentation to investors. Or a person on the job market might write what is known as an elevator pitch: a brief description of their work experiences that could ideally work to persuade someone to hire them.

In the land of audio, soundwriters could be asked to pitch their idea in a class or learning community or to a publication venue like a podcast, radio station, or audio journal. In this context, a pitch can be described as a brief synopsis of a project idea or plan that is meant to garner interest and invite feedback on the quality of the idea in relation to purpose, genre, audience, and possible place of publication. Many of those aspects will already be part of your project plan, but a pitch formalizes and crystallizes those ideas to deliver to an audience. While pitches may look different and have different purposes, they share these commonalities: they are brief, describe the most compelling or important parts of a project, and are presented in a clear, engaging, and accessible way. While pitches could conceivably be composed in any mode, we've found that pitches for audio projects still are most commonly written alphabetically.

There is no one way to write a pitch, but sometimes an instructor or publication outlet will provide guidelines for the format, nature, and content of a pitch. For example, radio show and podcast *This American Life* provides these guidelines:

> If you're pitching a story you're hoping to tell on the air yourself, let us know what happened in a page or two. For some stories just a few paragraphs are fine. You don't need to be formal about it, just tell the story the way you'd tell it to someone over drinks or coffee. If you have favorite moments in the story, let us know those. Tell us anything you think will help us understand what a great story it is. If the story happened to you and showed you something about the world you hadn't realized before or changed you (or the other people in the story) in some way, let us know that too. ("Submissions")

Similarly, the NPR podcast *Code Switch* provides readers with directions for pitching a story for the show (Raja and Thompson). Here's our summary of what *Code Switch* says your pitch should include. It should

- relate to the focus of the show: race, ethnicity, and culture
- be clear, free of jargon and [use] lots of description
- describe a story with a "riveting narrative" that has appeal and interest to a range of people. The story should focus on something that isn't or hasn't been exhaustively covered in the media, is thought-provoking, and offers varying perspectives
- be 250 words or fewer

Sometimes you might be given specific guidelines, but other times you won't. So what do you do in that case? You might do some online research to find guidelines and examples of pitches that correspond to the genre in which you're writing. For example, if you are writing an audio documentary or an audio feature story, the above guidelines from radio stories on NPR would be helpful for composing a pitch. Otherwise, you could reach out to your instructor or the publication venue to request guidelines. If you still can't find guidance, we offer guidelines for writing a pitch in Try-It 4.8.

> **Learn More**
>
> See our companion website for pitch examples.

Try-It 4.8 Writing a Pitch

Here's one way you can write a pitch:
- Title the pitch something provocative and eye-catching.
- Include a brief, compelling description of the project that will get your audience excited to learn the details.
- Describe your goals for pursuing this project (what you want to get out of the composition process), your project's purposes (what you want your audience to get out of it), and the target audience.
- Identify ways your project is compelling, different, and/or appropriate for the aural mode.
- Identify the sound elements that you expect will be incorporated into the project.
- Describe the sources you'll turn to for inspiration and guidance and the assets you hope to include in the soundwriting project.
- Note the possible challenges you may confront in composing the project.

SCRIPTING

Once a plan is set and a pitch is approved, soundwriters often begin writing a script—a written document of the actual words that will be read verbatim in the project. Some projects don't call for scripts (including some sound art pieces or soundscapes with fewer spoken words), and some soundwriters don't feel like they need a script, but don't be too quick to say you don't need one. There are often good reasons to do the preparatory work of writing out what you want to say and when you want to say it. After all, the visual/linguistic mode of a written script has a lot of affordances, mostly related to the time and energy you can spend by carefully choosing (and revising!) the language you want to use, the story you want to tell, or the content you want to present. Writing gives you the opportunity to focus your ideas and avoid digressions that may occur when speaking off-the-cuff, and it gives you the flexibility in trying out different ways to organize and structure your ideas. A script also makes writing transcripts a whole lot easier when you finish a project.

In general, we distinguish between two types of scripting: letting the tape lead and letting the script lead.

> **Learn More**
>
> Learn more about writing transcripts in chapter five, and see our companion site for examples of scripts.

- **Letting the Tape Lead**. This scripting process invites soundwriters to collect sounds and then use those sounds to guide the creation of a script. For example, when Tanya composed "Play It Loud," she wrote a script, but the script was developed very specifically to work with the tape she had already recorded and combed through from an interview. You could say that the "tape led" the script because her words followed the lead of the most interesting and compelling quotes that came from her interview and corresponded to her story idea. Kyle's podcast process in "Grumble, Grumble" also let the tape lead, but in a somewhat different way, since he had so many kinds of clips to include (long interviews, a short piece by his collaborator, and the gameplay sounds at the end). For the most part, those long clips stood on their own, but Kyle had to write a script that made them feel connected, choosing an order that worked best with what he had and showing listeners how they all connected.
- **Letting Your Script Lead**. This scripting process invites soundwriters to write a script before they collect sound. You might want to let the script lead your project when you only have a limited amount of time, when you want to gather sounds with focus (rather than staying quite so open to play or serendipity), or when you already have a strong idea of the main purpose and structure of your project. For example, Kyle's memoir was scripted out before he collected any sound. The script took the lead in his audio project, directing the choices he made about music and sound effects.

But regardless of which style of script you write, you need to be attentive to the kind of writing that works best for listening. It's different from the kind of writing that is meant to be read silently. Writing for listening calls for different ways to use language, sentences, paragraphs, tone, and content. At its core, it means writing the way you speak—writing the words and sentences that would occur in natural conversation with a friend or a family member on a day when your brain feels sharp and rested.

Writing in a conversational manner usually involves choosing words that are easy to understand; writing simple, brief sentences that are not grammatically complex; and breaking grammar "rules" when appropriate. When it comes to grammar, our motto is this: if it sounds natural and conversational when you say it out loud, go for it, even if you think your former English teachers would mark it with a red pen.

It's easiest to understand strong writing for listening by showing how it differs from writing for reading. Below you'll find sentences that work to convey similar content: the sentences on the left were written to be read with the eyes and the sentences on the right were written to be listened.to. These are excerpts from the alphabetic draft of Kyle's memoir "Pincushion" (when he expected it to be read completely on the page) and the form it ultimately took as the script he read from in its audio form.

Learn More

See interlude A for more about Kyle's composing process.

Table 4.1 Reading vs. Listening to a Memoir

Writing for Reading/Alphabetic Memoir	Writing for Listening/Audio Script
Excerpt 1: I actually really liked going to your house, and playing your games, and eating your mom's food, even though I sometimes told myself I didn't want to go....	Excerpt 1: I actually really liked going to your house, even though I sometimes pretended I didn't like you....
Excerpt 2: Let's say he was reading a library book, an image that reflects his symbolic meaning here as a renter instead of an owner, so different from me and Dustin and even his own father, all of whom would reach for what we wanted and cram reality itself into our vision instead of reading someone else's books.	Excerpt 2: Let's say he was reading a library book, something he rented instead of owned.

You can see that most of Kyle's decisions in these excerpts were about simplifying sentence structures to make them easier to immediately understand for a listening audience. The alphabetic version of Excerpt 1 adds a lot of details that drag out the sentence; the revision cuts the middle part and rephrases the end for a more direct, rhythmic punch that sounds more like he would have said aloud. Excerpt 2 was originally an attempt at sounding creatively weird, an effect that was overkill even in writing and certainly bound to be confusing out loud; the same idea was easily compressed from 56 words to 14.

Here's another example we wrote for you based on Brianna Holt's article, "How Does It Feel to Be Dating Again?" from *The New York Times*. The left column is the first three paragraphs of this article and the right column is one way it could be transformed for listening.

Table 4.2: Reading vs. Listening to News

Newspaper Copy	Audio Script
Even in the best of times, dating can be a nerve-racking experience. The isolation brought on by the coronavirus has left many singles even more apprehensive (and simultaneously, perhaps, more eager). Logan Ury, the director of relationship science for the dating app Hinge, calls the phenomenon F.O.D.A., or fear of dating again. "People are worried about their rusty social skills, not having anything to talk about," she said. Ms. Ury, who also ran Google's behavioral science team, also notes singles who suffered from loneliness during lockdown are now prioritizing dating over their career, family, and friends after realizing that their jobs were not keeping them warm at night.	Dating is scary. There's no doubt about it. It's even scarier when you've been cooped up in the house for more than a year because of a global pandemic. Logan Ury, who's a relationship scientist for the dating app Hinge, calls this foda—that's F. O. D. A…in other words, fear of dating again. She says people are nervous they won't know what to say, but they're also eager to get out there for some human connection.

As Kyle did with his audio version of "Pincushion," we simplified the sentence structures for the imaginary audio version of "How Does It Feel to Be Dating Again?" Many descriptive words are deleted and the sentences are shorter. The content is condensed considerably and altered to sound less formal and more conversational. Since parentheses denote secondary importance in alphabetic writing, we decided to simply delete that part. You'll also notice we marked up the script (more on that in the Recording Your Voice section below) in a couple of different ways to visually remind us to do different things while speaking: the extra spaces between each letter in F.O.D.A remind us to speak slowly; the ellipsis signals a brief pause and reminds us not to stretch the A (in F.O.D.A) out since it is not at the end of a sentence; and the underlined "other" signals pitch variation.

Yet even when you think you've got a hold on how to write effectively for listening, you'll undoubtedly, like us, revise your script multiple times before you ask for feedback or start recording. You can do this by simply reading it aloud to yourself and then listening to your recording with a printed script in your hand, changing the language, sentence structure, and content as you go just by noticing what *feels* and *sounds* right.

> **Learn More**
> See the Revising section in chapter five for more on working with revision feedback.

Check out the difference between Tanya's first draft and final draft of an audio script for "Speech, Invention, and Reflection: The Composing Process of Sound-writing" after she read it aloud multiple times to herself.

Table 4.3: Revising an Audio Script

Draft 1 of Audio Script	Draft 2 of Audio Script
After listening to my students' process notes, I realized I did the same thing in my car audio recordings. I would just sit in the car and blab on and on "blurting out" what I was going to include in this documentary, or how I was going to word something or where I should integrate music or where I should incorporate sound clips.... I would stumble and fumble and then I'd hit on something. Something that was good or something that was insightful or something that was totally horrible...whatever it was, it was something I didn't get to in any other medium. Sometimes these recordings were 20 minutes long. This free-speaking, if you will, this freedom to use language in a non-prohibitive way without limitations, it is no doubt valuable for student learning and no doubt valuable for teaching students how to write effectively.	After listening to my students' process notes, I realized I did the same thing in my car audio recordings, I would just sit in the car and blab on and on. I would stumble and fumble and then I'd hit on something, something that was good or insightful, or something that was awful and horrible. But whatever it was, I couldn't get there in any other way. This "freespeaking," if you will, this freedom to use language without constraints and limitations, it is no doubt valuable for student learning. And no doubt valuable for teaching students how to write effectively in any mode, but especially in the aural mode.

You'll notice the second draft is shorter than the first. Tanya recognized that some content was redundant in the first draft, like "blab on" and "blurting out." And other content wasn't all that important, like "sometimes these recordings were 20 minutes long." She changed sentences that she didn't think she would actually say in a conversation with a friend, like changing "whatever it was, it was something I didn't get to in any other medium" to "But whatever it was, I couldn't get there in any other way." Her script also introduces what many would call a punctuation error, with a comma splice (a kind of run-on) introduced in the first sentence; the thing is, comma splices often feel right when we read aloud, so she included it in her script without feeling bad about it. She even made slight tweaks to the script while recording, a practice that Kyle also uses. Reading the script aloud in both scenarios helped Tanya refine her writing for a listener.

Try-It **4.9 Practice Writing for the Ear**

Below are three activities that will help you practice writing for the ear:

1. Freewriting and audio process notes are great ways to practice writing for the ear. These genres can help a composer switch from a frame of mind where they carefully and torturously think through every single word toward a frame of mind where they write with the ease of how they speak. So first, follow our instructions above for freewriting and audio process notes. Then read over what you wrote and listen to what you said, with an eye and ear out for those phrases that sound like a natural, relaxed version of yourself. Then in the future, try using those phrases and sentences verbatim from your freewriting or transcribed from your process notes.

2. Find a newspaper article and rewrite it for the ear. Write a sentence, read it aloud, and ask yourself: Would I ever say this in conversation with a friend or at the dinner table? People who are d/Deaf or hard-of-hearing can ask, "Does this fit the natural vocabulary and rhythm I would use while signing with the people I know and love the most?" If the answer is yes, continue on. If the answer is no, revise: get rid of redundancies, shorten long phrases, simplify the grammatical structure. Try recording your rewrite aloud, perhaps further adjusting your language while recording.

3. Find the last piece of writing you composed for a class or a job. Read the writing. Then, from memory, imagine that you're telling a friend about it. Record yourself describing the content aloud. Listen to the recording after you finish. Take note of the words, tone, sentences, and sentence structure that you notice about your speaking voice—and if you have time, transcribe the whole thing! This kind of exercise will help you "get to know" your conversational oral speech habits and patterns.

INTERVIEWING

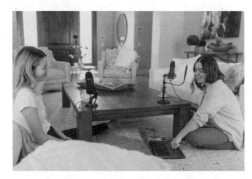

Figure 4.4
Conducting interviews is common in many soundwriting genres.

Many soundwriting projects will lead soundwriters to conduct interviews. Interviews are often the best way to gather information, opinions, perspectives, or even tape for experimentation or play. Yet we'll be honest: interviewing is hard. Generating good questions is hard. Creating an environment where your interviewee feels comfortable elaborating on responses, showing emotion, and speaking candidly is also hard. But it's certainly not impossible, as proven by the thousands of successful interviews you've heard on television, podcasts, and the radio. With some guidance and lots of practice, you'll be able to conduct interviews in a way that will yield great tape for your audio project.

The first thing you need to know about interviews is this: a good interview is not a rapid-fire question-and-answer session or an interrogation. A good interview is more like a conversation where questions, responses, and dialogue occur as naturally as possible. The interviewer may lead with prepared questions yet should strive to achieve a back-and-forth conversation, rich with spontaneous questions and even lively discussion. Leading that kind of interview is a skill that only comes with practice.

An interviewer has two main jobs: to *create a comfortable environment* and *to listen*. We don't mean listen like a soundwriter: we mean listen like a curious, present, and deeply interested and engaged person. Rund Abdelfatah, co-host and producer of *Throughline*, a history podcast, calls listening "*the* secret sauce of the interview" and says it's the primary means to get compelling tape (Migaki and Pierre). When an interviewer listens attentively, an interviewee tends to feel more comfortable, which often yields more honest, open, emotional, and interesting responses. Good listening enables interviewers to discover points of entry into discussion that they may have never imagined; questions that they never thought; and surprising, spontaneous, or interesting bits of information that may end up becoming central to an audio project.

Try-It 4.10 **Practice Interviewing**

Before you even begin generating a list of interview questions, it's helpful to conduct very low-stakes interviews just to get a feel for how you might engage in an interview like you would a conversation. Grab a friend or a person in your class and practice interviewing using these very basic questions:
- What was your first job like?
- What kinds of things did you learn at this job?
- What was the best part of working there?
- What was it like when you left the job?

After you hold this brief interview, take some time to reflect in writing: in what ways did the interview feel like a conversation? What did you do to foster a conversational environment? What more could you have done to make the interview more like a conversation than a rapid-fire question-and-answer session?

Now that you can imagine a conversational interview model and the roles of the interviewer, you're ready to start generating a list of questions, or conducting what is called a pre-interview. We'll explain both, starting with generating interview questions.

Generating Interview Questions

In most cases, you'll want to compile in advance a list of questions to possibly ask your interviewee. We say *possibly* because there's a good chance you might not ask all of the questions you write down. And, as we explained above, there's also a good chance you'll ask unprepared or spontaneous questions.

There are two general types of questions:

- **Closed questions** are questions that call for a specific, brief response, like "Where do you live?" "How long have you lived here?" and "How many children do you have?"
- **Open questions** are questions that elicit longer detailed responses, like "How did you feel when you were forced to leave your house?" or "What was your motivation for quitting your job?"

In most interviews, you'll ask *some* closed questions, yet in most cases, the majority will be open questions, for obvious reasons: you want your interviewee to be comfortable and to keep talking.

There are multiple ways to generate interview questions, and the kinds of questions you generate will largely be based on your rhetorical situation. We recommend first returning to your invention exercises, since most of them help you articulate the ultimate purpose of your project, which then can feed into your interview questions. Then, at the simplest level, ask yourself these questions: Why are you interviewing this person, and what do you need and want to know? Then, how does this interview fit in or function in your audio project? Often, your answers to those questions will lead naturally to a list of questions.

Here are a few other ways to generate questions (along with more suggestions in Try-It 4.11).

- **Do research**. While not all interviewees will have information about them online, some will. Your job is to find out as much information about them as possible. This is what Tanya did for "Play It Loud" (described in interlude D). She searched for her interviewee's name on the web and read magazine and newspaper articles about him as well as his personal/professional website, and she even listened to his music on Spotify. Tanya used all of this information to determine what she thought was most interesting about him, and from there, generated questions she thought could elicit more information about what she thought made him interesting.

- **Identify the heart of the project**. Audie Cornish, a host of NPR's *All Things Considered*, recommends interviewers "identify the primary bit of information that they want to know about more than all others" and boil that primary need down to a one-word concept, like *gender* or *race* (Rosenthal, "The Burning Question"). Once you have that word, you can use it as a guide to generate questions that directly relate to it, circling your core interest like a satellite.
- **Imagine question responses**. Audio producer Liz Mak encourages interviewers to anticipate possible responses to questions as a way to determine if a question would be worthy of asking (Rosenthal, "Interviewing for Emotions"). Imagine what an interviewee might say and think about how that response may correlate to your rhetorical goals.

Try-It 4.11 **Generating Interview Questions**

The following questions are helpful in generating lots of interview questions that you will later whittle down to a manageable number appropriate for the length of your interview and soundwriting project:

1. What is the ultimate purpose of this interview in your project? What will this interview tape give you that you couldn't achieve in another way?
2. How much time do you have for your interview? If you don't know, what do you think will be the ideal amount of time? Do you need to confirm this with your interview subject?
3. How open to a conversational model do you expect your interview subject to be? What can you do to help ensure that your interview has room for both planned and unplanned questions?
4. What closed questions should you ask? Plan to ask about basic facts that you already know (but that you want to hear your interviewee say on tape) and those that you don't know (because they'll help you contextualize the interview later when editing your project).
5. What open questions should you ask? Try to focus on questions that will get your subject telling evocative stories with lots of imagery.
6. What's the one thing you want to know more than anything else? Can you boil that down to a single phrase or word?
7. What are some answers you anticipate your interviewee will give? What questions would you then ask in response to keep your interview focused on your ultimate purpose?

Once you've generated a bunch of questions, you have to figure out which ones are the best. Consider using the guidelines below (and feedback from others!) to decide which questions to keep, how to best phrase your questions, and the order in which to ask them.

Choosing and Assessing Your Questions

- **Focus on your purpose and genre**. The interview questions should elicit responses that enable you to achieve your purpose within a genre. Return to your rhetorical and genre analyses (Try-Its 4.1 and 4.3) and check the questions against them. Delete the questions that are not directly or at least tangentially related to your purpose. Then delete the questions that elicit responses that aren't well suited to the genre.
- **Fish for detailed responses**. Most of your questions will likely be open-ended questions. Go through each question and ask yourself: Could a person respond to this question with a detailed response? If not, rephrase it in a way they could.
- **Eliminate redundancies**. Each question should be distinct and have its own purpose. Go through your list and delete questions that are versions of other questions or are likely to elicit the same or similar responses.
- **Stay simple**. Each question should be simple, straightforward, and easy to understand. Do not write two or three-part questions. Streams of questions like this are a big no-no: "When you were a child, what was your favorite thing to do, where did you do it, and who did you do it with?" Your interviewee will forget the second and third part of the question by the time they finish answering the first part. Or worse, they may try to answer all the questions at once, superficially addressing each of the three questions. The goal is to elicit rich, elaborate, detailed responses, and one good question at a time will enable you to do that.
- **Plan for time, and aim for fewer rather than more questions**. The number of questions you ask in an interview is dependent on context and the amount of time you scheduled for the interview. Remember, the interviewee is volunteering to speak with you, so you want to be respectful of their time. We don't have a secret formula that reveals exactly how long it will take someone to respond to one of your questions; that would be impossible. The length of a response is dependent on the interviewee's personality, the nature of the question, and more. Still, we do think it's safe to say that closed questions take under a minute and open questions could take anywhere from two to five minutes depending on how talkative or comfortable an interviewee feels. Yet—and that's a big yet—an open question may lead to several follow-up questions or maybe even an in-depth discussion. Then there's unexpected and spontaneous questions that are bound to arise from your good listening skills. This is all to say that less is likely more.

Ordering Your Questions

- **Organize with your project and the interviewee's comfort in mind**. After you decide which questions to ask, you'll want to prepare your list of questions to reference during the interview (perhaps on paper, a laptop, or a phone, if you put it in airplane mode to avoid distractions during the interview). It's a good idea to order the questions in the way you anticipate or would like the conversation to flow. You might even align your questions with how you think you might structure or organize your audio project. Whatever order you decide, be sure the first question is used to make the interviewee feel comfortable. In "The Art of the Interview," an episode of NPR's *The Students' Podcast*, Lauren Migaki and Jeff Pierre recommend asking questions related to topics like cars, pets, and holidays. For example, you might ask, "What's the coolest car you've ever driven?" or "What is your most memorable Thanksgiving?" or "What did you eat for breakfast today?" These "soft ball" questions will help everyone relax a bit and ease into the conversation.
- **Prioritize**. Identify the questions that are the most and least important on your list—you'll want to ask the most important questions first. You could number them in the order of importance, or you might ask yourself: If I could ask the interviewee only five questions, what would they be? Make the most important or top five questions a priority in your interview and keep the other questions accessible in case you have time to ask them too. You might also want to bold the important questions or mark them with an asterisk. This visual cue will support you in remembering which questions you should definitely ask during the interview.

The Pre-Interview

In some cases, you'll know exactly who you want to interview and for what reason. Say you're composing an audio story about how local businesses were affected by the COVID-19 pandemic: you'd obviously want to interview several local business owners. You'd use the guidelines in the previous section to generate questions. BAM; done. But in other cases, you might not know if the person you think you want to interview is the "right person" to interview based on the project goals. Say you're composing a story about the harmful effects of non-native plants in your neighborhood and find a person who may have that expertise, but you're not positive. Or maybe you were asked, like Tanya was, to compose a story about an "interesting" person and think you've found one, but can't be sure. How do you determine if you should indeed interview the person you think you should? This is where the pre-interview comes in.

A pre-interview is a brief unrecorded informal discussion over the phone or in person. The ultimate goal of this conversation is to determine if this person is the "right" person to interview for your project. The process for conducting a pre-interview is fairly straightforward. The interviewer gets in touch with the potential interviewee and requests a conversation. During this initial interaction, you would tell the person about the project, why you'd like to interview them, who might listen to the project, and the ultimate goal of the project. You should ask a couple of questions related to the project to get a general sense if they're a good fit. These questions might be from a list of questions you already generated or might emerge spontaneously during the pre-interview. After the pre-interview, ask yourself the questions below to help you decide if this is the "right" person.

- Will this person provide the information I need for my audio project, or would someone else be a better fit? Do they have knowledge or expertise or unique insight into the subject or topic in which they are being interviewed?
- Is this person who I imagined them to be? Could they play the role I imagined they would play in my audio project?
- Is this person capable of responding to questions?
- Is this person comfortable with being recorded during an interview?
- Does this person speak at a pace that listeners could understand?

After this conversation, you'll have a better sense of whether you'd like to ask this person for a more formal recorded interview.

During the Interview

Remember: your main job as an interviewer is to create a comfortable environment and to be a good listener. Of course, that's not the only thing you should remember. Here are other things to do and keep in mind during an interview:

- **Record the entire conversation**. There are tips for recording interviews below in the Recording Sound section of this chapter, but a few basic things are worth mentioning here. At the Transom Traveling Workshop, Rob Rosenthal suggested that you record an interview from the moment you enter the interview space until the moment you leave; you never know when something interesting may happen and don't want to deny yourself the opportunity to collect compelling audio.
- **Tell your interviewee the logistics of the project**. At the beginning of the interview, reiterate a description of your project, the goal of the interview, and the agreed-upon length of the interview. You'll also want to tell your interviewee who may be listening to the final version of your soundwriting—your professor, your friends, the world. This is also a good time for you to ask their permission to be recorded; this shouldn't be the first time they've heard about this and agreed, but it's always a good idea to have their verbal consent on tape.

- **Make your interviewee feel comfortable**. You can do this both with questions, as discussed above in the Generating Interview Questions section, and with body language. As soon as you walk in the door, get on the phone, or open a video chat, you want to project calmness. Laine Kaplan-Levenson, a producer at *Throughline*, talks about the importance of being relaxed. She says, "I don't put on any type of, like, professional airs or stiffness because they're going to mirror whatever energy I'm putting out. So I try to be as natural and relaxed and myself so that they can do that, which is going to get you the best tape because they're going to let their personality come out" (Migaki and Pierre). Be conscious of your body language and always begin with a soft ball question.

- **Don't chain yourself to your interview questions**. When beginning an interview, you should have your interview questions handy to reference. Yet continuously referencing a list of questions has strong potential to ruin the conversational vibe, so it's a good idea to try to memorize the list or casually reference it during the interview. Another trick is to create shorthand versions of your questions—brief phrases or words that correlate to your questions—and reference them as needed. Also, don't be afraid to ask interviewees to further elaborate on or explain responses. Questions like, "Can you tell me more about _____? Or can you talk more about _____?" generally work well. And as we said in previous sections, a conversational interview invites spontaneous questions, so be sure to listen well for opportunities to ask such questions.

- **Be flexible**. Sometimes interviews take a wildly different direction than what you imagined. For example, you might go into an interview thinking that your subject has an interesting story to tell about a recent trip to New Orleans, only to discover they have a *much* more interesting story to tell about their childhood in New Zealand. In this case, we'd encourage you to take a chance and pursue the New Zealand angle. Yes, the new direction may make your original list of questions moot, and that may be scary. Yet good listening abilities and open-ended questions—"What was that like? Can you tell me more? How did you feel? What did you think would happen?"—should assuage some of those fears.

- **Don't worry about messing up**. Seriously. You might stumble and fumble when asking a question, or a question might come out sounding silly or not-so-smart. No worries. In "Harnessing Luck as an Industrial Product," Ira Glass, host of *This American Life*, says he's more than willing to sound foolish in an interview, but not in stories he produces for the public (65). So remember, just because you say something and flub it up doesn't mean it has to be included in the audio project.

- **Be okay with uncomfortable moments**. If an interviewee stops to think, starts to cry, or has trouble articulating themselves, your first reaction might be to throw out a question, to console them, or even speak for them. Resist this temptation;

don't shut them up or shut them down. Sit in the discomfort and allow your interviewee to collect their thoughts or to feel their emotions. We strive for authentic reactions in interviews, so capturing this authenticity will be important.

- **Finish off well**. Toward the end of the interview, it's okay to scan your list of prepared questions and ask any that you missed. It's also generally good practice to end with open-ended questions that ensure the interviewee got to say everything they wanted to say. Questions like "Is there anything you want to say that I didn't ask you about? Did you get a chance to say all you wanted to about that?" work well. And don't forget this important final question: "Can I be back in touch if I have any follow-up questions?" Always leave the lines of communication open in the event you need to get more information later!

With all that said, there is no one way to interview or one right way to interview. No two people will ask the same questions or ask questions in the same way. Factors such as experience, mannerisms, and familiarity with a subject and interviewee all create different circumstances for each interview. It also takes time to get good at interviewing, so don't fret if your first experience isn't wildly successful.

After the Interview

You may walk out of an interview feeling a bit overwhelmed with how much tape you collected—maybe half an hour, or maybe four hours! You have a lot of work ahead of you, but before you even think about any of it, try out one of the best tips we've heard about what to do immediately after an interview. In NPR's *The Students' Podcast*, Sarah Gonzalez from the podcast *Planet Money* says to jot down three of the most memorable parts of the interview. "There's a reason why you remember them," she says, and that's likely because they are interesting, engaging, surprising, exciting, emotional, weird, or compelling—all of the things that make for good audio and strong audience engagement. Cognitive scientist Pooja Agarwal also emphasizes the importance of writing these moments down or even saying them out loud, since "our memories for pretty much anything fade really quickly" (Nadworny and Migaki, "How to Wade"). In other words, do this exercise as soon as you get to your car, hang up the phone, or end a video chat; it will work to alleviate the dread of tape overload and prepare you for the work ahead. These moments will likely play a role in other decisions you make about which tape to use or even the structure, content, or organization of an audio project.

> **Learn More**
> See Tip 4.6 below for tips on choosing interview quotes.

4.2 Interviewing That Supports All Bodies

As you plan and conduct your interview, do so in a way that makes the interview accessible to all bodies. Here are a few suggestions to keep in mind for any mix of d/Deaf and hard-of-hearing people, regardless of who is the interviewer or interviewee.

- Arrange the physical interview space to support everyone. For instance, the seating arrangements can be made to allow easy audio and visual access between individuals, with enough room for interviewers, interviewees, and interpreters. (See Janine Butler's "Principles for Cultivating Rhetorics and Research Studies within Communities" for more advice on arranging physical space.)
- Prepare your technology to support everyone. For instance, be prepared with cameras to capture signing along with spoken audio, and be ready to transcribe any signing later. And when filming sign language, don't turn off the mics; capture the natural sounds of movement and breath from both sides of the conversation, if applicable, which we find adds a humanizing touch. (For a video example, see the signed interviews in Jennifer J. Buckner and Kirsten Daley's co-authored chapter "Do You Hear What I Hear? A Hearing Teacher and a Deaf Student Negotiate Sound.")
- When interviewing in person or over a video call isn't feasible, interviews can be conducted in writing over email or in real time in a chat program or app. Later, the words of the interviewee can be read into recording software by an actor (a fact you'll want to acknowledge in your final product, and which can introduce emphases not intended by the author) or even read aloud by a text-to-speech program (though these programs often reflect speech rhythms poorly and sound robotic).

Make it your goal to follow the principles described by Margaret Price and Stephanie L. Kerschbaum in their description of how to reframe interview methodologies for research interviews (which we think applies to soundwriting interviews as well): "Crucially, our choices as researchers are not simply an effort to make the interview space more 'inclusive' by retrofitting previous interview methodologies. Rather, they compose a process of cripping the interview space itself—restructuring it and reconsidering the power dynamics that give rise to its normative structure" (20–21).

RECORDING SOUND

Figure 4.5
Recording can happen in any number of places, with any number of devices.

Of course, not all soundwriting projects will have you gathering interview tape; you could be recording audio in the field or downloading audio from any number of sources. It's hard to give generic recording advice in a book like this. After all, some of you have bought fancy digital recorders, while others of you will record with your phones. Even more complicated, the category of "recording" can include everything from technical tips on where and how to set up your microphones to delivery tips on how to speak in a way that will help you achieve your goals.

Because of those uncertainties, we'll keep our remarks here focused on three simple areas, all of which can apply to various technologies and contexts: how to approach recording various types of interviews, how to deliver your own vocal recordings, and how to record the world around you. We'll also briefly describe how to collect sounds from the internet, since so many soundwriting projects involve downloaded sounds blended with whatever you record yourself.

4.3 Saving, Storing, and Organizing Audio Files

We're begging you: please think about the importance of saving and storing audio files in a way that helps you easily identify and access them. This is especially important when you work with a lot of different assets in your audio project—and it's even more important for alleviating stress during the editing stage. We know all too well from experience that if you don't have good practices in naming and organizing files, you'll experience lots of frustration and aggravation.

Here are some tips:

- **Name your files** with descriptive titles that directly relate to the content of the file. For example, a file name like "Cafe Background Noise" works, while a file name like "noise" doesn't work. Even better: "BeaneryCafe_BackgroundNoise_ 4pm_24June2021"
- **Get your files off your recorder or phone right away**, since those devices often default to file names that won't make sense later. Get in the habit of regularly gathering your external recordings into your main computer space, naming them as you copy them.
- **Organize your files** using descriptive folder names. You might name these folders with the kind of asset that will be stored inside of them such as Voice, Sound Effects, and Music. Or maybe your project will lead you to have separate sub-folders for different interviews or different segments of your final project. But please, don't just plop them all into one spot, forcing you to wade through them later.
- **Backup your files** in at least one other place, like a cloud service or a portable hard drive. This is essential. Seriously. The last thing you want is to lose the precious audio you worked so hard to get.

Keeping your files organized and easily accessible will enable you to work more effectively and efficiently since you won't need to spend lots of time searching for files you need or want while working in the audio editor.

Recording Interviews

In the Interviewing section above, we shared all sorts of tips for preparing and conducting the interview, but what about recording it? Well, that depends on if you're interviewing a person sitting physically in the same room with you or not.

Here's advice for in-person interviews:

- **Choose the right room**. Aim for a fairly noise-free, non-echoey space. Avoid kitchens and bathrooms! A living room with a rug and furniture, for example, works well. (It might be weird to invite someone into your walk-in closet, but if you know someone well....)
- **Avoid extraneous sounds**. When you walk into the interview space, listen carefully for any sounds in the environment that could compromise the sound quality of the recording—like the sound of a fan, television, dishwasher, fridge, or furnace. If you hear anything, ask the interviewee to turn off the sound.

- **Record the "silence."** Record the sound of the room without anyone speaking for about 30 seconds; journalists do this for every interview. We know, this sounds like weird advice, but that "silence"—which is rarely *completely* silent—may help you later in the editing phase when you're trying to iron out transitions or add pauses to slow the pace of the interviewer or the interviewee. Yes, you can always insert into your project some complete, digital silence—the absence of all signal—but that kind of absolute silence usually strikes listeners as noticeable for its emptiness. You'll want to add this "room silence" instead, if necessary (Rosenthal, Transom Traveling Workshop).
- **Set up your microphone carefully**. As we wrote above, it's hard to give too many tips about mic placement, since you could be working with very different types of equipment. Still, a few basic suggestions that apply to most situations are worth making briefly:
  - Don't blow air directly in the microphone, unless you have a pop filter or microphone whose manual directs you otherwise. This goes for both you and your interviewee. If you blow air directly into the microphone, your speech will make a loud plosive sound that is difficult to alter in the editing stage. You can feel this air if you try holding your hand in front of your mouth while saying a sentence with lots of Ps and Ts and Bs. The air you feel shouldn't directly hit the microphone.
  - Prioritize the interviewee's voice over yours when considering mic placement. It's imperative that you get good tape from your subject, but if a question or response you make in the moment sounds quiet or distant, you can always shape your script later to add narration explaining what you said off-mic.
  - Monitor the recording with headphones. You want to catch any problems in real-time as they arise instead of being surprised by them later, whether they arise from unexpected sounds, volume imbalances, plosives, or anything else. Writing scholar Bump Halbritter writes about how the necklace of a famous interviewee once bumped against a lapel mic, making it sound like she was "in the back of a pickup truck... while someone shoveled gravel onto her" (118).
  - Pay attention to volume, since you don't want the recording to clip. "Clipping" refers to the distortion in a recording when the sound being recorded is too loud—perhaps the voice or other auditory signal is too loud, or perhaps the microphone's recording input level is too high (too "hot"). Many microphones will flash a red light at you or give some other visible signal when you clip, which is a sign that you should turn your mic level down, move your mic further away, or lower the volume of whatever you're recording.

Here is advice for remote interviews, when you can't be in the same physical room:

- **Instruct the interviewee as you would in person**. In some ways, distance interviews can be similar to face-to-face interviews: you'll want to find a quiet space, ask the interviewee to silence any extraneous sounds, and come prepared to facilitate or engage in conversation.
- **Seek a recording studio, if possible**. You may find that your university or company has access to a recording studio that is wired to easily record both sides of a phone conversation. We know that this is unlikely for many people, but it's worth a few minutes of investigation, just in case. If that's impossible and you need to record over the phone, consider finding an app that records calls or using a physical device that sits between your phone and your ear.
- **Get permission**. It's always a good idea to get permission from the interviewee to record, edit, and distribute the recording while you've got the tape running. This is good practice in person, too, but it's especially important on the phone, where your mic won't be visible and thus is easy for the interviewee to forget. You also might want to familiarize yourself with your state or province's law about recording voice (there are different laws in different locations) so you can share that information with your interviewee, if appropriate.
- **Lower your expectations**. Recorded phone calls will inevitably sound like phone calls, with a tinny, higher-frequency sound than a professional recording. Depending on your rhetorical situation, this might be okay—say, to emphasize that your interviewee is on-the-go or hard-to-pin-down—or it might be annoying or distracting. Similarly, many video chat programs and apps allow you to record video or audio from the call, but often these recordings don't sound great: they sometimes default to lower digital quality, include audible "hiccups" when someone's Wi-Fi blips, and are only as good as the users' mics, which are often just the (lousy) mics built into a laptop or tablet.
- **Consider asking each person to record their own side**. You might get better quality if you record your side of the interview, your interviewee records their side, and then you edit both high-quality recordings together manually, later. When you do that, the video call is simply a way to have a live person to respond to in the moment, not the source of audio you'll actually use. But if possible, try to make a backup recording at the same time (like recording your Zoom or Skype call), just in case the interviewee doesn't send the file or, heaven forbid, forgets to turn on the mic on their end! (Trust us: that's no fun at all.)
- **Practice!** You and your interviewee will both feel more comfortable if you schedule enough time for a practice run—either on the same or different day as the main interview. You want to make sure that everyone understands the technological constraints as well as possible.

Recording Your Own Voice

We get it: many of you hate the sound of your recorded voice. You're not alone. It's actually so common that psychologists gave it a name: voice confrontation. There are a couple of reasons why this can be so unnerving. First, your voice sounds different than you think it does. This is because when you speak, your body and bones play a role in the vibrations that carry your voice and ultimately how you hear it. These vibrations don't translate to a recording, so your voice sounds different to you, a lot of the time more high-pitched than you thought. Second, your voice may reveal emotions that you didn't know you were expressing, which may be surprising or even off-putting (Jaekl). We can't promise to completely ease your voice discomfort, but we can promise this: you can get used to your recorded voice and even grow to like it. Like any skill, though, it does take practice—and the tips below will help your practice lead you to more and more growth and comfort.

One way to help yourself feel comfortable: feel comfortable. No, really: set up your microphone in a quiet place where you won't be disturbed, but it's even better if it's a place you know and love, surrounded by things that make you feel comfortable. It's good news that soft things (sofas, beds, carpet, stuffed animals) are generally also good things for your recording quality, too! So turn off your phone, send everyone else in the house out on an errand, make a cup of tea, hug your stuffed animal, and hang out by yourself for a while in your living room or in a bedroom. You might consider setting up your microphone or propping up your phone in a store-bought or homemade portable vocal recording booth—a box, fabric or cardboard, lined with acoustic foam or whatever kind of foam you can find. The foam-lined box will make your voice sound rich and warm and eliminate any echoes or tinniness.

While a comfortable setting is ideal, we have both foregone comfort for set-ups that we know will give us really good audio quality. We often record in our respective bedroom closets, sitting on the floor or a stool while surrounded by hanging clothes with the door shut. The space is ideal: it's small, full of echo-absorbing clothes, and shut off from people and other noisy spaces in the house. Other people we know drape towels, blankets, or coats over their head while speaking into a microphone, creating a similar kind of tiny closet environment. The most inventive set-up we've ever heard of is the use of "pillow forts." Don Gonyea, an NPR reporter, uses this strategy all the time: he props up pillows behind and around his computer with his microphone positioned in front of the computer (Nadworny and Migaki, "Do You Want"). This method, in our opinion, sounds the closest to a studio recording as you can get.

After determining how to best record yourself, then what do you do? Remember, our advice above in the Scripting section about writing in a conversational way? We're hoping you already have a script or plan that will help you sound the way you want to: casual, relaxed. Yet it's often difficult to feel relaxed when you're in front of a microphone knowing that people will later listen and possibly judge your voice

Figure 4.6
Make your own pillow
fort to improve your
recording quality.

or delivery. "Mic-fright" is real. It can make people read or speak quickly or space out while they're talking. Or worse, it can make people sound stiff and robotic. No listener will connect to the sound of a robot, so it's important to try to sound natural. Here is some advice for how to do so.

- **Write on the script**. If you're working from a script, underline or capitalize words you want to emphasize when you read aloud, add spaces where you want to pause, note where you want to speak slowly or quickly in the margins—and then *practice, practice, practice*. Practice reading through the script aloud, noting any other places that you think should be marked. After practicing a couple of times, hit the record button and practice delivering it while recording. Fair warning: do not have high expectations of yourself just because the red recording light is on. You'll likely need to practice delivering the script many times while recording before you sound natural. With lots of practice, you'll likely end up memorizing the script or parts of it and simply reciting it without needing to look at the script much. That's a good thing: reciting from memory leads to a more natural delivery.
- **Imagine a friendly face**. Sora Newman, a voice trainer at NPR, recommends visualizing a friendly listener or even looking at a picture of someone you know to sound more conversational (Kern 133). Imagining like you're talking to someone makes it much easier to actually sound like you're talking to someone, which is the ultimate goal.
- **Repeat yourself**. Of course, you might have a sneaking suspicion in the midst of recording that you sounded... off when you said something. If you're even the slightest bit unsure, go ahead and repeat the sentence (and then repeat it again for good measure). You can always edit out mistakes later, which will be easier than setting up your mic again later. And we suggest rerecording entire sentences, not just words or phrases. You don't want to find yourself trying to

edit parts of two sentences together that simply don't fit in a natural, unnoticeable way; better to have an entire sentence that sounds the way you want it to.

- **Record all in one sitting**. A human voice sounds different all the time, from day to day and even from hour to hour. This means that recording narration on different days and splicing them together will likely sound awkward. So try to record all in one sitting. You may even want to record the same lines on different days and later determine which version of your voice you think sounds better.

- **Use your body in the same way as you would in a conversation**. You might shrug your shoulders when you don't know the answer to something or raise your voice when you ask a question. You might smile while you're talking or pull your shoulders back when you have something important to say. Pay attention to what you do with your body when speaking to someone in a real-life conversation, and allow your body to mimic those moves when you speak into the microphone. Yes, it may feel silly to do that alone in a quiet space, but trust us, it will help with a more natural delivery. You should see how much we gesture with our arms and hands when recording; it's pretty hilarious.

- **Prepare your breath and voice**. In *Sound Reporting*, Jonathan Kern reminds us that speaking is a physical process that involves your "lungs, diaphragm, your vocal cords, and the resonance of your entire upper body" (137). If you're nervous or tense, everything tightens up and interferes with strong vocal delivery, so try to relax your back, shoulders, neck, and jaw before you begin speaking and during the recording. And don't forget to breathe. Take some deep breaths before you begin speaking and take natural breaths through the entire recording. When you forget to breathe, you inevitably speak more quickly, so unless quick talk is part of your rhetorical plan, be conscious of your breathing.

- **Slow down**. Listen to the amount of space between sentences in a professional audiobook or a high-profile, edited podcast; you may notice that there are more, longer pauses than you initially thought before you paid attention to it. That's because, often, a professional, knowledgeable, friendly voice is also a voice that isn't rushing—and people new to recording (especially those new to reading scripts) often find themselves wanting to rush. If you don't believe us, just give it a shot: record some extra-long pauses between sentences while recording, and then feel free to delete those spaces between sentences later if they seem too long. But we think that if you try to read just a bit slower than you initially assume, you'll often like the effect—and so will your listeners.

- **Be yourself**. Don't try to make your voice sound different or imitate someone else's voice; your own accent (yes, we all have accents), vocal habits, and vocal personality are all part of what make you sound like an embodied human, a real person your listeners want to get to know. If you do anything to your voice, try taking one more piece of Ira Glass's advice: lower the tone of your voice just a bit so it sounds a touch deeper (Abel 102). Sometimes this conscious choice can make you sound a bit more like *you*, which we think is different from putting on a vocal coat that doesn't fit your shape.

- **Get feedback.** Ask someone else to listen to your recording to give you feedback on your delivery: your teacher, your peers, friends, family members, university writing center, or really anyone willing and able to listen. You can even give them guidance on what kind of help you need: "Do I sound like a robot? Do I sound conversational? Is there any part where I say something that doesn't fit with the content (like an excited voice when talking about something sad)?"

> **Learn More**
> See the Peer Review section in chapter five for more on good feedback practices.

4.4 Microphones

For up-to-date advice on which microphones to buy, it's always best to do a current search online; we especially like the advice at Transom.org. Still, we know it can be intimidating to browse terms and make decisions without even a basic introduction. This list, then, is simply a brief overview of the types of mics we find ourselves using regularly in different contexts.

You'll notice we're not including "the mic built into your laptop and phone" on our list. That's not because those mics are bad—though actually, the mic on your laptop is probably pretty bad for your high-stakes soundwriting—but because this list is more for people looking for ways to go beyond those simple, everyday mics. We've had students record podcasts and interviews using their phones that sound great for beginners, especially when they've taken the time to make a few test recordings as we describe below in Try-It 4.12. But what other easy, useful options are out there?

- **Earbuds or USB headsets**: If you're recording directly to a computer, you'll find that just about any external microphone will sound better than the little mic built into your laptop. If your phone came with a set of earbuds with a mic, try plugging that into your computer and recording with it. Or you can buy USB headsets on almost any budget, sometimes with the mics on little arms placed next to your mouth (to avoid the plosives from breathing directly into the mic), and sometimes with mics only visible as teensy holes on one side of the headphones. Gaming headsets work great, too.
- **External microphones for your phone**: There are many varieties of microphones designed to improve the quality, flexibility, and reach of your phone's mic. Some snap on, and some are attached to a cable or wand; some need a headphone jack, and some use USB-C; some are built to work with a proprietary app, and some work with your phone's default voice memo app.

- **Portable digital microphones**: These are standalone devices (usually a bit bigger and chunkier than a phone) with built-in microphones that allow you to record directly to a built-in drive or removable SD card. They come in various configurations and styles (depending on how much money you want to spend, naturally). You might prefer an external mic for a number of reasons: they typically allow you to monitor your recording through headphones in real time, provide visual cues if your mic is too hot and the recording is clipping, sound better than a phone microphone for many purposes, allow you to plug in external microphones and stands, and keep your phone free for other things. Many are also Wi-Fi-enabled for easy file transfer and have multiple inputs to make it easy to record multiple interviewees or sound sources at the same time.
- **Lapel microphones**: These are small, clip-on mics that are clipped to the main speaker's clothing, leading to consistent volume (as long as they don't turn their head too much). They can often be connected to whatever device you want to use to actually record—your phone, computer, or a portable digital microphone.
- **Shotgun microphones**: These mics are often at the end of a "wand," sticking the mic itself away from the person holding it and allowing for quick, directional focus of the recording source (like if you want to flip it quickly back toward you when you ask a question). Their sound quality is often excellent and professional (though of course, they're available at different price points) and can often be plugged into different devices.
- **USB microphones**: Finally, we should mention USB mics—those mics that plug directly into your computer, often sitting on your desk on a built-in stand. These mics are so varied that it's hard to describe them as a single category; their main similarity is that they're all designed to work simply and easily, without the need for any adapters or mixing boards between your mic and your computer. Many of these use fancy words (condenser! cardioid! dynamic!) to describe the types of hardware under the hood and the range and types of audio they record best; if you're shopping seriously, you should acquaint yourself with the best models at your price point, including getting to know the words used to describe them. Kyle does much of his recording with a Yeti microphone made by the company Blue, which he likes for a few reasons: he sounds good talking directly into it alone, but he can also change a setting to record two interviewees or an entire room; it has a headphone jack that allows him to monitor his recording in real time; and it has volume and gain controls right on the mic, allowing him to fiddle with changes physically, not always in the software. Other USB mics have some or all of those features in varying configurations.

Recording Sound Effects

Figure 4.7
Try recording
the world
around you.

Have you ever plugged headphones into a digital microphone and just walked around, listening to the world digitally amplified? We find this always leads to magical discoveries: footsteps that sound more complex than you ever realized, birds that you didn't know sang so well, traffic that seems closer than it looks, wind chimes that come from around the corner.

That principle of listening to the world is at the heart of recording your own sound effects for your digital projects. Sure, these days you can find just about any sound you can imagine online with a license you can use. (See Collecting and Downloading Sound below!) Still, there's also something satisfying about making your own recordings by gathering ambient sound or inventing your own sounds like the Foley designers we discussed in chapter three—plus, it can give you control over getting *exactly* what you want.

Here are a few basic tips that we think will apply no matter what kind of mic you're using:

- **Plan, but not too much**. As with every part of your project, what you record should be based on the needs of your rhetorical situation. If you've been following our advice so far, you probably have a detailed plan of what exactly you need, and there's something great about taking your recorder to get exactly those sounds—like footsteps, a door slam, a car starting, or a cat purring. But try turning on your mic and headphones a while before and after you actually record, just in case some unusual sound catches your ear.
- **Repeat if possible**. In the moment, it can be tempting to think, "Okay! I got that sound on my first take! Done! Where's lunch?" But trust us: you'll be glad later if you have many choices to choose from. If you're recording a sonic event that you created yourself, repeat. Slam that door again. Scribble with your marker for just five more seconds. Don't leave the football game until your team has scored at least twice, so you get two versions of the cheering crowd.

- **Aim for a recording that's as loud as possible—but not too loud**. As we explained in the Recording Interviews section above, a mic that's too hot can clip, leading to distracting distortion. But on the other end, you don't want your sound effect to be so quiet that you can't hear anything. Keep adjusting and repeating the action you're recording until it sounds loud in your headphones without going into the red.

- **Ambience is easier to capture than specifics**. A warning: if you have your hopes set on a particular, perfectly isolated outdoor recording—say, a basketball bouncing or swishing through a net—you may find yourself increasingly frustrated without professional equipment, as the sounds of wind, cars, and passersby get in the way. But on the other hand, you may find that recordings of general ambience come through exactly right, in contexts where you *want* everything else: the crowd at the basketball game, or the collection of sounds as your train approaches and you get on, or everything echoing around the fountain at the indoor mall. Just be sure to familiarize yourself with your state's recording laws; we suggest doing your best to record general hubbub, not individual speakers' words.

4.5 Audio File Formats

It's easy to feel overwhelmed by all the file types that can be used to export and share digital audio. What are you supposed to do when people start talking about WAV, MP3, OGG, M4A, FLAC, and more? (These types of files are marked by the suffix on a digital file name, the letters after the period—like interview.wav or effect.mp3.)

> **Learn More**
> Learn more about exporting audio to share it, and how exporting is different than saving, in chapter five's section on Exporting.

You can find detailed descriptions of all these file types online, but we think a few basic tips are good to know for beginning soundwriters, especially when you begin recording, editing, sharing, and converting files. Thus, we'll only skim the surface here; yes, audiophiles, we know that there's a lot more to say about sample rate and bit rate, but we think most amateurs won't need to dive that deep.

- **WAV** is a common uncompressed audio format that tends to be very high quality and very large. If your digital recorder or recorder app lets you record straight to WAV (and if you check the settings, it usually will), choose that setting when you really want the recording to sound as good as possible. But because WAV files are so big, beware recording to WAV if you're low on digital storage space or if you want to record something that's really long.

- **MP3** is also common and is often seen as the smaller, worse-quality cousin of WAV files. (For instance, many digital recorders let you choose to record straight to WAV or MP3 with no other options.) MP3 files are smaller than WAV files because they're compressed, which inevitably leads to the loss of some audio information—but in many cases, not enough that most people will notice the loss. Not all MP3 files are alike; those that are more compressed (smaller file size) can sound noticeably worse than those that are less compressed (bigger file size); you'll see MP3s described as being compressed from the worst-quality 96 kilobits per second (kbps) all the way up to the best-quality 320 kbps. If you're not sure what file format to use when sharing your audio, MP3 is a safe, versatile choice due to its popularity and manageable size. It's also generally safer to use MP3 to record spoken voice than something more complex, like music.

- **M4A** is a file type native to Apple products. Practically speaking, that means if you record on an iPhone using the voice memo app, the default file type is (at the time of writing) M4A. That can be a problem if you're trying to get that phone recording into some audio editors. You have two solutions if you want to edit M4As on those computers: 1) look for a way to convert the M4A into an MP3 or other file format using one of the many online converter sites or programs, or 2) search online for instructions about how to install a plugin to your audio editor that will allow you to import and edit M4A without the need to convert first.

Here's an example of how Kyle uses file formats when podcasting: to preserve high-quality audio, he uses as many assets as possible that are WAV files. For instance, if a friend records a segment on another computer, he asks them to use WAV. Then, when he's done putting everything together in his audio editor, he exports to a MP3 file at 320 kbps (the highest-quality MP3) and uploads that MP3 to his podcast host, since he knows that most people will think that MP3s sound good enough and he wants his filesize to be manageable.

You don't have to stop with these three, of course. For instance, many people prefer to save high-quality audio in FLAC format instead of WAV because you get the same quality in a smaller file size, and many prefer OGG over MP3 since it compresses files smaller yet sounds better. You can experiment with these file types by exporting audio from your audio editor into various file formats at various rates of compression and then comparing the exported files' size and audio quality. (The MP3 format was developed using Suzanne Vega's song "Tom's Diner"; that might be a good place to start!)

Try-It 4.12 Experiment with Microphones and Recording Locations

One of the best ways to learn how to get good sound from the mics available to you is simply to make lots of recordings and listen to them next to each other, hearing the nuanced differences. Here's our recommendation for how to do so:

1. Choose at least three different microphones that are portable, depending on what you have access to—perhaps your phone, laptop, or tablet, and ideally also a portable digital microphone and at least one mic you can plug into another device, like a USB headset and/or a set of earbuds.

2. Then choose at least three different spaces you can record in. Try to choose spaces where you might actually find yourself trying to record narration one day (so don't pick the loud kitchen at the restaurant where you work): maybe an empty classroom on campus, your living room, a walk-in closet, or even inside a car.

3. Then record something using each microphone in each space—so if you have three mics in three spaces, you'll have nine total recordings. Begin the recording by explaining where you are, what mic you're using, and how far away the mic is from your face, and then add a standard sentence or two from a favorite book or poem, for consistency.

4. Get all the recordings onto a single listening device, like a computer. You can play them one at a time using that computer's default music program—perhaps in a new playlist—or if you're familiar with basic audio editing, you could import each recording into an audio editor and drag them next to each other in a single audio project. That way you'll be able to hit play once and listen to them all next to each other without needing to stop, and you can export the entire file to share all the recordings at once with others.

> **Learn More**
> See the Editing Basics section in chapter five for some pointers for beginners.

5. Ideally, listen to the recordings with other people, talking about which mic and space sounds best. (In a classroom, it can be great to listen to multiple classmates' recordings together, where the best mics and spaces will stand out clearly.) Try listening to your recordings in different spaces, too—say, once in your car, once in headphones, and once through your best computer or TV speakers.

COLLECTING AND DOWNLOADING SOUND

There are times when you will know exactly what kind of sound you want to incorporate into your audio project and other times when you only have a general sense.

You might even find times that you want or need *some* kind of music or effects but have no idea what kind of sound would work best. Regardless of the situation, you need to know how to find different kinds of tape online—voices, sound effects, and music.

Here's the thing: finding tape and then determining how to use it ethically and legally can be complicated. Here are a few general guidelines that we think should guide your use of downloaded tape, but remember that it's always worthwhile to talk to a professor, librarian, or audio professional about this matter too.

- **Follow the ethical guidelines of your rhetorical situation**. If you're doing an audio project for class, cite using the academic style your professor wants. If you're making a radio feature, cite your audio assets in the way followed by professionals in that arena.
- **Be nice**. Don't ask yourself, "How much can I get away with?" Instead, ask yourself, "How does the person who created or uploaded this audio want me to use this audio, and how might they want to be attributed?" If you're not sure of where the line is, ask a professor, colleague, or someone with more soundwriting experience than you.
- **Know your Creative Commons licenses**. Many people have shared content online with particular kinds of Creative Commons (CC) licenses, which give you detailed instructions on what you may or may not do. Don't assume that just because something has a CC license that you can do whatever you want with it; follow the guidelines of the license.
- **Know your fair use rights**. If you follow certain precautions, you can be fairly certain that certain uses of copyrighted work are legally allowed under the part of US copyright law called "fair use." Sometimes people are more afraid to exercise these fair use rights than they should be. Fair use is the law! Use your rights!

Let's pause for a minute on those last two, since we've noticed that they're sometimes confusing.

When someone uploads sound to certain websites, they might choose a particular kind of Creative Commons license as a way to say, "Please use my work, even without asking permission! Just please follow these guidelines as you do so." For instance, when uploading to Freesound or the Free Music Archive (two of our favorite places to search for audio in our projects), the uploader can decide if future downloaders of that sound may remix the sound into something new, if the sound can be used in commercial projects, and if any new sounds should also be licensed by Creative Commons. Those options lead to abbreviations that soundwriters should get used to, like CC BY (you may remix, share, or sell this sound, as long as you give attribution) or CC BY-NC-ND (you may distribute this sound as a whole, as long as you don't change it, don't use it commercially, and give attribution). Check out creativecommons.org for all the details you need to understand these licenses, in everyday language that non-experts can understand!

The lesson is clear: follow the intentions of the sound's creator and owner.

But what about when you have an idea for the perfect sound, but it's not labeled with a Creative Commons license? Here's the thing: any sound you find online, rip from a YouTube video, or capture from a streaming audio service is almost certain to be protected by copyright law, with all of the owner's rights reserved. So does that mean they're off-limits for your soundwriting projects?

Well, depending on how you want to use the copyrighted work in your sound-writing piece, you may have a fair use right to use it. We say "may" because fair use is purposefully a slippery, uncertain concept; in the United States, ultimately only a judge can declare if a use was indeed legally fair or not. But that doesn't mean we don't have guidance! For instance, the Columbia University Libraries website hosts one of the first "fair use checklists" ever made, which composers of any kind (including soundwriters) can use to help determine if their use of a copyrighted work is likely to be fair or not (Crews and Butler). The checklist walks you through the same "four factors" that a judge would use if they were determining if your use is fair or not. Here's our brief summary of those factors:

1. **The purpose of the use**: Your use of copyrighted work is more likely to be fair if you're using it for the purpose of criticism or commentary. In sound, that often means that you're using the copyrighted sound as an example of a larger point ("Check out the unusual way the key changes in this excerpt!" or "You've got to hear this person I'm critiquing to believe he said that"), rather than just as background music or "auditory frosting."

2. **The nature of the copyrighted work**: Your use of copyrighted work is more likely to be fair if you're using nonfiction, already-published work (say, audio clips from historical news recordings). That means, sadly, that any use of copyrighted music is less likely to be fair. (So we don't recommend layering Beyoncé under your narration unless you're doing so for criticism or commentary, as described in factor 1.)

3. **The amount of the copyrighted work you use**: Your use of copyrighted work is more likely to be fair if you only use a small amount, especially if the part you use isn't the central, most important part of the work. It's a longstanding rumor that there's an automatic length of time that's automatically safe/fair. Yet there's no number of seconds that makes you automatically immune to getting a cease-and-desist letter from a copyright owner. In sound, that means you probably don't want to play an entire copyrighted song in the background of your project, even if you're critiquing it; when possible, just edit in the parts of the copyrighted work you want to comment on.

4. **The effect of the copyrighted work on the market**: Your use of copyrighted work is more likely to be fair if your use won't hurt the owner's ability to sell copies of it—and you're *extra* safe if the work you're using is difficult to legally get permission or a license for. So you might want to ask yourself, "Could someone take my audio project, extract the copyrighted stuff out of it, and thus avoid buying it legally?" If the answer is yes, like if your podcast ends with an entire song at the end with nothing else layered with it, you're closer to infringing copyright law.

You might have noticed that some of these factors almost seem to contradict each other. That is, you might want to use a copyrighted song as part of a larger critique you're making, which is *more* fair according to factor 1, but it is also a creative, musical example, which is *less* fair according to factor 2. That's the nature of fair-use judgments: they're often complicated, with some leaning in your favor and others leaning away from you. In the unlikely event that a copyright owner sues you, the judge would look at all four factors, deciding which matter more or less in your particular case.

In practice, what does all this stuff about Creative Commons and fair use mean for soundwriting? Here are a few quick tips that won't apply to every situation, but which will generally help you out:

- If you're looking for background music, look for something with a Creative Commons license that allows you to remix it—that is, any CC license without an ND, which stands for "no derivatives."
- If you're looking for sound effects, the same CC rules apply as with music—and it's even safer to just record them yourself.
- If you're using an audio clip to discuss it or comment on it, you're almost certainly going to be okay, even if it's copyrighted—but to be extra safe, don't use more of the audio than you need or in a way that could conceivably hurt the market.

CHOOSING TAPE FOR YOUR PROJECT

With some projects, you'll find yourself constantly popping in and out of your editing program as you gather more assets and adapt your plans. But some projects benefit from another step that will guide you in making decisions about which of those recordings really fit in your project, which need to go, and which need to be edited to fit. Making these choices isn't easy, especially if you have hours and hours of tape to wade through.

The rhetorical situation of your project should guide you here. If your voice as narrator is "leading" the project as a way to help you achieve your purpose for your audience, and you're using other tape to "dance" with that narration, for example, then you might already know the kind of tape or the exact recording that you want. For example, in Tanya's "Peaceful Warriors" she searched for media clips of Trump saying what many would consider problematic statements about women, people of color, and people with disabilities. Once she found the media clips, which were anywhere between five-minute and one-hour news segments, she knew she'd only use brief parts of the clips and disregard the rest. At the same time, she also knew that these clips could adjust her narration or even beckon a different kind of asset to go along with it. So she was prepared to change plans if needed. Flexibility is key when working with tape.

4.6 Choosing Quotes from Interviews

Finding good quotes from interviewees to incorporate in your project is hard, especially if you're working with several hours of tape. While your genre will likely dictate what constitutes a good quote, here are some general guidelines for making that decision (Rosenthal, Transom Traveling Workshop). An effective quote:

- Provides insight that isn't obvious
- Offers an opinion or reflection
- Offers a statement that is especially meaningful coming from the person who said it, as opposed to someone else
- Captures an unexpected, spontaneous, chaotic, accidental, surprising, or emotional moment
- Offers a pithy, witty, and/or complete thought
- Paints a vivid visual

But let's say you're letting the tape lead. In that case, you might approach your tape with less of an exact eye for what you want; you might instead listen creatively, trying to find connections, surprising moments, or content that matches your initial ideas or goals.

If that seems scary or time-consuming, try creating a "roadmap" of your recordings and using that roadmap to help you make decisions about what to include in your project. We suggest two ways to create your roadmap: logging and/or transcribing.

Roadmap Option 1: Logging—In Jessica Abel's *Out on the Wire*, radio journalist Ira Glass describes "logging" as listening to tape and taking notes about its content without stopping the recording (29). These notes can be one word or one phrase or one sentence, not a word-for-word transcription of everything said on the tape. With audio projects, the way something is said may perhaps be just as important as what is said, so familiarizing yourself with the tape through logging will help you become more familiar with it and thus assist in determining what parts would work well for your audio project. It's really hard to find connections in something you haven't even listened to yet.

Roadmap Option 2: Auto-Transcribing—Transcribing tape is documenting the content in its entirety. In the Transcribing section of chapter five, we'll discuss tips for creating transcripts for your audience, giving them a written way to access your work—but that's not what we mean here. Now, at this early stage in the soundwriting composing process, we're talking about transcribing as a way to use the affordances of the visual mode to support your planning. But because you're working with raw tape, it's not a good use of your time to transcribe *the whole thing* on your own, especially if you have a lot of tape, like from an interview or long field recordings. There are multiple free transcription programs that provide fairly accurate documentation of audio content. Several of them also provide timestamps throughout the transcript, which will enable you to know exactly what is said at different moments in the recording. While an auto-transcription in itself doesn't enable you to dwell in the audio, it does give you a visual map that can guide you to the parts you want to listen to more closely. And the good thing about words on a page or a screen is they can be annotated: printed out, cut up, highlighted, notated, and scribbled on.

Try-It   **4.13 Making and Analyzing Your Roadmap**

This activity guides you in creating and analyzing your roadmap to help you make decisions about what tape to use in your audio project.

1. Open a raw audio asset, ideally one with a lot of words in it; the recording of an interview works well. (If you're not working on a soundwriting project right now, try searching the web for an oral history recording to download for practice.) Then make a roadmap using one of our two suggested methods: logging (taking notes while listening to the tape, but without pausing it) or auto-transcribing (uploading the audio to a free or cheap site or playing it for a real-time transcription app—at the time of writing, perhaps Otter, Rev, Google Docs, or anything else you can find online).

2. Once you have your roadmap, take notes on these questions to help you choose the best tape for your rhetorical situation:

   a. What are the assignment expectations (if any) about how tape should be used in this project?

   b. What is your purpose for this audio project, and how might your tape allow you to achieve these purposes and goals?

   c. What other factors of the rhetorical situation might play a role in the tape you choose, or the kind of tape that would be helpful to include in this project? Consider the needs of your audience (both intended and actual), your broader context, and the expectations that go along with your genre.

d. Are there moments in your roadmap that give you an emotional reaction? We're thinking of those spots that make you laugh out loud, feel a pit in your stomach, or get chills on the back of your neck. Can you find a way to work those in?

Key Chapter Takeaways

- We all have our own ways of finding ideas that will help us achieve our rhetorical goals—the process that's called "invention." When we're stuck on a project or starting out, invention techniques are helpful for moving our projects forward.
- Soundwriting projects are more likely to get off on the right foot when they've been carefully planned—ideally, in plans you make for yourself and in pitches you present to others for feedback.
- Writing scripts to be read aloud is different from other kinds of writing: you should strive for simple sentence structures, repetition of key points, and notes on your script that remind you how to say certain words and phrases aloud.
- Interviewing is most productive when it's thought of as a conversation rather than a rapid-fire question and answer session. Do your best to create a comfortable environment for discussion and be sure to listen attentively. Interviews go smoothest when you've prepared your questions and are not afraid to ask spontaneous questions.
- Recording sessions (both for interviews and your own narration) go best when they're in places that are conducive to recording voices, and when all the people involved feel physically and emotionally comfortable.
- When downloading sound files hosted online, respect the people who recorded them by following the terms of whatever license they used to share their work. When working with copyrighted assets, know your fair use rights, but don't abuse them.

Discussion Questions

1. When you're making something—maybe an essay for a class, maybe art for yourself, maybe soundwriting—how much do you tend to plan, and how much do you just tend to dive in and start working or writing? What successes and problems have you faced with your default method? Which of the invention and planning techniques in this chapter (if any) seem like they might be useful to you?

2. Think of a time you read, watched, or listened to an interview of any kind, in any context. What made the interview seem successful or unsuccessful to you? To what extent were you the composers' intended audience?

3. If you had to name your "default" recording context—the place and mic that you expect you'll default to unless there are reasons not to—what would it be? What informal checklist of things might you go through each time you record there to make your recording session as successful as possible?

Works Cited

Abel, Jessica. *Out on the Wire: The Storytelling Secrets of the New Masters of Radio.* Broadway, 2015.

"About the Podcast." *Lore,* www.lorepodcast.com/about.

Buckner, Jennifer J., and Kirsten Daley. "Do You Hear What I Hear? A Hearing Teacher and a Deaf Student Negotiate Sound." *Soundwriting Pedagogies,* edited by Courtney S. Danforth et al., Computers and Composition Digital Press/Utah State UP, 2018, ccdigitalpress.org/book/soundwriting/buckner-daley/index.html.

Butler, Janine. "Principles for Cultivating Rhetorics and Research Studies within Communities." *Present Tense,* vol. 8, no. 1, 2019, www.presenttensejournal.org/editorial/principles-for-cultivating-rhetorics-and-research-studies-within-communities.

Crews, Kenneth D., and Dwayne K. Butler. "Fair Use Checklist." *Copyright Advisory Services,* Columbia University Libraries, 14 May 2008, copyright.columbia.edu/basics/fair-use/fair-use-checklist.html.

Elbow, Peter. *Vernacular Eloquence.* Oxford, 2012.

Glass, Ira. "Harnessing Luck as an Industrial Product." *Reality Radio,* edited by John Biewen and Alexa Dilworth, The University of North Carolina Press, 2010, pp. 54–66.

Halbritter, Bump. *Mics, Cameras, Symbolic Action.* Parlor, 2013.

Holt, Brianna. "How Does It Feel to Be Dating Again?" *The New York Times,* 24 June 2021, www.nytimes.com/2021/06/24/style/how-does-it-feel-to-be-dating-again.html.

Jaekl, Philip. "The Real Reason the Sound of Your Own Voice Makes You Cringe." *The Guardian,* 12 July 2018, www.theguardian.com/science/2018/jul/12/the-real-reason-the-sound-of-your-own-voice-makes-you-cringe.

Kern, Jonathan. *Sound Reporting: The NPR Guide to Audio Journalism and Production.* U of Chicago P, 2008.

Migaki, Lauren, and Jeff Pierre. "The Art of the Interview." *The Students' Podcast*, NPR, 8 Mar. 2020, www.npr.org/2020/03/06/812934447/the-art-of-the-interview.

Nadworny, Elissa, and Lauren Migaki. "Do You Want to Build a Pillowfort?" *The Students' Podcast*, NPR, 10 Jan. 2021, https://www.npr.org/2021/01/09/955339564/do-you-want-to-build-a-pillowfort.

———. "How to Wade through All That Audio." *The Students' Podcast*, NPR, 15 Mar. 2020, www.npr.org/2020/03/13/815531186/how-to-wade-through-all-that-audio.

Price, Margaret, and Stephanie L. Kerschbaum. "Stories of Methodology: Interviewing Sideways, Crooked and Crip." *Canadian Journal of Disability Studies*, vol. 5, no. 3, 2016, pp. 18–56.

Raja, Tasneem, and Matt Thompson. "How to Pitch to Code Switch." *Code Switch*, NPR, 1 January 2014, www.npr.org/sections/codeswitch/2014/01/01/258689701/how-to-pitch-stories-to-code-switch.

Rodrigue, Tanya K. "Speech, Invention, and Reflection: The Composing Process of Soundwriting." *Amplifying Soundwriting: Integrating Sound into Rhetoric and Writing*, edited by Michael J. Faris et al., WAC Clearinghouse, forthcoming.

Rosenthal, Rob. "The Burning Question." *Transom*, 21 Nov. 2012, transom.org/2012/the-burning-question/.

———. "Interviewing for Emotions." *Transom*, 30 Sept. 2019, transom.org/2019/interviewing-for-emotions/.

———. Transom Traveling Workshop. *Transom at WDET*, Dec. 2019. Workshop materials.

Stedman, Kyle. "Listening like a Fan." *Technoculture: An Online Journal of Technology in Society*, vol. 7, 2017, tcjournal.org/vol7/stedman.

"Submissions." *This American Life*, WBEZ, www.thisamericanlife.org/about/submissions.

Winn, Ross. "2021 Podcast Stats & Facts (New Research from Apr 2021)." *Podcast Insights*, 10 Apr. 2021, www.podcastinsights.com/podcast-statistics/.

Interlude D

Working within the Limitations of a Structured Writing Process: How Tanya Composed "Play it Loud"[1]

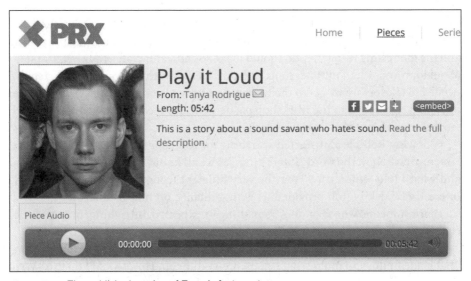

Figure D.1 The published version of Tanya's feature story.

INTRODUCTION

A couple of years ago, I searched for a class I could take to learn more about audio storytelling and soundwriting production. At that point, I had taught myself everything I knew about soundwriting and felt like I needed guidance from an experienced radio professional or established podcaster to grow as a soundwriter. In my search, I found the Transom Traveling Workshop, an intensive eight-day crash course in the nuts and bolts of audio storytelling, led by experienced producer and teacher, Rob Rosenthal. This interlude tells the story of my experience in this workshop, where I created a piece of soundwriting in response to an assignment, just like many of you will do. I'll share some of the challenges I encountered during different parts of the composing process, some of which had me feeling stifled and restricted. I hope this

---

1   The published version of this story can be heard at Detroit's WDET 101.9's website, https://wdet.org/posts/2020/02/28/89283-ben-collins-finds-suffering-solace-in-sound/, or on PRX.

interlude will help you recognize that the constraints and limitations of an assignment and a structured composing process for soundwriting can be more helpful and productive than you could ever imagine.

BEFORE THE WORKSHOP: FINDING A SUBJECT, CONDUCTING RESEARCH, AND WRITING A PITCH

Before the workshop began, Rob emailed us our assignment. The assignment was bare-boned and straightforward: "profile someone who does something interesting and the interesting thing they do should make sound," and craft a radio feature story about four-and-a-half minutes long. Rob provided us with guidance on the steps we needed to take before we got to the workshop: find a person to profile; write a formal pitch and circulate it to the workshop participants for feedback; and after the pitch feedback, confirm the interview details.

Following Rob's lead, I started searching for someone who could be considered "interesting." Now, the word "interesting," as we all know, is pretty subjective—who and what I find "interesting" may be very different from who and what Kyle finds interesting. Luckily Rob provided us with guidance on how to interpret the word (in short: someone who is or does something unexpected, intriguing, or out-of-the-ordinary) so I drew on that during my quest to find a person to profile.

The workshop wasn't in the city where I live or in a place where I knew anyone. That made finding an interesting person pretty difficult. How would I do this? Well, I'm pretty good at researching, so I started there. I went online and searched in newspapers, online forums, and magazines for a person, an event, an issue—anything that might point me to someone that could qualify as interesting. I stumbled across an article in a magazine about a musician/music producer with three ear disorders that made hearing sound nearly intolerable, both physically and mentally. I was fascinated and confused. Why would a person who is continuously assaulted by constant ringing and loud sounds that sometimes make him feel physically ill be a musician? This person, I thought to myself, no doubt qualified, at least from my perspective, as interesting. I chose him to profile for my story, then scoured the internet once again to find out more about him and his conditions. I looked in newspapers, magazines, medical journals, and websites. And while doing so, I took lots of notes, writing down important information, possible story angles, and possible interview questions.

The next step in the process was to write a pitch. I was so thankful Rob provided us with pitch guidelines because this kind of writing was certainly new territory for me. The pitch was to include three paragraphs: the first paragraph being a compelling description of the story; the second being a one-or-two-sentence distillation of the story in the form of a focus sentence or x/y formula statement (which are two

Learn More

See chapter four for more on pitches and how you might write one.

kinds of story idea "test" methods); and the third being an explanation of why the story was timely. The required contents of the second paragraph would have really thrown me for a loop if I hadn't read Jessica Abel's book *Out on the Wire* and Rob hadn't provided us with a brief, accessible explanation of a focus sentence and x/y statement. In short, they are different ways to both generate story ideas and to "test" if story ideas are compelling. Take the focus sentence, which Rob discusses at length in Abel's book. It's a sentence template that helps determine the subject and conflict of the story, or in other words, what makes the story a *story*. The sentence shell is: somebody does something because _____(this is their motivation for doing that thing), BUT _____ (this is the challenge they have to overcome) (Abel 52). The x/y statement, as explained by podcaster Alex Blumberg in Abel's book, is a bit more straightforward, with a sentence shell like this: I'm doing a story about **X** (topic of the story). And what's interesting about it is **Y** (the thing that actually makes the story compelling) (56).

I tried to write the second paragraph of the pitch first because, after all, I needed to figure out what the story was about before I could write a compelling description of it for the first paragraph. I knew that one of the story "test" methods would surely help me do that. While I had read about these story "test" strategies before and understood them in theory, I became paralyzed when I tried to sit down and write one. I was completely out of my comfort zone. I had never come to identify a main idea in writing—either in alphabetic writing (like a news story or a scholarly argument) or soundwriting—before I started writing. My regular practice is to do quite a bit of writing and thinking after learning more about something or someone, so by being asked to identify the essence of a story before I learned more about the subject of my story felt very uncomfortable. I also wasn't quite convinced that there was a ton of value in knowing and being able to identify a story at this very early stage in the writing process. Nor am I the biggest fan of sentence templates like the focus sentence, though I have used them to teach writing and know they can be productive sometimes. My instinct was to resist, but I wanted to learn, and I trusted Rob, so I tried my hardest to distill what I thought was a story into an x/y statement. After multiple drafts, this is what I came up with:

> **Learn More**
> You can read Tanya's pitch in its entirety on the companion website.

This is a story about Ben Collins, a sound-maker and sound-engineer who has three ear disorders: tinnitus (constant ringing in the ears), hyperacusis (everyday sounds that are extremely loud), and misophonia ("hated" sounds that trigger an emotional and/or physiological response). This story is interesting because Ben Collins lives in two intersecting, conflicting acoustic worlds, and he manages to ground himself amidst sonic chaos and continue a deep engagement with sound.

The language is way too academic-y for radio, but it certainly got to the "thing" that made Ben interesting. I circulated the pitch, received some feedback, and got the green light to pursue my idea. After that, I pre-interviewed Ben—in other words, I briefly spoke

> **Learn More**
> See chapter four for more on pre-interviews.

with him to determine if he was as good a story subject as I thought he was. He checked the box in that his career choice was certainly unexpected and surprising, so we set up a day and time for a formal interview, and a couple of days later, I hopped on a plane across the country, having no idea how important my x/y statement would later become for my story.

AT THE WORKSHOP: A STRUCTURED COMPOSING PROCESS

The workshop was true to its description in its intensity and commitment to teaching participants the various aspects of audio storytelling. I could describe the rest of the experience in any number of ways, but the part that is most memorable is another instance of resistance. This time it was my resistance to the multiple steps of the composing process of the major assignment—the radio feature story. And this time my resistance was even more intense than what I experienced with the pitch.

Let me fast forward a bit and pick the story back up after I interviewed Ben on the third day of the workshop. Rob, over the next couple of days, introduced us to a multistage chronological writing process for crafting a radio feature story. The steps included: create an outline of topics or themes that emerge from the interview; log tape (or in other words, create a loose transcription of the recording in written form); choose a limited number of compelling quotes to possibly include in the story; organize the quotes according to topic or theme; determine a story structure; and write a script

> **Learn More**
> See chapter four for more on logging tape, for guidelines on how to choose possible quotes for a story, and for more on "letting the tape lead" scriptwriting.

"around" the quotes. (This kind of scriptwriting is often referred to as "letting the tape lead." In short, the writer uses the quotes to determine the content of narration and how the narration and quotes can work together to tell the story.) Throughout each stage, workshop participants received feedback from the teacher and others in two groups of four to five people.

With the exception of giving and receiving feedback, this writing process was new to me and counterintuitive to the way I approach writing and teach it. The seemingly discrete and rigid stages, doing one thing at a time in a specific order, felt suffocating, formulaic, and uncomfortable. Writing is messy and chaotic! And that's what makes it so great! With that said, though, I resisted the urge to hop back on a plane to Boston and followed Rob's lead.

I'm so glad I did.

As the workshop progressed, my resistance slowly transformed into an understanding and appreciation of what I was doing and learning in the workshop. The first time I felt my resistance begin to dissipate was when I set out to wade through two and half hours of interview tape. I was overwhelmed and stressed. I had worked with more tape in previous audio projects but never had a deadline to complete the project. This was a different story. I had four days to produce a "broadcast-quality" radio feature story. Time was not on my side. I did not have the luxury of spending hours and hours agonizing over ideas or words or sounds.

But you know what I did have? I had my x/y statement, which I had revised multiple times based on feedback from Rob and the other workshop participants. The statement became my guiding light, or what we called "the north star" during the workshop. I also had my outline of themes and my newfound knowledge about what makes a quote compelling. These things became my sounding board. While thinking about possible quotes to use, I used my x/y statement to help me determine if the quote in some way contributed to the telling of the story I had wanted to tell. I used the outline to determine if the quote worked to help tell an aspect of one of the themes in my story. And I used my newfound knowledge about what makes a compelling interview quote to determine if I should indeed include the actual quote or if I should summarize it in my narration. Then, I drew on what I learned about scriptwriting to compose a script that guided me in recording my narration and crafting my story in an audio editing program.

> **Learn More**
> You can read Tanya's script on the companion website.

I also had a "living" sounding board—smart people around me who were more than willing to interrupt their own work to help me rework my introduction to sound less academic-y or to help me figure out how to fade in music at just the right moment. My material and living soundboards proved essential in enabling me to complete the task, as they paved a direct path to the finish line. Without this guidance, especially as a developing soundwriter composing in a foreign genre, my path would have been more like an overgrown garden: I would have felt lost and overwhelmed.

> **Learn More**
> See chapter five for more on giving and receiving feedback and working with feedback to revise your soundwriting.

My resistance further dissipated when I recognized the "writing stages" weren't as rigid as I initially thought. The continuous and welcoming feedback at each stage of the process blurred the seemingly concrete steps of the composing process, as the other workshop participants and I naturally moved back and forth between choosing quotes, writing narration, and employing sonic strategies in conversation. And even when I wasn't talking with others, I recognized I was also moving across the stages without realizing I was doing so. For example, I rearranged the quotes in my story during the editing stage. The messiness and chaos I yearned for was indeed there, yet it was organized chaos, and that proved more helpful than complete mayhem.

I remember thinking the writing process introduced at the workshop could be described much like how a former student described the sentence templates I used in class to teach academic writing. He said they were like training wheels that help you learn how to write so you can eventually do it on your own. The structured composing process—from interviewing, to using the story "test" methods, to organizing quotes methodically, to scriptwriting through "letting the tape lead"—functioned in the exact same way. It gave me the knowledge and practice in making the moves called for in many soundwriting genres, preparing me for the soundwriting work I would do in the future when I didn't have a guaranteed support network like I had at the workshop. It also helped draw my attention to the writing process, making me much more cognizant of the kind of soundwriting composing process that would work best for me for any given soundwriting project.

And in the end, I did indeed successfully craft a radio feature story. I even submitted it to Rob a couple of hours before the deadline! My story, "Play It Loud," was later played on WDET 101.9, Detroit's local NPR station, and on PRX Remix, a show that plays on over 20 radio stations across the country. In listening to it now, I can hear many things I could have done differently or things I would do now to make it better. Yet I'm proud of what I accomplished during that time and incredibly grateful for the experience. And just like my audio project "Peaceful Warriors," I continue to draw on the lessons I learned from this experience as I grow as a soundwriter.

Interlude Takeaways

Here are some lessons I learned from the workshop:
- Constraints are helpful because they provide support and guidance for accomplishing a task and meeting a deadline. Oftentimes they aren't as rigid as they initially seem.
- Use guidelines to compose a pitch (created by an instructor or identified for a particular podcast). If you don't have guidelines or can't find them, use the guidelines presented in Try-It 4.8: Writing a Pitch in chapter four of this textbook.
- Make a plan (or follow a plan) for steps you might take to accomplish a soundwriting task. Be willing to move freely between and among these steps and to revise or maybe even completely alter your plan during the process.
- Identify the kind of scripting approach you will use with your audio project: "letting the tape lead" (collecting sound before you begin writing) or "letting the script lead" (write a script before collecting sound).
- Get feedback at every stage of your process. Informal talk sessions with people responding to the same assignment are particularly valuable in the writing process.

Genre Conventions: Radio Feature Story/Narrative Journalism

There are various ways radio producers name this genre: audio documentary, narrative journalism, and radio feature story. Because these stories are much shorter than narrative journalism you hear on podcasts like *Radiolab* and *This American Life*, they might best be described as a radio feature story. Below I identify the genre conventions of a radio feature story, yet they are generally the same as other kinds of narrative journalism with the exception of the story length. With that said, the genre analysis below can guide you in composing either a radio feature story or a longer piece of narrative journalism.

Here are some genre conventions:

- **Where It's Heard**: this genre is usually heard on national and local radio programs (like NPR's *All Things Considered*, for example). (Other narrative journalism can be heard on podcasts.)
- **Length**: These stories are usually between four and eight minutes. (Other narrative journalism can be up to an hour.)
- **Content**: The stories focus on one individual. That individual is unique in some way and/or has a surprising, out-of-the-ordinary, or interesting life experience. Interview clips and narration are the primary elements in the story. The narrator is commonly objective and their role is to frame and move the story forward. They usually do not play a large role (if any) in the story. Narration and interview clips are used together throughout the story, neither one playing for long bouts of time. (Longer narrative journalism features more than one person, yet it is still character-driven.)
- **Structure**: The structure reflects a traditional alphabetic story structure in that it's a sequence of events, commonly with rising action, conflict, and resolution. In other words, a person encounters a challenge or conflict, confronts or overcomes it, and changes as a result. A common way to organize the components in this kind of story is to use what is known as the "e" structure, explained above. Another common structure used is a chronological narrative that tells how an event or experience unfolds (as Ira Glass would say: this happened, then this happened, then this happened...).
- **Language**: The narration is conversational and descriptive. The language (and other sonic strategies) should work to immerse the listener in the story, evoking strong visuals in the mind's eye, and creating a strong connection between the character(s) and the listener.
- **Opening and Closing**: The start of the story hooks the listener immediately and can do so with any kind of sound element—voice, scene, music, sound effects. It indirectly or directly poses a question (or questions) that keeps the listener interested in knowing the answer(s). The end of these stories usually

offers something to every single listener: a universal lesson, a piece of advice, a hard-hitting reality, or something thought-provoking or philosophical.

- **Script**: These stories invite the "let the tape lead" approach.
- **Sonic Rhetorical Strategies**: The predominant strategy used in these stories is usually voice—the voice of the narrator and the voice of the interviewee. Yet they are often sound-rich and deeply immersive, with the use of ambient sound and music.

For more advice on how to compose narrative journalism soundwriting, check out Jessica Abel's *Out on the Wire* and Transom.org.

Works Cited

Abel, Jessica. *Out on the Wire: The Storytelling Secrets of the New Masters of Radio*. Broadway, 2015.

Rodrigue, Tanya K. "Play It Loud." *PRX*, 2019, https://exchange.prx.org/pieces/302723-play-it-loud.

———. "Ben Collins Finds Suffering, Solace in Sound." *WDET*, 8 Feb. 2020, https://wdet.org/posts/2020/02/28/89283-ben-collins-finds-suffering-solace-in-sound/.

Chapter Five

EDITING, REVISING, AND SHARING

INTRODUCTION

Figure 5.1
Audio editing software makes soundwriting easy.

This chapter builds on what you've learned in previous chapters by diving deeper into audio editing on your computer, but it's more than that. It also guides you through what happens after you've crafted your first draft—all the revising, transcribing, and sharing that you'll do to finish up and get your soundwriting into the world.

We know that some of you will read straight through this book from start to end, while some of you will probably pop into this chapter for specific editing advice before reading earlier chapters. Those approaches are both great! Use the Table of Contents and Index to help you find what you need, when you need it.

ORGANIZING ASSETS IN AN AUDIO EDITOR

We'd first like to introduce you to two important terms we'll use a lot in this chapter: tracks and clips. Both terms refer to ways that your audio assets—your raw material—can be organized in whatever audio editing program you're using.

Tracks

Let's start with tracks. In many programs, a track is a horizontal bar that can be empty or filled with audio assets, which look like squiggly waves of differing lengths and heights. When you import or record audio into an audio editor, the sound will manifest itself in a horizontal bar—a track. It's helpful to think of tracks like timelines, in that they show you in the visual mode what a listener hears in the aural mode, as time passes; what comes first is on the left and what comes later is on the right.

Tracks can also be layered atop each other, displayed in your audio editor with one above the other. The various tracks all have their own particular audio information in them, but when you play your entire audio project, you hear them all at the same time.

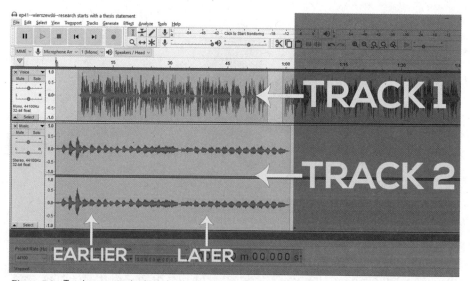

Figure 5.2 Tracks are stacked vertically. Audio information shows a timeline, with audio that plays earlier starting on the left.

In practice, you will use tracks to organize different assets that you might want to edit separately: perhaps one or more tracks of voices speaking, one or more tracks of music, and one or more tracks of sound effects. If you have more than one track, you'll want to be sure to give each track a descriptive name so you can easily differentiate between the assets. The key is to think of tracks as tools to help you organize your content and to edit discrete parts of your audio, without having to make changes to everything at once.

Tracks are just for you as the soundwriter; when you share your soundwriting, you'll export your work as a file that is easy to *listen to* but no longer able to be *edited* by the listener. That means that the audience doesn't have access to your tracks. For instance, if you have a project with a voice track and a music track, it's easy to delete the music track to let the voice play alone. But if you've exported your project to a shareable file format like an MP3 and then try to open that MP3 file in your audio editor, you'll no longer be able to delete or edit the music track. The key is to always differentiate your project files (the files you use while editing) and your exported files (the ones you share when you want feedback or want to share your finished work).

One more thing to learn about tracks: sometimes they're in stereo (with different audio played in each ear) and sometimes they're in mono (with the same audio played in each ear). Here's how it plays out visually: you may notice that some tracks include a single horizontal waveform line, while others have a double line, as in Figure 5.3.

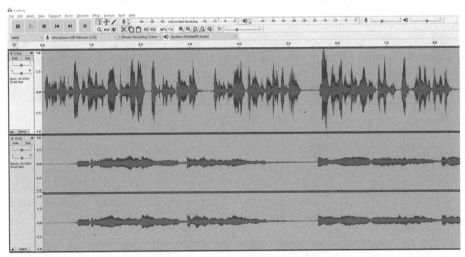

Figure 5.3   A mono track that plays at the same time as a stereo track.

Notice how the top track (a spoken-voice recording) is made up of one horizontal line, while the bottom track (a musical recording) is made up of two horizontal lines. That's because the Voice track is in mono and the Music track is in stereo; if you listen to this project, you'll hear the voice speaking as if it's right in front of you or right in the middle of your head, while the music will have some parts that happen more toward the right or left (perhaps different instruments). A single project can have tracks that are both mono and stereo, but some programs won't let you copy and paste audio from one type to the other.

Clips

Clips are smaller than tracks; they are sections of audio that can be easily moved along or between tracks. Clips are often used as selections of audio "clipped" from a larger track, like a picture you clip from a magazine with scissors. A horizontal track can be made up of one or several clips.

Figure 5.4   Two clips on the same track.

Soundwriters create clips so they can line up different sections of audio with precision. For example, if your project has one narration track and one music track, you might find yourself wanting your narration to start and stop at the exact right moment in relation to the music. In that case, you might split your narration track into multiple clips, each of which can be dragged left and right (forward and backward in time for the listener) to line up with the music track.

Clips also enable soundwriters to get a handle on audio files that are really long. Say you've imported a raw recording of a two-hour interview into your audio editor and you want to use at least five different parts of that interview in your final audio documentary. If you split the track into multiple clips, you'll be less overwhelmed and better able to manage the content. Many programs will also let you label the clips with a word, phrase, or number that corresponds to parts of your script (if you have one) to keep yourself even better organized. Those labels will help you avoid repeatedly listening and relistening to remember the content of each clip; it's a way to use the affordances of the visual mode while producing work to be ultimately experienced in the aural mode.

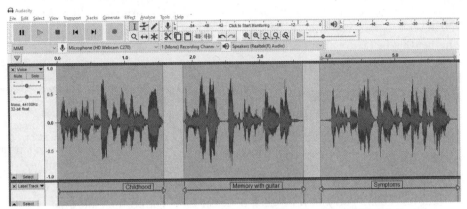

Figure 5.5   We know what audio is in each of these clips without needing to listen to them over and over, since they've been so clearly labeled.

EDITING

Now let's learn some basic and intermediate skills in your audio editing program. You'll see that we've split these editing tips into four subsections: Editing Basics, Editing Voice, Layering Together Multiple Tracks, and Adding Effects. These sections guide you through a commonly used workflow for multitrack projects with narration, such as a podcast or an audio documentary. We encourage you to figure out a workflow that works best for your project and to move around to different sections in this chapter in a way that makes sense for you.

Even though this section may get a little technical, remember that these aren't just skills to practice for the sake of practicing them; these editing skills help you capitalize on the exciting affordances of the aural mode, all those unique things you can communicate and express when using sound. So remember that editing audio is just as rhetorical as brainstorming, planning, recording, and downloading assets—it's another step toward helping you craft an immersive experience for your audience that achieves your purpose.

While we'll focus on editing moves in general, we know that in practice you'll be executing these moves in particular programs, all of which do things a bit differently. Our screenshots and the tutorials on our companion site focus on a particular audio editor called Audacity, an open-source audio editor that we like because it's free, powerful enough for most users and projects, popular in the classroom, and available on Mac, PC, and Linux. There are many other audio editors out there if you don't use Audacity: at the time of our writing, Macs come bundled with Garage-

Band (though it's unavailable on PC), subscribers to Adobe Creative Suite can install Audition, and there are plenty of other free and cheap alternatives, including some simple browser-based editors for those who don't want to install software. You can probably make a good decision on which one to use by simply searching for online articles that compare and contrast programs and playing around in different ones. Whatever program you choose, be sure to familiarize yourself with the program, whether that be reading any "getting started" manual or watching online tutorials.

Editing Basics

Most audio editing programs have a few basic features that will feel familiar to soundwriters who have practiced alphabetic writing in a word processor—things like selecting, copying, and pasting.

> **Learn More**
> See our companion website for animated gifs showing how to select, zoom, cut, paste, and more in Audacity.

- **Select**: Selecting is one of the most commonly used moves in an audio editor, since it's the first step in performing several other basic editing moves. Often, you'll have to click a "select tool" button first, allowing you to then click and hold your mouse button to drag a selection that is small or large (including perhaps an entire track or material on multiple tracks) before doing something else to that selection. Your editor probably also allows you to zoom in, enabling you to choose the exact right beginning and end of your selection; you may also be able to adjust the length of your selection to perfect it.
- **Copy**: If you choose to copy your selected audio, the same thing will happen when you copy in any program or app: the audio you selected will stay where it's at, but the computer will invisibly save a copy of the content you selected in its memory, ready for you to tell it where to paste it. Remember, you won't initially see anything happen when you copy; the computer will then be waiting for you to tell it where to paste it.
- **Cut**: Cutting is like copying, in that it allows you to put content somewhere else, but it's different in an important way: when you select content and choose "cut," the content will immediately disappear from its original place.
- **Paste**: After selecting content and then copying or cutting it, you'll then need to take a final step and put it somewhere! This "putting it somewhere" is called pasting. If you try to paste and nothing appears, you may not have copied or cut properly first.
- **Trim**: You might find that you don't need any of the material on your current track other than what you've selected. In that case, trimming allows you to select what you want and in one click, delete everything to the right and left of your selection.
- **Delete**: Of course, you might not want to trim or put the material you selected anywhere else—you might just want to delete it! Well, that's easy: select the audio you want gone, and hit the delete button on the keyboard.
- **Repeat**: Many programs will allow you to copy audio content and then paste it multiple times without needing to recopy. For instance, let's say that you want

a particular one-second sample from a song to repeat four times in a row. You can select the one second, copy it, click where you want to paste it, and then paste four times in a row.

- **Undo**: Be bold when editing! Anything that you do can instantly and easily be undone, just as in any other computer program! Look for an "undo" option and redo option in the menu. Many audio editors also include what's called "non-destructive editing," which allows you to easily reintroduce any audio that you trim while editing; search your editor's manual to see if this option is available to you!

5.1 Common Keyboard Shortcuts

The more you edit audio, the more you'll want to memorize keyboard shortcuts that save you the trouble of finding particular menu commands over and over. Search online for the name of your audio editor and the phrase *keyboard shortcuts* to find a more complete list; the ones provided below are just the basics. (Note that these are written with a PC audience in mind; Mac users should replace the CTRL key with the COMMAND key, which will usually be marked with a four-pointed cloverleaf icon.)

Shortcuts you'll use in many different programs:

- CTRL+A: Select all the material in the project (in some editors, across all the tracks)
- CTRL+C: Copy the content currently selected
- CTRL+X: Cut the content currently selected
- CTRL+V: Paste the copied or cut content at the place where you last clicked
- CTRL+Z: Undo your last action
- CTRL+Y: Redo an action you recently undid
- Spacebar: Play or pause audio
- CTRL+S: Save your project

Shortcuts that are especially useful in Audacity:

- CTRL+D: Duplicates the content currently selected on a new track
- CTRL+L: Silences the content currently selected
- CTRL+T: Trims the content currently selected, leaving what you selected and deleting all the content on either side of it
- CTRL+I: Splits the current clip into two clips at the place where you last clicked
- CTRL+B: Adds a label at the place where you last clicked
- CTRL+J: Selects all the material in the current track to the left of where you last clicked
- CTRL+K: Selects all the material in the current track to the right of where you last clicked
- CTRL+F: Fits the entire horizontal length of your project onto a single screen, so you won't need to scroll left and right to see everything

If you're new to audio editing, many of these basic editing moves make most sense in the context of an example. In chapter three, we asked you to imagine you were interviewing a bunch of college students complaining about cafeteria food for an audio documentary. Now say you're working on that project and have gathered all your assets—your interview, your narration, and the sound effects you plan to use. You decide you want to start the documentary with a 20-second clip from the interview recording, and you also want to start gathering the other clips that you'll probably end up using.

Here's how the basics we've described above might come into play as you work on this goal. First, you'll import your long, raw interview recording into your audio editor on a **track** of its own, and then you'll create a new track where you'll store and organize the various interview **clips** you actually want to use in your final audio documentary. You **label** the top track "raw interview" and the second track "interview clips" so you can easily identify their contents later. You **zoom** in on the raw interview track to identify the exact beginning and end of a section you want to use, **select** that portion of the track, **copy** it, and then **paste** it as a new clip on the interview clips track. Then you find another segment you want from the raw interview track, select and copy it, and paste it as another clip to the right of the previous clip. As you continue, you'll have a track filled with pre-selected clips that are ready to drag into place to align with your narration.

These kinds of basic moves will feel easier and easier the more you soundwrite!

Editing Voice

Often, we find ourselves cleaning up voice tracks before we do anything else. That's because voice recordings often have an inherent messiness to them: varied volume, false starts and retakes found between usable takes, pauses where you had to return a text, and so on. You can save yourself time later if you start your project by getting your voice tracks in good shape and then building sound effects and music around them. (This won't apply to all soundwriting projects, since you won't always use voice in the same way, if at all.)

Depending on what audio editor you use, you may need to do more or less voice editing manually to get the sound quality you're aiming for. For instance, a paid program like Adobe Audition or Hindenburg Pro comes packaged with presets designed to make your raw voice recording sound as good as possible for your podcast or other voice-heavy projects, while an open-access program like Audacity will require you to apply voice edits a bit more manually.

Noise Reduction

If your recording conditions weren't ideal, you might want to run a noise reduction effect over your entire voice recording before doing anything else. This can help reduce any steady, regular background noise, like a consistent fan blowing or refrigerator rumbling.

Learn More

See our companion site for a gif showing how to use the noise reduction feature.

Figure 5.6   A short vocal recording that was made in a noisy environment.

Check your audio editor's manual for noise reduction instructions, which some-times require two sequential steps: identifying the audio you want to reduce and then identifying the audio from which you want to subtract the noise.

However, use noise reduction sparingly and carefully. Some small noises are bet-ter left untouched, and sometimes noise reduction can change sound for the worse, adding an unnatural tinniness to your vocal tracks that is more noticeable than a bit of natural background noise. (Best, of course, is to get a clean recording without noise in the first place.)

Try-It   5.1 Noise Reduction

This activity invites you to practice using noise reduction in the audio editor with a messy sample recording. Once you clean up a practice recording, you'll know how it works when you're editing audio for your real projects. Try it for yourself following the steps below:

1. Make a "noisy" recording that has a regular sound in the background, like a fan that's blowing near the mic. Be sure that the recording has a few seconds of just the fan blowing without you talking.

2. Say or read something into the microphone while the noise is still going; any-thing will do. Shoot for at least 30 seconds.

3. Try reducing the noise using whatever technique your audio editor's online manual suggests. If you're using Audacity, use the two-step process of select-ing just the noise and then selecting everything you want to subtract that noise from, following the instructions in the Noise Reduction effect.

4. Play with the settings to hear what overly noise-reduced audio sounds like. Try to find the sweet spot where the noise is lessened without introducing any additional problems.

Compression

You might find that when you listen to your voice recordings, there will be moments when you're too loud or too quiet, like if you accidentally moved your head closer or further from the microphone, or if you got tired as your recording session dragged on. There are lots of ways to fiddle with volume in your projects; however, sometimes, you want to even out the volume over an entire selection or track, and that's when you need dynamic range compression.

The simplest way to understand compression is that it makes the quieter parts louder and the louder parts quieter, *compressing* the volume so that it's all a bit more even. "Dynamic range" is a fancy way of saying, "the distance between the loudest and quietest volume"—so a large dynamic range has very soft quiet moments that contrast with extremely loud moments, as in a classical symphony. This effect "compresses" that dynamic range, squishing it together, so listeners don't have to fiddle with the volume control as much while listening.

Figure 5.7   One track with dramatic volume variation and a copy of that track with those variations compressed.

You'll want to search online for the best settings to use for your compressor effect, which can have a scary amount of settings (all designed to help you get the effect you want without overdoing it).

5.2 Isn't Compression Bad?

In popular music recordings, dynamic range compression gets a bad rap, and for good reason. Popular music audiences tend to react positively toward whatever music sounds loudest, so audio engineers have found ways to squeeze as many changes in volume as possible out of musical recordings, so even parts of music that would be quieter live (perhaps when some instruments stop playing or when the singer quiets down) don't actually quiet down on the recording. This can lead both to artistic problems—with the natural drama of dynamic changes lost, which is especially a problem in classical music—and to quality problems. For instance, in a 2009 NPR piece, engineer Bob Ludwig bemoaned the sound of a compressed snare drum, which goes from sounding "sharp" to "more like somebody padding on a piece of leather or something like that" (Siegel).

But for beginners trying to clean up their voice recordings, dynamic range compression can be a life-saver—and at least to our ears, the quality rarely suffers in the way that Ludwig described. By highlighting a section of audio, we can immediately even out our volume in a way that will keep our listeners from needing to turn their volume dials up and down, all while making every word clearer (even those last words of sentences that are so likely to be said just a bit too quietly).

Try-It 5.2 Compression

This activity helps you learn more about compression in the audio editor so you have a better idea of what it does and how you might use it in your own soundwriting. Try it out by following the steps below:

1. To hear the effects of dynamic range compression, make a recording of your voice or someone else's that has uneven volume—perhaps with some whispering, some quiet talking, and some loud, projected talking. Try dropping the volume for entire sentences and for just a word or two here and there. You should be able to visually see that your recording is unevenly loud just by looking at the waveform, which will have HUGE MOUNTAINS and itty-bitty bumps.

2. Then apply your audio editor's compressor effect. If you don't like the results, undo it, play with the settings, and try again. Or, you can simply run the compressor effect over your audio multiple times, which will even volume out even further. Remember, you can find guidance online with suggestions about the settings if you don't understand them.

3. Now, appraise your newly compressed audio with your eyes and your ears. Does your waveform look more even? Does it sound more even? What parts did it successfully even out, and did it introduce any new problems?

Editing Out Vocal Mistakes

It's natural to find that your vocal recordings are messier than you'd hoped, filled with misreadings of the script, coughing, or dogs barking. That's okay; you'll rarely (if ever) have shareable audio from a single take of recording your voice. So give yourself a pep talk ("You can do this!") and a lot of time to edit the mistakes out of your raw vocal recording.

Here are some common steps you might find yourself taking as you clean up your audio recordings.

- **Back everything up before editing**: We like to save a high-quality file (usually a WAV file) of our raw vocal recordings exactly as they were before editing anything. Sometimes we even upload those raw recordings to the cloud. Just in case.
- **Beginnings and endings**: You'll probably find that you have lots of empty space to cut at the beginning and end of your recording, especially if you're like us and just leave the mic rolling through all of your better and worse takes. (Kyle has a weird habit of saying, "Let's do this!" loudly at the beginning of every project; he has to edit it out every time.) So a first step for editing might be to cut all that chatter.
- **Choose between takes**: If you took our advice in chapter four's Recording Your Own Voice section, you probably have a few sentences that you tried speaking more than once. Now that some time has passed since you originally recorded, you're in a good position to choose which delivery style sounds better in context; select the takes you don't want and delete them. (Remember, if you backed up your raw recording, or if you're using a non-destructive editor, you're never 100 per cent losing anything; be brave and cutthroat with your deleting!)
- **Pauses (adding and deleting)**: You want your voice tracks to sound as natural as possible, as if you just happen to speak perfectly clearly and brilliantly on your first try. That often means lots of cutting of those extra-long pauses between words or sentences (perhaps when you were scrolling your script down to the next page). Don't over-do it: if you cut too much space between a sentence, that can sound unnatural too, or it can take away the audience's need to pause and reflect on especially important sentences. Editing voice is about making a cut, relistening, relistening again, un-doing, trying the cut again, relistening, and relistening again before moving on. Use your eyes and your ears.

  > **Learn More**
  > See the Silence section in chapter three for practical advice about how to effectively use silence between sentences and sections.

- **Body sounds**: You might be surprised at how much of your body you hear in your raw recording: licking your lips, sighs, belly rumbling, burps. You'll want to edit the sounds that are distracting, but not all of them. After all, your listener knows that the voice they're hearing is from a live person with a real body.

Breaths are a good example: unless the breath is unnaturally loud or long, it's usually best to leave it in.

- **Fine-tuning**: You have the power to re-record mispronounced words, add names you forgot to mention, or repeat entire sentences that just don't sound right. But as we advised in chapter four, we find it's always better when we don't need to rerecord those details. Mess with the natural delivery of sentences at your peril; it's easy to change something in a way that sounds worse than the natural flub you were trying to fix.

Try-It 5.3 Cleaning Up a Reading

Try this activity to practice editing recordings so they sound like a natural, perfect first take (even though they weren't!).

1. Find a page or two from any book and read it aloud into your audio editor, or ask someone else to do so. When you make mistakes, just pause for a second, reread that entire sentence, and continue on.

2. Then edit out all the mistakes, redundancies, or parts of the recording that don't sound like a smooth, polished reading. Be sure to keep track of time! Note how long the original messy recording is, how long it took you to edit it, and how long the final, edited audio is. Try to get a sense of what your editing speed is—not because faster is better, but so you have a realistic idea of how much time to set aside for your soundwriting work.

For more advice, you might want to skim the advice online for readers at LibriVox, a site where volunteers read and distribute books that are in the public domain ("About Recording").

Layering Together Multiple Tracks

The previous section focused on editing voice clips—but many soundwriting projects will include much more than just voice! Whether you're working on the audio documentary about the cafeteria we discussed above or if you're putting together a new episode of your podcast, you'll often find yourself layering multiple tracks with narration, interviews, sound effects, and music. What kind of editing tricks will help you manage all that?

The advice in this section is focused on how to make sure your audio is heard *when* you want it, *at the volume* you want it. The next section will focus more on what kinds of effects you can add to change the actual sound of your different audio clips. You can find guidance on how to do the editing moves in Audacity in both the Tips sections in this chapter and on our companion website.

Cutting and Lining Everything Up

In many audio genres, you'll find yourself adding new audio tracks to your project one at a time, lining up and adjusting the new track, and then repeating with your next track. We know that not every project demands that kind of workflow, but that's the generic assumption we're working under in this section.

For instance, let's say that you've recorded the narration for a podcast episode and cleaned up that vocal recording, following our advice above; it's on a track labeled "Narration." But let's also assume that there's a piece of music that you want to play quietly under a certain section of your words, and when the music swells at an emotional moment, you want the narration to pause for a moment, letting the music do its work. How can you make that happen?

Import your audio. In many programs, you can simply drag an audio file (like your music asset) into your project window, automatically making it appear as a new track. If that doesn't work, look for an "import" option.

Move the new track to its rough position and do an initial trim. You probably have a basic idea of where you want your new musical clip to start—say, right when your narration starts to hint at the deeper emotional implications of the story. So start by dragging your music clip to the rough place where you think you'll want it to be, repeatedly testing how it sounds with the other tracks around it. Leave yourself open to surprise as you line it up; you might be shocked to find that a certain moment in the music matches the vocals better than you expected.

This is also when you can delete any extreme beginnings and endings to the new clip that you're sure you won't use—but be careful as you cut. It's easy to think, "Oh, I'm sure I won't need this long ending to the musical clip," only to find later that once you adjust other things in the project, you'll wish you had just a few more seconds of that music. Better to leave the clip longer than necessary at this point, especially if you're using a "destructive" audio editor that makes it harder to recover deleted selections.

If necessary, split and arrange other tracks to match the new track. For this podcast episode, you want your music track to "take over" for a few seconds, right? (See Figure 5.8 below for a preview of how this might look when you're done.) That means that you'll need to insert a new pause to your vocal clip that wasn't there before. To do so, find the spot on your "Narration" track where you want to add a pause and split the clip in two (following the instructions for your editor). Then you can drag the two clips to the right and left, adding time between them for the music to take over.

Once your tracks are lined up as perfectly as possible, it's time to make sure they can be heard in just the way you want.

Adjusting Volume

You can adjust the volume of an entire track or just particular moments in clips on that track. Here are a few basic suggestions for adjusting volume, but remember that your particular audio editor will probably have even more options. Let's continue to assume you're working with the same hypothetical podcast episode we discussed above.

Initial adjustments to the entire track. Let's assume that your narration track is the correct volume; you've compressed it and made it as loud as possible without any clipping. That means you want anything you layer with your vocal track to be perceived as quieter than that vocal track, allowing the voice to be clearly understood. (This is why we tend to start by editing our voice recordings first.) And that means that the most common first step is to make the music quieter, across the entire track, since it's very common for music to be initially so loud that you can't hear any layered voices at all. Look in your audio editor for tools that let you lower the volume of an entire track, clip, or selection.

Fading selections in and out. You'll also often find that there are at least two ways to fade a track's volume in or out: automatically or manually. When layering sounds, you'll often find yourself using various kinds of slow or quick fades, helping your audience's primary attention move to what you want them to notice most at any given moment. Many programs allow you to fade automatically or manually, with varying degrees of specificity:

- **Automatic fade**: The basic function of this effect is simple and expected: highlight a selection of audio, select the Fade In or Fade Out effect from your editor's menu (or in GarageBand, add a "volume point," before or after which everything will fade in or out), and the sound fades in or out. No big deal. But the more you use it, the more you'll find yourself using the effect in more subtle ways. For instance, the more audio you select (or the location of your GarageBand volume point), the longer your fade will take, so if you want a long, dramatic build-up of music before a climactic moment, just highlight a longer stretch of music before fading it in, and your sound will seem to grow and grow. Or you could layer one slow fade out over another track with a slow fade in, giving your listeners a pleasant, fuzzy, transition effect (as long as the two tracks sound good when blended that way). You can also fade very briefly at the beginning and end of clips, highlighting just a fraction of a second to "smooth out" entrances and exits that might otherwise sound abrupt. Play around!
- **Manual fade**: Many programs will allow you to "draw" the volume of a clip, letting you drag a clip's changing volume with your mouse, such as with Audacity's Envelope Tool or Audition's ability to draw linear, logarithmic, or cosine fades.

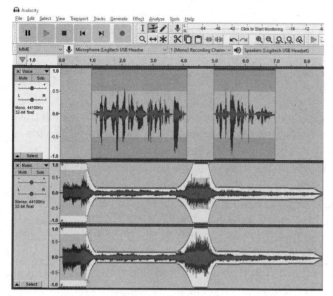

Figure 5.8   A vocal track layered with a music track that has had its volume manually adjusted with Audacity's Envelope Tool.

The podcast episode we've been discussing should now be in good shape if you've been following these tips! You aligned the music to sound at the right moments in relation to the narration, and then you adjusted the volume of the musical track in multiple ways: lowering all of it to make sure that the narration could always be heard above it, raising it when the voice wasn't speaking, and adding quick and slow fades to make volume changes feel natural.

5.3 Adjusting Volume in Audacity

All audio editors will give you multiple ways to adjust the perceived volume, since layering and mixing tracks is such a key component of any soundwriting. Here are a few ways to do so in Audacity, many of which have analogs in other editors. See our companion site to see animated gifs showing all of these volume adjustments applied in Audacity.

- **Lower the gain:** To the left of every track in Audacity, you'll see a slider with a minus and plus sign, which lets you adjust the "gain" of that track—a tricky, technical term that we won't get into here. In practical terms for beginners, lowering this slider won't change the look of the waveform on your track, but it will make that track sound perceivably quieter. (You don't want to *raise* the gain of a track, though, which will risk clipping, giving you a distorted sound.)

- **Use the Amplify effect**: Even though this effect is called "amplify," it can be used to *lower* the volume of a selection, too. Just select the audio you want to raise or lower, choose Amplify in the Effects menu, and in the Amplify menu drag the slider to the left to lower the volume and to the right to raise the volume of the selection. (Note that unless you check "allow clipping," you can't use this tool to make a selection so loud that it clips, or distorts.)

- **Use the Envelope Tool**: In an audio editor, an "envelope" is usually a line that represents some sort of change to the audio over time. Audacity's Envelope Tool allows you to draw lines ("envelopes") that affect the volume of a clip in precise ways, following the lines you draw. To use it, hit the F2 key or click the Envelope Tool button (in the set of five main tools), and then start clicking and dragging the waveform of your clip. Each click creates a pivot point, and subsequent clips let you drag the volume before and after those pivots up and down.

Try-It 5.4 Layering Multiple Tracks

This activity invites you to use various assets to practice layering tracks and creating different kinds of rhetorical effects, like using music to evoke emotion in a story. Try it out following the steps below:

1. Record your voice telling a story or ask someone else to do so. It's easiest to record straight into the audio editing program using a built-in microphone or one that's plugged into your computer, but you can record on another device and import the audio into your editor if you prefer. If you did Try-It 5.3, where you cleaned up a reading, that's the perfect audio to use for this one too! This exercise works best with a vocal track that is the loudest thing you hear, so try compressing your audio to even out the volume.

2. Find a spot where you want the music to swell and split the clip right at that spot, giving you two clips. Drag the right clip a bit to the right so you can visually see where the two clips split.

3. Import your music by dragging the file into the project or using your editor's import command.

4. Move the clip on your music track to the left and right to find a perfect moment that lines up with your split in the vocal track above it. If the time between the two vocal clips is too long or short, drag the clips to the left or right to adjust.

5. Decide when you want the music to start and stop playing beneath the vocal track. Should it be playing softly under most of the vocal track? Just a bit before and after? Try both and see which you like best. Trim the beginning and ending of the music clip to make it start and stop at the right time.

6. Adjust the volume of the music clip, perhaps by lowering the entire music track's volume, fading in and out, and making the volume swell to be louder when the speaking stops.

Adding Effects

The above skills in adjusting the length and volume of your tracks and clips are like the bread and butter of audio editing—but what about taking your project to the next level? Below are just a few of the effects that we've found ourselves using regularly, though every audio editing program will have different ones that work better or worse for your project. As always, use these effects rhetorically, with the needs of your audience in mind.

Equalizers

You may notice that a voice or other type of content sounds like it is too tinny, or too bassy, or just not as crisp and distinct as you'd like. To adjust the sound of your clip, emphasizing high, medium, or low parts of your recording, you can play around with equalization settings, often abbreviated to "EQ."

For the beginners reading this book, chances are that you'll only want to play with EQ on a surface level, without diving too deep into the many, many tricks you can pull off with various EQ settings. For instance, in "Real World EQ," radio producer Jeff Towne describes some of the many reasons soundwriters play with EQ. He points out that EQ adjustments can be used when your audio sounds "too bright," "too boomy," or "too dull or thin," but also that it can be used to remove "low rumble interfering with the intelligibility of your interview," "to pull a voice out of the murk," to "reduc[e] the effect of wind or plosive distortion from P-pops," to "reduc[e] tape-hiss or other high-frequency irritations," "to tame excessive sibilance" from lots of S sounds, to adjust "hums and buzzes," and to improve the sound of phone audio. Since this book is aimed at those new to soundwriting, we're not going to dive into that level of EQ adjustments, but you should know that advice on those things is only a web search away.

We tend to go simpler by starting with our audio editor's presets and going from there. We recommend you start by checking if your program has built-in ways to improve the sound of your voice or whatever other kind of audio asset you're working with—but we also know you might want to try adjusting things yourself, too. So use your editor's EQ presets, but go beyond them with manual adjustments, too! Eventually, you may find a setting you like that you can apply to your vocal recordings right away every time, helping you sound just a bit more the way you want to sound, like adding a filter to your photos on social media.

5.4 Adjusting EQ in Audacity

In the current version of Audacity, there are two different options that let you achieve similar EQ results: the Filter Curve effect and the Graphic EQ effect. They work like any other effect in Audacity: you highlight what you want to adjust (perhaps an entire track or multiple tracks, or perhaps just a short section), choose the effect from the Effects menu, preview what your changes will sound like before you commit to them, and then apply the effect (and perhaps undo what you did if you find you introduced a problem!). Both the Filter Curve and Graphic EQ effects have presets to give audio a "bass boost," "treble boost," or "low rolloff for speech," all of which can be helpful when editing your voice to give it a richness missing from raw recordings. But they also have fun effects like "AM radio," "telephone," and "walkie-talkie," all of which can be especially useful when you're producing radio dramas or other creative projects.

Our companion website features animated gifs showing both of these effects in action.

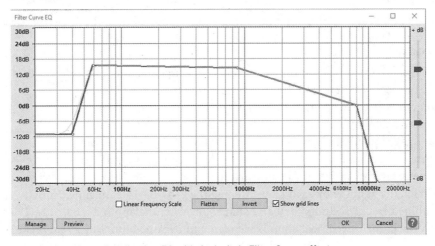

Figure 5.9 Manually adjusting EQ with Audacity's Filter Curve effect.

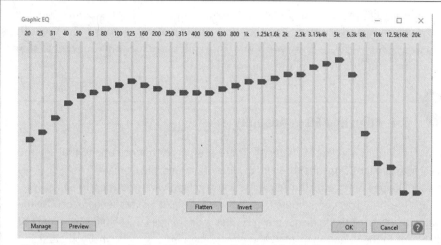

Figure 5.10   Manually adjusting EQ with Audacity's Graphic EQ effect.

Try manually dragging things in both of these EQ effects! The best way to learn is to adjust something, listen to what it did, adjust something different, listen again, and so on.

Reverb

Reverb effects digitally mimic the sound of recording in a different, reverberant space, adding a sense of largeness to your sound. The *Audacity Manual* says Reverb gives an "impression of ambience" ("Reverb").

The main reason we use the Reverb effect is to make a conversation, musical instrument, or singing voice sound like it's in a bigger room, thus smoothing out the harsh edges. Or you can use Reverb to more subtly affect a clip by adding a bit of warmth to a voice that was recorded in a very dry environment or even to change the nature of a sound effect you downloaded or recorded yourself. For instance, Kyle was once layering individual recordings of a symphonic Beethoven piece as recorded individually at home by each player during the COVID-19 pandemic. Initially, the combined tracks sounded dry and sharp, but when he applied a bit of reverb to each track, the instrument sounds blended and became more like a real orchestra playing in a room together. As always, play around with your settings and consider your rhetorical situation.

> **Learn More**
>
> See our companion site for a link to a video Kyle made showing you some of the tricky things to keep in mind when applying Reverb and Echo in Audacity.

Speed, Pitch, and Tempo

In many soundwriting projects, you won't adjust the speed of any of your clips; after all, a podcast that assembles narration, interview, and music is generally more about layering, cutting, and adjusting volume than making any part speed up or down. But we can also imagine other times when adjusting the speed of a clip might fit your rhetorical goals, like if you're editing sound effects for a particular emotional response (e.g., making them eerier or awe-inducing), adjusting music to make it feel more languid or frantic, or disguising someone's voice.

The fun thing about editing the speed of audio digitally is that you're not constrained by what would happen if you slowed down or sped up audio using physical media, like when you spin a vinyl record at the wrong speed or play magnetic tape slowly or quickly through a cassette player. With that physical media, when audio plays slower, two things happen: it takes longer to play, and the pitch is lowered proportionally to how slow you're playing it. Speeding up recordings on physical media makes it play faster and sound higher. But with digital audio, you're not necessarily held to that physical reality.

5.5 Adjusting Speed in Audacity

To adjust the speed of clips in Audacity, look for effects called Change Speed, Change Pitch, and Change Tempo:

- **Change Speed** affects your highlighted audio in the same way physical media works: you can make your selection play a percentage faster or slower, and the sound is also pitched higher or lower.
- **Change Pitch** affects your highlighted audio by making it sound higher or lower, even though it still takes the same amount of time to play—so you could make a singer sound like a chipmunk without changing the length of the song. However, you can only adjust pitch so much before you introduce noticeable problems, so use this effect sparingly.
- **Change Tempo** affects your highlighted audio by changing the amount of time it takes to play but without affecting its pitch. This can be useful when you want a clip of any kind to take an exact amount of time—but like Change Pitch, it can introduce distortion if used extremely.

You can get used to these effects easily by playing around with recorded music. Import an MP3 or M4A into Audacity and see what happens when you play around with the speed of the clips in different ways.

Try-It 5.5 **Effects**

This activity encourages you to play around with various effects for the purpose of recognizing their rhetorical functions. Here's how to do it:

1. Record yourself or someone else reading a brief passage from any source—just two or three sentences is best. If necessary, clean it up: trim empty audio from the beginning and ending and/or compress the audio. Or, ask someone to record a couple of sentences for you, or grab audio from an online source.

2. Add a new track to your project, copy the clip containing your original recording, and paste your new recording to the new track. Paste it so it will play after the original track finishes; for example, if the original is 10 seconds long, paste a copy of it at the 10-second mark.

3. Add any effect you want to the new track! You could play with the EQ settings, add reverb or echo, change its speed or pitch or tempo, or add any other effect that your audio editor allows you to add! If your audio editor allows you to name your tracks, rename your new track as a record of what effect you used.

4. Add a new track, copy the original again, and repeat with a different effect. Eventually, you'll have a recording where you can hear your initial recording changed in multiple ways, with every change labeled clearly so you can remember later what you did!

REVISING

Jessica Abel's book *Out on the Wire* emphasizes how much time the best radio shows and podcasts spend revising. (See Figure 5.11.)

It's comforting to recognize how much time soundwriters spend perfecting the shows you hear on the radio and on their podcast feeds. It means you can trust that what you hear—the phrasings, the music, the interview clips—were chosen collectively by a smart group of professionals who worked tirelessly to give us all the best audio possible.

Think about that dynamic between creator and audience: when audiences know that they're hearing soundwriters' best work honed through multiple drafts, they're assured that what they're hearing is worth spending time on. Revised audio eases the fears of audiences who don't want to waste their time. Revised audio comforts.

This section suggests ways you can help comfort yourself and your audience through careful revision of your soundwriting projects. We're assuming that at this point you have a draft of real audio to listen to, even if it's rough; we're not discussing revisions to a words-only script or plan, though we do have some guidance for

Figure 5.11
Discussing a story on the show *Snap Judgment* (Abel 192).

revising scriptwriting in chapter four. We suggest how to get good feedback from others, how to revise your own work when alone, and how to use your audio editor to make those changes easy and manageable.

Peer Review

You can probably already guess what the scariest—but also the most effective—way of revising is: play your draft for a group of people who will be honest with you.

In some ways, we want to just leave our advice at that: play actual audio (not just a script) for a group of people (since a group gives them the opportunity to talk to each other as they build their response) who will be honest with you. Almost any spin-off of that formula can lead to magic. They'll help you hear your work with new ears. Our students have told us that in-class soundwriting peer review has been one of the main motivators to push them to improve their projects.

Don't forget the deeper, rhetorical purpose of peer review: since rhetorically effective audio is audio that works for real audiences, you can only really know if you're achieving your purpose if you test it out on real audiences. Those audiences don't have to be experts on your project's subject matter (unless you're creating it for an audience of experts); they just have to be smart, kind, and willing to creatively brainstorm ways to make your work better than ever.

Of course, there are also a few ways to help make a peer review session go better:

- **Choose people who know your genre**: If you're blending sound effects and quick interview clips to simplify a complicated subject in a style inspired by the show *Radiolab*, find people who listen to *Radiolab*. If you're working on a piece of audio art for a gallery installation, find artists or museum curators.
- **Prep your focus group some, but not too much**: Before clicking play, tell your group about the purpose of your audio project—what you're hoping to achieve in this piece—but don't give them a play-by-play of every choice you made until they've had a chance to listen and respond. You want to know if they think you achieved your purpose, but sometimes too much prep can distract them from that key question.
- **Get feedback both out loud and in writing**: Sharing feedback out loud helps feedback be rich and complex, with all the affordances of conversation: communicating tone, facial expressions, body language, and unfinished thinking that can be bounced off by others in the group. But sharing feedback in writing lets you return to it later and honors those who process information better alone. So give your group chances for both, perhaps by asking them to write responses to certain questions as they listen, then giving them a chance to revise those notes into fuller overall comments, and then asking them to explain what they wrote to you. (See Tips 5.6 and 5.7 below for more detailed instructions for reviewers.)
- **Have a script ready (if you have one) so you can revise out loud together**: If someone says, "Toward the beginning, I thought there was a line that seemed awkward, but I didn't write it down," you want to be able to pull up your script and say, "Oh, was it when I said this?" Then together, you can try to figure out what didn't work; perhaps there's a bulky sentence that could be said more naturally or a long sentence that could be revised to let you breathe better.

These instructions of course are biased toward having a live group of people in the room to talk about your draft, but we know that that's not always feasible. But even if it's impossible, you can still try creative ways to get at least *some* feedback from others before publishing your work or submitting it to a reviewer. For instance, you might ask friends on social media if they want to give feedback, and then you could share a file and written instructions with anyone who volunteers. Or you could set up a virtual peer review session, since many video-chat programs allow you to share the system audio from your computer directly with others on the call. Or maybe you have a former teacher who could help you out, or a friend from class or your job, or a writing center on your campus; most people will feel flattered that you asked them and will try to do their best to give you advice.

5.6 Overall Tips for Peer Reviewers

Often, a peer review group will go best if you give the reviewers some guidance on what kinds of feedback will help best. Here's some draft language that you can modify and hand out to those in your group.

- **Always praise *and* critique**: Be brave enough to search hard for what's working best in this audio but also for what's working *least* well. And feel free to explain when something is messily in the middle, perhaps with phrases like, "I like how this section _____, but I was a little rattled when it suddenly shifted to _____."
- **Ask specific questions**: One of the best ways to critique is by asking the soundwriter to explain their choices. You might ask questions to soften a harsh blow (e.g., "Can you tell me why you started with that sentence?" rather than, "I hate the beginning"), but you also might ask them simply because you want the soundwriter to think about that idea (e.g., "Do sections one and two feel sufficiently connected to you? Did you consider adding a more explicit transition?"). Ask questions about big-picture issues like topic and organization but also about small editing fixes like phrasings, uneven volume, or awkward pauses.
- **Always add a "because"**: Your praises and critiques should never leave the soundwriter wondering what you had in mind, so always explain the reason for your point. Never just say, "I loved it"; say, "I loved it because _____."

5.7 Specific Questions for a Peer Review Session

Learn More

See a printable version of these peer review guidelines on our companion site.

- **Ideas and Focus**
  - Is the main point or idea clear?
  - Does the piece seem to stray from what its original purpose seemed to be? If so, does that change of focus seem purposeful and effective, or distracting and accidental?
  - Is every segment here necessary to help achieve the purpose?
  - Are there any gaps that could be filled or transitions that could be eased with a new segment?
  - Will the project's primary audience get what they need? When actual audiences hear this who aren't the primary audience, are they likely to react well or poorly to any particular segments?
- **Organization**
  - How effective is the first sentence? The last sentence?

- Are transitions clear and effective? Did you ever wonder "where you were" in the project?
- If the project uses music, does it help organize different parts of the project into distinct sections?

- **Imagery**
  - Can listeners "see" the scenes you describe?
  - Are there any places where a field recording or downloaded sound would help listeners envision the setting?

- **Nonverbal Audio**
  - Is the music just right? Does it draw too much or too little attention to itself?
  - Were any alternative musical pieces considered that we could hear and compare to what made it into this draft?
  - Are there too many or too few non-musical sound effects? If you're not sure, how do other pieces in this genre use them?

- **Editing**
  - Are voices always clear and easy to understand?
  - Is there any awkward background noise that could be edited out?
  - Is anything too loud or too quiet in relation to other parts of the project, like music that drowns out speaking?
  - Is the overall project too quiet? How loud is it compared to other audio or music you play on the same device without adjusting the volume?
  - Are there any unexpectedly sudden aspects, like music clips that could be faded in more smoothly or sentences that start or stop too close to what comes before or after?
  - Are pauses and silence used purposefully, with neither too many nor too few?

Self Review

The suggestions above are all designed to give you real feedback from real people, but we get it: sometimes you're working close to a deadline or your friends are all unavailable. The following tips can help you hear your work in fresh ways to spur revision, even when no one else is available.

- **Take a break**: You've probably heard this tip before when talking about writing text, but it works for soundwriting, too: always let your work rest at least overnight before submitting or publishing it. Fresh ears help you notice those weird pauses, those strange dynamic jumps, that embarrassingly bad background music, that lousy joke.
- **Listen through different speakers**: If you've been soundwriting through a particular set of speakers—maybe your earbuds, or your laptop speakers, or your

best professional gear—don't send out your work before listening on other speakers first. You've probably got lots of options: try different styles of headphones (even if you have to borrow them), different kinds of computer speakers (even if you have to use a friend's set-up), and different locations. Don't forget to listen in your car, on the cheap Bluetooth speaker you keep in the kitchen for washing dishes, or with your phone propped up in a cup, especially if you think that's where your listeners might listen.

- **Know your quirks**: If you've done any soundwriting before, you probably know a few things about yourself. Maybe your transitions are too quick, or your voice recordings have too much volume variation, or you use too many cheesy effects, or you *sound like you're reading* when you read scripts, or you tend toward wordiness. If possible, listen to previous soundwriting you've done, note the problems you don't want to repeat this time, and then revise your new project with that list in front of you.
- **Listen from an audience-based perspective**: Imagine that you're someone else hearing this piece for the first time—ideally, someone who will encounter this work wherever it's eventually going to live (on the radio, on a particular publication's website, on your SoundCloud, in your professor's grading queue). As you listen, make notes about what that person might need to know and how they might feel.

Revising in Your Audio Editor

We know that the prospect of revising digital audio can have a steeper learning curve than simply revising text in a word processor, especially when your project has multiple tracks that could be easily misaligned. Still, we promise that this fear will get easier to handle with practice (even if it never goes away)—and revising is worth it!

Revising is different in every program, but here are a few basic suggestions on using your software that might guide you in the right direction when you need to make a change, big or small.

- **Don't misalign everything**: It's easy to delete a piece of audio, forgetting that your deletion affects the timing of everything else later in the project. This is especially a problem in Audacity, where the default behavior when you delete is to shift everything in a clip to the left (earlier in time) to fill in the space you just deleted—which might mean your perfectly aligned music later on is now off by a few seconds!
- **Zoom in and out often**: We recommend regularly zooming in to do detailed revision work and then regularly zooming out to see the entire project. If you have multiple tracks lined up, it's possible that you'll instantly be able to see when things are aligned well.

> **Learn More**
>
> See our companion site for tricks that will help you avoid misaligning everything in Audacity, using tools like the Silence button, the Split Delete command, and the Sync-Lock option.

- **Make changes of the exact same length**: When replacing a clip of audio, it can sometimes save you trouble if you replace that clip with new audio of the exact same length. For instance, let's say you mispronounced a single word in a project that's *practically done* and you want to replace just that word without messing anything else up. If that happens, highlight just that word, making a note of exactly how long it is. Then rerecord a replacement word in a new project file, trim it to be the exact length as what you need to replace, and edit it back into your main project.
- **Replicate your original recording conditions**: It makes us sad to say this, but it's true: as we mentioned in the Recording Your Own Voice section of chapter four, if you're rerecording even a very short bit of narration, it'll usually sound noticeable if you rerecord in a different place or using a different microphone. Trust us; we've tried to record quick redos on our laptop mics or Zoom headsets from our offices or wherever we happened to be sitting. But if we originally recorded using our Blue Yeti in our walk-in closet, the best way to revise is to record with the same Blue Yeti in the same walk-in closet. Sorry.

EXPORTING

A common mistake that beginning soundwriters often make is to mix up two commands in their audio editor: saving and exporting. Here's the super-simple overview:

- **Save** when you want to return later to a snapshot of your audio editing progress at that moment in time, with your ability to edit tracks and clips intact. Save to a file type used by your audio editor alone, like AUP in Audacity, SESX in Audition, and BAND in GarageBand.
- **Export** when you want to share drafts or final versions of your audio with anyone else. Export to a filetype that others can listen to, like WAV or MP3. This "locks in" the edits you've made to your file, creating a file whose individual tracks and clips can no longer be individually edited.

> **Learn More**
> Learn more about common file formats in Tip 4.5.

The mistake people sometimes make is to save and then try to email or share their project file (AUP or SESX or BAND) with someone else, even though those project files are only needed by anyone who is actually going to edit the audio, not by someone listening to it. This is actually a common problem for beginners working in many image, audio, and video editing programs; it's always a good idea to get used to what file extensions are used for the project file you save to while editing and for the shareable file you export to when finished.

In practice, this can complicate your life if you're trying to work on an audio project on multiple computers or collaborate on an editing job, since the project files you save might be very large and associated with a number of other smaller files in folders that need to be shared along with the project files. That means that if you're trying to get a project file from one computer to another, you'll want to read the audio editor's manual first for the most up-to-date advice.

TRANSCRIBING

Chapter four discussed tips for writing a script, which we define as the written document you prepare as part of the plan for your soundwriting, usually with words that you plan to read verbatim.

But we distinguish a script from a *transcript*, which is the document you prepare to accompany your final, shared work. A transcript allows your audience to experience your work through the linguistic and visual modes. This might be especially important for d/Deaf and hard-of-hearing individuals or for those who are more familiar with consuming information via words than audio, perhaps because of cognitive differences in the way their brains process information or perhaps just because they'd rather read words in a given time and place. A transcript can also help listeners and researchers search your work by searching for specific words (something that is still frustratingly hard in most audio interfaces), and it allows you to give careful, specific credit to all your sources and assets. In short, transcripts are not just helpful, they're crucial and equitable.

You might ask, "But isn't my script the same as my transcript? I already wrote out what I was going to say before I started recording!" We would say that the two are often closely related, but they're not the same. Remember, a script comes before the soundwriting happens and the transcript comes after, and a lot can happen in that time. Maybe you changed lines as you read them or added new segments that you never planned for. Plus, the script probably doesn't include as much description of all the audio that eventually made its way into the project. For instance, our scripts often include vague lines like, "Add music here," but the transcript will describe the mood of the music, quote its lyrics, and cite it in a way that's appropriate for its context. That's because transcripts give readers as full an experience as possible through words alone. The transcript, then, might *start* by copying the old script into a new file, but it's then perfected by double-checking the words that are heard and by describing the sounds that are heard. Some transcripts go even further by adding detailed time-stamps, explaining various stereo effects, or using creative visuals to help readers get the full experience of the audio project.

Here's an example from the transcript to a piece that Kyle composed called "Listening like a Fan," which was a hybrid personal/academic essay, in sonic form. You can hear it at an online journal called *Technoculture* (Stedman).

Narrator: [male voice, speaking in a friendly, casual voice] So maybe you've heard of the series of videogames called Final Fantasy. So most versions of Final Fantasy games include this melody that's called "The Prelude." So on the original Nintendo—you know, like the NES from the 80s?—it sounds like this.

[Music: ascending arpeggios on an obviously low-fi, old-school videogame system (Uematsu)]

Ok, whatever, right? But here's a clip from Camille Saint-Saëns' Piano Trio No. 1 in F Major, which was composed way back in the 1860s:

[Music: a strikingly similar ascending arpeggio played on a piano with an orchestra behind it (Saint-Saëns)]

Do you hear that connection?

…

Works Cited

Saint-Saëns, Camille. *Piano Trio No. 1 in F Major*, Op. 18. Performance by Joachim Trio, Naxos Records, 1995.

Uematsu, Nobuo. "The Prelude." *Final Fantasy*, 1987, www.vgmpf.com/Wiki/index.php/The_Prelude.

> **Learn More**
>
> We know labeling a voice as "male" or "female" can replicate problematic stereotypes, so if Kyle were publishing this today he would have used another term—perhaps "voice toward the deeper end, but not too deep" or "tenor voice."

Just looking at the excerpts from this transcript, you can see a few choices Kyle made that could also guide your own transcript-writing:

1. **Describe the experience of the sound**. That includes letting readers know that the narrator (Kyle) is "speaking in a friendly, casual voice." Describing the experience of the sound also includes the sound of the music—not just by writing "music," as some incomplete transcripts do, but by actually describing its instrumentation and effect. In more recent transcripts, Kyle has started describing

music as being in a major or minor key and by adding how fast or slow it is. If you do not have the musical vocabulary to identify the instrument or key, focus your energy on describing its effect and mood.

2. **Adjust your transcript to match what is actually said in the final project**. For instance, you might have noticed that the first three sentences of this transcript all begin with the word *so*, which wasn't in the original script. Yet when Kyle prepared the transcript and checked the script against the recording, he found that he had inadvertently added those *so*'s into the recording; they had felt natural in the moment when recording. Since they were in the audio, they had to go into the transcript, too.

3. **Cite in a way that's appropriate for your context**. This publication required formal citations in MLA style, which are peppered throughout the transcript in parentheses (even though they weren't said aloud). This helps a listener who hears a sound or a quotation and thinks, "Ooh, I want to learn more about that! I hope the transcript tells me where it came from!" Notice too that the citations are formal whether they're for music, sound effects, or a written quote; academic citation styles are flexible enough to allow you to cite all of those types of assets. If this piece were published on a podcast, MLA citations would have seemed overboard, so the sources would have been listed or linked more informally.

5.8 Transcribing Tips

There's a lot of advice available for those who are dedicated to creating soundwriting projects with accessibility in mind! Here are just a few of the many resources you could check out, all from scholars of rhetoric:

- Dev K. Bose, Sean Zdenek, Prairie Markussen, Heidi Wallace, and Angelia Giannone, "Sound and Access: Attuned to Disability in the Writing Classroom": Includes a great overview of why soundwriters should keep disability in mind and offers instructors ideas for teaching students about transcripts.
- Leah Heilig, "Transcription as Play," found on pp. 79–81 of "3,000 Podcasts a Year: Teaching and Administering New Media Composition in a First-Year Writing Program" (Faris): An instructor describes playful ways to use fonts and color to shape meaning in audio transcripts.
- Sean Zdenek, "Designing Captions: Disruptive Experiments with Typography, Color, Icons, and Effects": Argues for "enhanced captions" that creatively go beyond what we typically think of as captions.
- Mariana Grohowski, "Transcribe.wreally: Methods for Digital Transcription of Audio": A brief, practical article about using a specific transcript tool.

> • Sean Zdenek, "Accessible Podcasting: College Students on the Margins in the New Media Classroom": An argument claiming that "Accessibility is virtually invisible as a topic in mainstream podcasting discourse," along with advice about how to make podcasts more accessible through transcripts.

SHARING YOUR WORK

Here's a fear we have: that you'll take the advice throughout this book, create amazing soundwriting, and then leave your work in a lonely, unloved file on your computer, never to be heard outside of your own earbuds. Your work deserves to be heard by others! This applies even if you're just a beginner playing around for the first time—actually, it applies *especially* if you're a beginner, since sharing work for audiences is perhaps the best way to improve and to get the motivation to keep creating more and more.

We've also felt the allure of how sharing a little leads to the desire to share more. When Kyle published his earliest audio work in 2011 and his first podcast in 2014, for example, the positive responses from friends and other scholars motivated him to want to share more—and that encouragement led him to keep trying and improving his craft.

But still, the question remains: Where and how should we share our audio? In some ways, the answer is similar to the question of where and how to share your alphabetic writing: by submitting to a publication or by publishing it yourself. We'll share a few ideas below on both of those solutions.

Submitting to the Radio

We admit it: it's often difficult for novice soundwriters to get their work published on the radio. Most often, radio stations employ their own audio producers or elicit freelance work from experienced producers. While that may be the case, there are indeed radio stations that may be willing to publish your audio stories and documentaries.

There are two ways you could try to publish your work. The first way is to search online for radio stations that accept freelance audio projects. Most of the time, radio stations will want you to send a story pitch rather than a fully produced project because many producers like to contribute to the production of the piece. So you'll want to find the proper contact person and email them your pitch. If they are interested, they will ask you to move forward in producing your work (likely with their guidance).

> **Learn More**
> See Pitching Your Idea in chapter four for advice on writing a pitch.

The more likely way to get your soundwriting played on the radio is to upload it to the Public Radio Exchange (PRX), an audio marketplace where radio stations and podcast creators search to find work to play on their programs. The marketplace houses hundreds of stories and podcast episodes from people with varying levels of experience, from novice soundwriters to established radio producers. The downside is that you'll need to pay for a membership and create an account. The upside is that established producers and radio stations or programs might ask to buy or play (if you don't charge a fee) your work. Since Tanya uploads all her work to PRX, she has benefited from the upside, as several of her pieces have been broadcasted on the radio, both on programs (PRX Remix) and at stations across the country. And while there's no guarantee your project will garner interest on PRX, it will at least have a public place to live on the internet. That means more people will be able to access and listen to it.

Submitting to Literary and Artistic Magazines and Contests

An increasing number of online publication venues are eager to publish exciting and innovative audio work—often including styles and genres that wouldn't fit on the radio.

In the literary publishing world, these venues often (but not always) simply publish audio versions of pieces you might find in printed literary magazines that publish creative nonfiction, fiction, and poetry, without extra music or sound effects added. For instance, *The Drum* literary magazine exclusively publishes audio, but if your story is accepted, listeners will only hear your voice, not any other soundwriting tricks. Other publications open the door wider; for instance, the respected literary journal *The Missouri Review* hosts an annual audio contest called The Miller Audio Prize, which invites anyone to submit soundwriting in the genres of poetry, prose, humor, and audio documentary.

The list of available venues is constantly changing, so it's important to do your own internet searching for the best venues, perhaps by searching the excellent list of literary magazines at the *Poets & Writers* website ("Literary Magazines") for the word *audio*, or by noting where work was originally published that ended up being showcased on the Third Coast International Audio Festival's podcast *Re:sound* or on one of the many review episodes of Rob Rosenthal's *HowSound*. Or, you could simply search online for something like *audio publication venues*.

Sharing on Your Own Social Media Pages

Maybe all this talk of submitting to professional places is scary and you feel like it's out of your league. You might be wondering, "Aren't there other ways to share my work that are less ... official?"

Of course—that's what social media is for! Just keep in mind that if your eventual goal is to publish your work on a radio show or in a literary magazine, those venues might only consider work that has never been shared online previously, though every publication is different. For instance, when Kyle completed "Pincushion," he originally published it to his own SoundCloud account and shared links to it on Facebook and Twitter. Then, when it was accepted by *Memoir Magazine* (which explicitly allowed him to submit work that had been previously published), he took it down from SoundCloud.

But if you're sure you want to share, how can you share well? Here's our advice:

- **Post it on a single site**. If your piece takes off, you want there to be a single link where people can find it like SoundCloud, YouTube, or PRX. Plus, you might want to track the number of listens it gets, which is easier on a single site. Use other sites to link to that one online home.
- **Use metadata wisely**. Even though the web is full of multimedia material, we all know that searches are primarily text-based. That means you should make sure your post is full of text as well. If the site you're posting at allows you to post a description and tags, use that space well. Think broadly about any word or idea your piece might be associated with, predicting the sorts of things people might search for.
- **Send people to listen to it**. Obviously, you'll tell your family and friends to check out your new audio piece, when appropriate. But be strategic, too: look for online groups, discussion boards, and similar social media accounts that seem to welcome links from people like you. Don't be creepy, but do try to get online conversations going about your work. Often, people will appreciate discovering that you've created the thing they've been looking for all along.

Podcasting

Figure 5.12
Make your own podcast to feature your soundwriting.

Some of you might be reading this book because you want to start a podcast—and no wonder, since podcasts are huge. Market research firm Statista reports that the 88 million podcast listeners in 2019 will nearly double to 160 million by 2023 (Watson). That's a lot of listeners and a lot of podcasts!

Quick reminder: podcasts, as we mentioned briefly in chapter one, are shows that are *episodic*—audio that is released as episodes that are part of a larger show, as opposed to soundwriting that can stand alone like an audio essay, a radio feature, or an art installation.

However, giving general podcast advice is difficult, especially since this book focuses so much on making decisions that match your rhetorical situation. Think about it: we could give you lots of specific advice in this section about how to design your sound-writing just right for a podcast, like how to use complex layers of music, vocals, and sound effects throughout. But you might find that for your purpose and audience, an unscripted, unedited style is more appropriate. (But hey, if that's you, you should still transcribe your episodes to make them accessible!) It all comes down to our point from chapter one: the effectiveness of any piece of communication depends on how well it achieves its purpose with its audience.

Where does that leave us in this section, then? Well, there are still a few things we can share about the basics of hosting and sharing podcasts, but again, we're worried: that advice will age really quickly. So with a warning that you'll want to look up the newest information on podcasts before making your own, here are a few basics:

> **Learn More**
>
> Learn about podcast genre conventions at the end of interlude C, where Kyle writes about composing a podcast episode.

1. **Choose a host** by comparing the current options (and deciding if you want to pay anything). These days your host might be Anchor, Libsyn, PodBean, Sound-Cloud, or any number of other options. Some will be completely free, some will give you extra options for a small fee, and some require payment up front—often with added features that might be important for your show.

2. **Create an account** at one of those sites and follow the steps they require to set up the details for your show.

3. **Record a short trailer** for your show, explaining to listeners what they'll hear when your regular episodes start releasing. This has two benefits: it lets you start a buzz early, ensuring people will listen when your full episodes come out, and it makes the distribution step described below go more smoothly. Create your trailer using all the soundwriting tips we've given throughout the book, export your audio to a shareable file format like a high-quality MP3, and upload it to your hosting site. When you upload, you'll be given options to give the trailer a title and description (sometimes called "show notes") and perhaps other options (like season and episode numbers, and a way to mark whether you use explicit language).

4. **Distribute your show**. Most people listen to podcasts in apps that are designed to pull lists of recent episodes from hosting sites, saving the listeners the trouble of going to all their favorite shows' websites to download episodes one at a time. Your hosting site knows this, so it will have automatic or manual options to get your show listed in various apps and online directories (like the powerful Apple Podcasts and other directories like Stitcher, Spotify, Google Podcasts, and

more). If your host will automatically distribute your podcast, simply direct it to list your show in whatever places it has an agreement with—a process that goes smoother if you have a trailer already posted, since some distributors want to make sure your podcast has actual content up before adding it to their lists. But you may have to follow your host's instructions for manually distributing your show, which consists of copying a line of code (called a "feed") from your host and sharing that feed one at a time at the most popular distributors, all of which will walk you through the steps at their site.

5. **Set up your web presence**, if you want. Hosting sites will often offer simple, bare-bones sites that listeners can visit to hear your shows or link to in a web browser, but many podcasters choose to create their own websites that feature more engaging content, like extras, an about page, images, and so on. Whether you make a flashier site is up to you and your rhetorical purpose. If you design a site, look for a template that's designed for podcasts, which will ensure that when you release a new episode, you can easily embed the audio from your host and add whatever extras you want.

6. **Record new episodes** regularly, if possible, posting them to your host the same way you posted your trailer. Once your distribution is set up, you won't have to do anything but post new audio to your host; once it's there, new episodes will magically appear in your audience's apps soon after they are released! Aim for a regular schedule, rather than releasing episodes whenever you feel like it. Be sure your show notes for each episode include basic information that someone might search for, citations for any sources or assets you used, thanks to anyone that helped you produce the show, and a link to a full, rich transcript so it's accessible to everyone.

Conclusion: What's Next?

It's hard to end a book like this. After all, we hope that the soundwriting you've practiced through these tips and exercises is just the beginning of your journey recording and editing audio. And the book isn't really designed to just be read through once, front to back; once you hit the end, we expect you'll still page back and forth to jot new notes and try exercises you skipped.

Still, we have some ideas on what we hope you might take away from this book:

- **New habits of mind**: Your soundwriting—and any other composing you do, in and out of class—will be marked by a new courage, willingness to play, and thoughtful reflection.
- **New avenues for listening**: You'll dive deeper into podcasts more fully than before, exploring genres you hadn't considered and looking for shows with rich transcripts. You may even start listening to more public radio, audiobooks, and other genres of soundwriting.

- **New, rhetorical ways of listening**: Grounded with new understandings of rhetoric and listening like a soundwriter, you'll notice the specific choices soundwriters make as they use their genre to affect their audience in their particular context.
- **New cross-genre models for composing**: The steps you practiced here will affect the writing and making you do in other contexts, helping you move through rich exercises for brainstorming, drafting, revising, and sharing in everything you do.
- **New directions for your academic interests**: Sound studies is a multidisciplinary academic field; we bet some of you will start digging into the ways sound is part of the scholarly world of your major or intended career. Or if you're planning to learn more about the disciplines of rhetoric and writing, we hope you'll use the citations throughout this book as a starting place to better understand the growing, booming, danceable world of studies in sonic rhetoric. Look up some of the articles and chapters we mention (especially the ones that are online and include audio clips), and then look up the citations in *their* work, and so on.

Key Chapter Takeaways

- Whatever audio editing program you use, be sure to get to know its basic layout, features, and terminology including how it organizes tracks and clips.
- When working on a multitrack soundwriting project, a common order of work is to clean up and maximize the volume of your narration and then layer other tracks of music and sound effects. Be attentive to *when* the tracks play and *how loud* they play; this kind of attention will ensure your audio sounds the way you want it to.
- Revising soundwriting will undoubtedly make your soundwriting better. Find a peer review group and provide them with guidance on how to give you productive feedback. You can also give yourself feedback by imagining how your audience might engage with your soundwriting and by listening in different places to your soundwriting through different speakers. Don't be afraid to make changes.
- You can share your soundwriting on the radio, online, or on a podcast. Acquaint yourself with various places you might submit your work as well as their submission guidelines. Always prepare a transcript for any soundwriting you plan to share.

Discussion Questions

1. What audio editors do you have experience with, if any? Try searching the web for advice on the best programs to help you compare and contrast features. Be sure to search for both free and paid programs and for programs you install on a computer versus services you can use in a web browser. If you like editing on a phone or tablet, search for those programs too. Which look promising, and why?

2. When you're editing audio, which parts of the process feel similar to writing and editing words on the page or screen? Which parts feel completely unlike writing with words?

3. What barriers can you imagine or have you faced when it comes to sharing your soundwriting with others for feedback? What have your previous experiences been when it comes to getting feedback on any of your work, whether created for school, a job, or for your own enjoyment?

Works Cited

Abel, Jessica. *Out on the Wire: The Storytelling Secrets of the New Masters of Radio.* Broadway, 2015.

"About Recording." *LibriVox: Free Public Domain Audiobooks*, librivox.org/pages/about-recording/.

Bose, Dev K. et al. "Sound and Access: Attuned to Disability in the Writing Classroom." *Tuning in to Soundwriting*, edited by Kyle D. Stedman et al., enculturation/Intermezzo, 2021, intermezzo.enculturation.net/14-stedman-et-al/bose.html.

Faris, Michael J., et al. "3,000 Podcasts a Year: Teaching and Administering New Media Composition in a First-Year Writing Program." *The Proceedings of the Computers and Writing Annual Conference, 2019*, edited by Chen Chen and Lydia Wilkes, The WAC Clearinghouse, 2020, pp. 71–82, wac.colostate.edu/docs/proceedings/cw2019/chapter6.pdf.

Grohowski, Mariana. "Transcribe.Wreally: Methods for Digital Transcription of Audio." *Kairos: A Journal of Rhetoric, Technology, and Pedagogy*, vol. 21, no. 1, 2016, praxis.technorhetoric.net/tiki-index.php?page=PraxisWiki%3A_%3ATranscribe.wreally.

"Literary Magazines." *Poets & Writers*, www.pw.org/literary_magazines.

"Reverb." *Audacity Manual*, 13 Apr. 2021, manual.audacityteam.org/man/reverb.html. Accessed 28 June 2021.

Siegel, Robert, host. "The Loudness Wars: Why Music Sounds Worse." *NPR*, 31 Dec. 2009, www.npr.org/2009/12/31/122114058/the-loudness-wars-why-music-sounds-worse.

Stedman, Kyle. "Listening Like a Fan." *Technoculture: An Online Journal of Technology in Society*, vol. 7, 2017, tcjournal.org/vol7/stedman.

Towne, Jeff. "Real World EQ." *Transom*, 11 Mar. 2003, transom.org/2003/real-world-eq/.

Watson, Amy. "U.S. Podcasting Industry—Statistics & Facts." *Statistica*, 8 June 2020, www.statista.com/topics/3170/podcasting/.

Zdenek, Sean. "Accessible Podcasting: College Students on the Margins in the New Media Classroom." *Computers and Composition Online*, Fall 2009, seanzdenek.com/article-accessible-podcasting/.

———. "Designing Captions: Disruptive Experiments with Typography, Color, Icons, and Effects." *Kairos: A Journal of Rhetoric, Technology, and Pedagogy*, vol. 23, no. 1, 2018, kairos.technorhetoric.net/23.1/topoi/zdenek/index.html.

PHOTO CREDITS

Figure 1.1   Photo by Dekler Ph. Source: https://unsplash.com/photos/5ZFwlzb-0UQ

Figure 1.2   Photo by Luca Bravo. Source: https://unsplash.com/photos/uDwtAiRRvs4

Figure 1.3   Illustration by W.B. Robinson. Source: https://babel.hathitrust.org/cgi/pt?id=nyp.33433090924402&view=image&seq=104 (PD book)

Figure 1.4   Photo by Soundtrap. Source: https://unsplash.com/photos/c_S99FlDqSw

Figure 1.5   Photo by sindrehsoereide. Source: https://pixabay.com/photos/headphones-audiobook-technology-3658441/

Figure 1.6   Photo by Soundtrap. Source: https://unsplash.com/photos/CF8fATqx6VM

Figure 1.7   Photo by Free-Photos. Source: https://pxhere.com/en/photo/12419

Figure 1.8   Photo by Ron Kroon. Source: https://commons.wikimedia.org/wiki/File:Nina_Simone_1965_-_restoration1.jpg (public domain)

Figure 1.9   Photo by Jason Corey. Source: https://www.flickr.com/photos/mrcolantuono1/8327996804/ (CC BY 2.0)

Figure 1.10   Photo by William Neuheisel. Source: https://commons.wikimedia.org/wiki/File:Sunday_Drum_Circle_(4676809653).jpg (CC BY 2.0)

Figure A.1   Source: Screenshot by Kyle D. Stedman. Used with permission.

Figure 2.1   Photo by Eric Nopanen. Source: https://unsplash.com/photos/8e0EHPUx3Mo

Figure 2.2   Photo by Vincent van Zalinge. Source: https://unsplash.com/photos/nq5bgxSg8gE

Figure 2.3   Photo by James Drury. Source: https://www.flickr.com/photos/30000124@N04/9118416416 (CC BY 2.0)

Figure 2.4   Photo by Gerd Altmann. Source: https://pixabay.com/illustrations/vibrations-interference-wave-545138/

Figure 2.6   Photo by Anthony Intraversato. Source: https://unsplash.com/photos/za1Blqqbslw

Figure 2.7   Source: https://pxhere.com/en/photo/52574 (PD)

Figure 2.8   Source: Created by Kyle in Photoshop using no-attribution-required assets from https://undraw.co/ and https://uxwing.com/

Figure 2.9   Illustration by Edmon De Haro. Source: https://www.mindful.org/how-to-practice-mindful-listening/

Figure 3.1   Photo by Andrey Popov/iStock.com

Figure 3.2   Photo by João Marinho. Source: https://unsplash.com/photos/yCwtZhYcQxs

Figure 3.3   Photo by Josh Sorenson. Source: https://unsplash.com/photos/MjIMc6uhwrE

Figure 3.4   Photo credit: Vancouver Film School. Source: https://www.flickr.com/photos/38174668@N05/5815457665 (CC BY 2.0)

Figure 3.5   Photo by Ivan Pretorius. Source: https://pixabay.com/illustrations/girl-silence-portrait-woman-face-2179466/

Figure 4.1   Photo by Soundtrap. Source: https://unsplash.com/photos/SwObqQUc_vk

Figure 4.2   Photo by Annie Spratt. Source: https://unsplash.com/photos/QckxruozjRg

Figure 4.3   Photo by Photostockeditor. Source: https://photostockeditor.com/image/human-man-wearing-brown-cordless-headphones-headphones-84764

Figure 4.4   Photo by Kate Oseen. Source: https://unsplash.com/photos/XQKUIPjPl-s

Figure 4.5   Photo by ConvertKit. Source: https://unsplash.com/photos/BOI9jki3nzY

Figure 4.6   Photo by Tanya Rodrigue. Source: personal photo.

Figure 4.7   Photo by Paul van de Velde. Source: https://www.flickr.com/photos/dordrecht-holland/33870840882/ (CC BY 2.0)

Figure 5.1   Photo by Mic JohnsonLP. Source: https://www.flickr.com/photos/186095195@N02/49399738563 (CC BY 2.0)

Figure 5.11   Abel, Jessica. Graphic novel excerpt from *Out on the Wire: The Storytelling Secrets of the New Masters of Radio*, copyright © 2015 by Jessica Abel. Used by permission of Broadway Books, an imprint of Random House, a division of Penguin Random House LLC. All rights reserved.

Figure 5.12   Photo by Christina Morillo. Source: https://stocksnap.io/photo/woman-podcast-WKR3QXHW3U (PD)

INDEX

From the Publisher

A name never says it all, but the word "Broadview" expresses
a good deal of the philosophy behind our company. We are
open to a broad range of academic approaches and political
viewpoints. We pay attention to the broad impact book
publishing and book printing has in the wider world; for some
years now we have used 100% recycled paper for most titles.
Our publishing program is internationally oriented and broad-
ranging. Our individual titles often appeal to a broad readership
too; many are of interest as much to general readers as
to academics and students.

Founded in 1985, Broadview remains a fully independent
company owned by its shareholders—not an imprint
or subsidiary of a larger multinational.

To order our books or obtain up-to-date information,
please visit broadviewpress.com.

broadview press
www.broadviewpress.com